◇ ◇ ◇

OUTSIDE OURSELVES

◇ ◇ ◇

OUTSIDE OURSELVES

Landscape and Meaning

in the Greater Yellowstone

by Todd Burritt

© 2018 by Todd Burritt
All rights reserved

ISBN 978-0692959459

Ordering Information:

gentian.press@gmail.com
Livingston, MT

One of the great dreams of man must be to find some place
between the extremes of nature and civilization
where it is possible to live without regret.

—Barry Lopez

INTRODUCTION . . . IX

Part One. MODERN MOUNTAINS . . . 1
The Wind River Range

Part Two. ON RUNNING AWAY . . . 55
Dubois
The Washakie Wilderness
Cody

Part Three. THE COMPROMISED WILD . . . 121
The North Absaroka Wilderness
Yellowstone National Park

Part Four. NEW WORLD, OLD WEST . . . 185
Cooke City
The Absaroka-Beartooth Wilderness

Part Five. WHERE WE'RE GOING . . . 243
Gardiner
The Gallatin Range
Bozeman

NOTES . . . 305

INTRODUCTION

> In 1959, my brother John and I and a number of colleagues began a long-range study of the grizzly bear in Yellowstone National Park and parts of four adjacent national forests. This area comprises 5 million acres, and in terms of its natural character and the life forms it supports can be considered the greater Yellowstone ecosystem.
>
> —Frank C. Craighead Jr., *The Track of the Grizzly*

Craighead's definition of the Greater Yellowstone Ecosystem (GYE) came first. It outlines a boxy, seven-sided area—centered on Yellowstone National Park, but two-and-a-quarter times bigger. Nobody needed to tell this adventurous scientist that straight boundaries on maps are confessions of ignorance. He was already doing as much: winging a grand vision based on the seven most peripheral pieces of grizzly bear sign that he and his brother, John Craighead, could confirm. Clearly, this was a working draft, destined to grow with additional research and the recovery of the great bear. Less clear, perhaps, is that the concept was a visionary one.

Yellowstone Park's first boundary came almost a hundred years earlier. Slightly off square, seven miles taller than wide, it should be seen as a preliminary announcement: *there appears to be something special here*. For preserving public access to unusual hydrothermal features, the box functioned quite well. But for erring on the large side—encompassing river valleys and high plateaus distant from the famous geysers—it was ahead of its time. Because it wasn't just hot water leaving impressions on Yellowstone visitors: the scenery and wildlife held just as much power to enthrall. As these types of secondary attractions succumbed to development throughout the rest of the country, and the populace became increasingly urbanized, park offerings looked more radiant with contrast. The meaning of Yellowstone kept enlarging until, finally, it became emblematic of all that the natural world has to teach us. Today's park boundary sports only slight amendments—impish ears, a couple bite marks—but much more dramatic changes, to accommodate its conceptual expansiveness, have been imagined.

Hindsight makes history seem inevitable, so it is important to remember how many accidents brought this tract of country to where it is today. In 1886, fourteen years after its designation as the world's first national park, Yellowstone had no budget. Ungulates vanished among poachers, an "Improvement Company" hustled to sell 4,000 high-visibility acres to developers, and a powerful general—a man who once advocated extinction for bison and genocide for Native Americans—had a change of heart. Philip Sheridan ordered the cavalry to go save Yellowstone as a souvenir of the American West his military campaigns nearly eradicated, and they stayed there thirty years.

As Sheridan saw it, one way to protect the park from the exploitation impinging on all sides was to make it bigger. He suggested nearly doubling Yellowstone's area to include wildlife habitat south and east. Although this proposal failed, that same terrain later inspired a different kind of federal protection, and timberland reserves—the precursor to national forests—would one day wrap almost all of

Yellowstone's perimeter. Other special places adjacent to Yellowstone received separate designations: contiguous John D. Rockefeller Jr. Memorial Highway and Grand Teton National Park suggest that Yellowstone could have—and in a sense, does—keep running another forty miles south. (Emerson Hough coined the term "Greater Yellowstone" in 1917, while pushing to make just such an expansion official.) Still other parks in the area have been proposed: the Wind River Range, roof of the GYE, is one long-time nominee.

A geography of government oversight offers only the most superficial explanation of what we're calling Yellowstone. Few natural areas have inspired as many or as varied attempts at definition; this doesn't suggest that it has been summarily defined so much that it refuses to be. Perhaps the nearest thing to a consensus says that, whatever Yellowstone is, it's not limited to Yellowstone-the-Box. The migrating animals, the geothermal energy, the receptive human minds—even the name comes from without: golden cliffs along the Yellowstone River, over a hundred miles downstream from where it exits the northern boundary.

That's the enduring lesson of the Craighead study, which lasted over a decade before park management—overwhelmed, perhaps, by the terrific complexity emerging from within its jurisdiction—rashly terminated the project. After initially intending to demarcate the Yellowstone grizzly population, the Craigheads realized that, strictly speaking, there is no such thing. Their wooly piece of the puzzle is "hitched together with everything else in the universe," as John Muir would say. Today the GYE is often described as 22.6 million acres: more than four times the Craigheads' 1979 version, and eleven times Yellowstone-the-Park's boundaries. We hope this new definition encompasses enough of what we love to survive in perpetuity. Yet not only are the acres in question managed inconsistently or hardly at all, it would be silly to suggest that anything about Yellowstone just stops there, either—or for that matter, anywhere else.

You could spend all day trying to wrestle this thing into a pigeonhole. But we're talking about land, here—infinitudes of sensory possibility. At some point you have to get out, see what you see, and start making it up for yourself.

◊◊◊

In 1967, a twenty-two-year-old British art student named Richard Long cut across a field on his way home from class. Maybe he took that shortcut every day, or maybe he'd never noticed it before, and the realization struck him. Whatever the reason, upon reaching the trees on the other side, he turned around and retraced his steps. Then he walked it again. When his footprints matted a trail through the grass, Long framed it in a photograph, and "A Line Made by Walking" kicked off a long career of major works inspired by that simplest mode of human transportation.

Why is this significant? While other artists journeyed ever deeper down the wormhole of human artifice and self-reflexivity, here was a reawakening to the latent power of raw creation: what is hidden in plain sight. Employing landforms as both subject and medium, "land artists" such as Richard Long subverted the modern institution of art. Often inconvenient—if not impossible—to exhibit, and therefore fashionably anti-materialist (the movement was first described in the 1960s), land art simultaneously harkens back to some of humankind's earliest surviving expressions of the mysterious: ancient standing stones and geoglyphs that can still be encountered on all the inhabited continents.

Landscapes come most naturally to photographers. Perhaps in no other discipline are the documentary and poetic so indistinguishable. Even more conventionally, "landscape" is a genre of painting as well as its most banal subject; it is shorthand for a horizontal orientation of the frame. And in modern literature that ostensibly ignores landscape and place, the absence reverberates as a theme upon itself. So this ancient world gets treated by master after disciple after master, layman and savant, generation upon generation—yet there always seems to be something more to add, something we have to try saying for ourselves.

It's good to remember that "Line Made By Walking" does not, of course, commemorate a unique occurrence. Our history as a species is written in lines made by walking.* Rather, the photograph is important for the clarity of its articulation: how revelatory it can feel, on a personal level, to start looking at your feet as a pen and the landmasses of the planet as a blank page. How easy it is to get lost in ideas on a scale you haven't previously imagined. This metaphor of writing our story through motion is both a cliché and, I believe, an invaluable starting point for a life's worth of journeys. Because the greatest landscapes of all are the ones we hold in our heads. If this world is going to sustain us, we must regard it with an equally inexhaustible imagination.

◊◊◊

My own connection to the GYE began with fascinations my parents developed for the area, long before me moved there. Their interests manifested in different ways, but parts of each, I believe, passed on to me. We moved to Bozeman, Montana, about an hour from Yellowstone's northern boundary, in 1990.

I don't remember where it was, somewhere in the mountains south of town, that I first saw a trail sign marking a destination more than ten miles away. That stuck with me. It was the double-digits, somehow, that wove the spell: the thought that it goes and keeps going, further than my short legs could. Around fifteen years later this feeling found a parallel when I drove down to Dubois, Wyoming, to begin my first season with the Forest Service. It was the first time I ever saw the Wind River Range, the first time I ever saw the southeast corner of the same ecosystem where I grew up, and when I looked in the direction of home, all I could see was the unnameable. The majestic.

Now I can say that for the last couple decades a compulsion to be outside has been the defining force in my life. It wrenches me around, abandons me in the cold, and most of all, places deep, abstract convictions about the inherent importance of exposing oneself to

---

* In 1912, Antonio Machado elevated this subject into the realm of dreams. "Wanderer, your footprints are/ the path, and nothing else;/ wanderer, there is no path,/ the path is made by walking./ Walking makes the path,/ and on glancing back/ one sees the path/ that will never be trod again."

natural phenomena in my head—convictions that get challenged by all the other types of responsibilities in my life. This is the story of an exercise for those convictions, an exploration of how the land rises to our interests and feeds them in return. More specifically, it's the story of a two-month diagonal across the Greater Yellowstone I walked with my then-girlfriend (and now-wife), Jen. As such, it is a piece of "adventure writing," and it is my regret if it's nothing more.

I have tried to dwell as little as possible on the physical difficulty of our walk. Not only were the technical challenges insignificant by the standards of today's celebrity adventurers (I still whine, at least once), what difficulty there was is really beside the point. We conceived our trip as an act of homage to the landscape, not as a demonstration of human prowess. I should explain that the book itself, then, developed from an after-the-fact realization that the walk rewarded our efforts to a degree I did not expect. As intimate as the experience was, and as precarious as it can feel translating such things for an audience, I hope that sharing what I can will draw respectful attention to both the mightiness and fragility of our common heritage of land.

As I was writing this book, a coworker asked me what still needed to be said in "nature writing," and immediately I thought: maybe it has all been said. But we need to keep reminding ourselves. Only later did that begin to make sense to me. I believe in sharing stories about where we are and what it means to us. We need to keep the names for Earth on our tongues. It sounds old hat: *Okay, simple enough*. But as Jen and I found on our walk, with so many louder and more colorful designs competing for our loyalties, cultivating this sort of attention can be a slow and effortful road.

T. B.
Livingston, MT
February, 2018

Part One. MODERN MOUNTAINS

Wherever we go, there seems to be only one business at hand—
that of finding workable compromises between the sublimity
of our ideas and the absurdity of the fact of us.

—Annie Dillard

1

After years of imagining, months of preparation, and days of anxiousness, it was funny to watch my boots go one in front of the other up the trail, the same as almost every other day that summer. The sun, the soil, the plants, the stone—it was all there, uncannily normal. And why shouldn't it be, I had to wonder.

There were four of us at that time, setting off into the late-morning heat of August. Jen, her mom Tammy, brother Sam, and me. Tammy's car, receding behind us, sat in a gravel parking lot called Bruce's—that's an elbow where the Loop Road doubles back on itself, a place I know well. Since my first season with the Forest Service in Wyoming six years earlier, I'd been working to internalize its environs as a kindred dimension of the same ecosystem where I grew up, though hundreds of miles separate the two. The Sinks Canyon Guard Station, where I lived one summer, sits just a quarter mile from Bruce's, and more than once I finished a week of backcountry work by walking straight to its door—pulaski in one hand, key in the other.

When Jen visited me we'd hike from the doorstep, or ride our bikes seven miles downstream into Lander, a little town straddling the transition between Wind River Range and Wind River Basin. In the intervening years, we dissected the surrounding wild lands on dozens of eight-day hitches with the Forest Service, often alternating these work trips with six-day backpacks of our own. This was compulsive, insatiable exploration, and every trip strengthened our fantasy of a time we wouldn't have to come back "out." With no car to return to, and no obligations, we could put it all together. We could give physical meaning to this impossible place, or concept, or dream. And that day—August 8th, 2015—was different because we were doing it. It was the first day of sixty that Jen and I would spend inventing a squiggly route between the southeast and northwest corners of the Greater Yellowstone, immersed in its elements.

Getting to that point required planning and deliberation, overwhelmingly so at times. The previous winter we began dehydrating discount produce; I wangled an unheard-of two months of leave-without-pay from my (seasonal) job; Jen broke with convention by deferring the exam that capped her graduation from a nursing program at MSU—and then we had to steal Tammy away from her busy life, for a seven-hour ride down.

Now, as I began to unwind from the stress of putting the logistics in place,* some rather obvious questions began popping up for the first time. What did I hope to achieve? How was this different from all the other summers? What was this thing we were doing? "It's a journey," said my first thought, and as I tested that word on the low and familiar canyon walls a cloud of similarly inadequate ideas swirled in response.

---

* More accurately, Jen put the logistics in place. I stressed out.

I'd have to wait and see if any of them fit. And until then, I'd have to keep walking.

◊◊◊

Bruce's is the lowest elevation trailhead in the Wind River Range, and for me, that is much of the appeal. By starting the morning in sagebrush, transitioning to aspen, camping in lodgepole pine, and reaching whitebark pine before lunch the next day—all while some of the greatest mountains of the Northern Rockies grew around us—we'd get to see just what they are made of. That said, there are more obvious places we could've started. South Pass, a couple dozen miles away, is no less than the key that unlocked the West to the Oregon Trail. The Continental Divide, so long a soaring and serrated spine, wanders vaguely there into a land of shallow washes, and that's what allowed pioneering wagon trains to transition almost imperceptibly from the headwaters of the Atlantic to the headwaters of the Pacific.[*] Once boosted as the next Strait of Gibraltar, this landmark was forsaken by modern highways and, not unlike Yellowstone's symbolic gateway arch in Gardiner, Montana, is shunted and bypassed today. Nevertheless, you couldn't find a clearer spot to point to and say: *this* is where Greater Yellowstone starts.

Then, the natural boundary at South Pass is anything but definitive to hundreds of Wind River elk that cross South Pass a couple times a year to winter on the Red Desert, and every starting point proves subjective in the end. We chose Bruce's. As Jen pointed out, Tammy was nice enough to drive us the seven hours down from the endpoint of our trip, and with only one night to join us on the trail, it would be gracious to lead her up a forested creek before turning her around rather

---

[*] There's practically a *river* flowing across the divide. The Sweetwater wraps the southern toe of the Wind River Range's hundred-mile crest in a superb example of antecedent drainage. By maintaining its course throughout the excavation of thousands of feet of surrounding sediment, the Sweetwater "descended" over the granite crest, eroding it top down, so that on maps it appears to have broken willfully from the Pacific to the Atlantic rather than quietly obeying gravity. Further downstream, the Sweetwater slices through Devils Gate, a narrow doorway in a fin of bedrock, which has become a textbook example of this phenomenon.

than so many miles out one of the parched and blustery jeep roads from South Pass. I agreed. I'm suspicious anyway of the symbolism imposed on journeys such as ours; I assume through-hikers who contrive drop offs and pick-ups at political boundaries have geography in mind less than making a statement. Wherever we started, Jen and I would be out for a long time—that's what I cared about.

I also appreciate that Sinks Canyon, the location of Bruce's, bridges the front- and backcountry in a way I know and understand. Since we hoped to finish our hike in Bozeman, hometown to us both, and we'd pass through two other communities where one or both of us had lived, Jen and I indulged the thought that our walk was less a vacation than a definition of homeland. We weren't out to cherry-pick unflawed aesthetics—we'd done that on plenty of previous trips. We wanted to see how the entire functioning landscape stitched together, and transition zones—like boisterous Sinks Canyon—would be a vital part of that.

◊◊◊

If I did have any misgivings about starting in Sinks Canyon, as the lower Middle Fork of the Popo Agie River is known, they would've disappeared that first morning. Sinks is one of the great portals into the Rocky Mountains. I've had that in my head since reading A.B. Guthrie Jr.'s *The Way West*, throughout which the trailblazer (modeled on the trapper Jim Bridger) ceaselessly regales his party with the mythology of the Popo Agie.[*] Our drive up the canyon began in a fluvial cottonwood grove. We ascended arid benches populated by erratics—boulders deposited by receding glaciers, in this case onto incongruously bright sandstones and shales—before passing through a narrow gateway of Tensleep Sandstone. Dun-colored cliffs ramp steeply before breaking off into the sky, only to be succeeded by white walls of limestone and

---

[*] When I finally got there myself, it was a trick to stop mispronouncing this confusing name (a French spelling of the Crow term for "headwaters") the way it looks, and say it right. *Puh-PO jah.*

dolomite, which hold on a bit longer before disappearing in turn. These shells of sedimentary rock lay flat when the granite core of the Winds was undistinguished within the earth's crust. Since lifting, they've eroded quickly, along with so many other soft strata that hardly interrupt the level of the plains today. There's a good reason why these bands pitch as steeply as they do: all told, the Wind River geologic block rose 60,000 feet. While most of this growth was paced by erosion (there have never been eleven-mile tall mountains here), it still represents one of the greatest such uplifts known to science.

Sinks Canyon is named for a place where the Middle Fork, in all but the highest water, disappears beneath a wall of dolomite before reemerging a quarter mile downstream. This suggests a rather obvious correlation of cause and effect—in one side, out the other—but in a fitting introduction to Wyoming geography, it's not as straightforward as you'd expect. As a National Geographic guide explains,

> Tracer dye poured into the river above The Sinks turns up in The Rise as expected, but it takes two hours to get there, and the water comes out warmer than it went in. There is also more water coming out than entering, suggesting additional underground sources and a complicated network of passages—perhaps a large subterranean reservoir.

A small state park offers interpretation on this oddity, and between the park, extremely popular sport climbing on the vertical walls ("550 routes," my guidebook announces, "an easy weekend trip from Salt Lake, Jackson, or Denver"), and the trailhead we were heading to, Sinks is a bustling little outdoor venue. By no means does it feel like the middle of nowhere. In fact, the first mile and a half up the Middle Fork may be the most popular day hike in the range, with a trail wide enough to hold hands, all the way to the first waterfall. It was curiously quiet that day for us. I remember exchanging a few words with an older couple out looking for mushrooms (trail encounters don't get nicer than that), and after we passed the turn for Popo Agie Falls, use fell off altogether. From there we had a few exceptional miles of quiet scenery before a junction funneled in traffic from another trailhead called Worthen Meadows. That's where most backpackers start: they "save" 2.9 miles by driving up the hill and then dropping into the Middle Fork on a stack of steep switchbacks in generic lodgepole. They also miss the transitional beauty that comes with a slow start at Bruce's—whalebacks of glacier-smoothed granite speckled with starbursts of stonecrop, swales of rustling aspen replete with more solitude than can be found over many a tract of Wind River backcountry.

Past the junction the lodgepole close in. We camped our first night at Three Forks Park, an apparent misnomer for where Deep Creek joins the Middle Fork. It is a dependably popular place to camp. We arrived just behind an outdoor education class (NOLS, to be specific: recognizable for their mandated use of ankle gaiters, even in hot and dry conditions) and a gang of cows. As the guided party turned the opposite way, I led us out to a humdrum spot where the trail crew usually camps. We all ignored the more aesthetic but illegal sites sandwiched between the trail and the creek[*]—those were filled by groups that arrived later. Yes, we were in the wilderness now, but merely in the political sense of the word. The only backcountry savvy I employed that first day was crowd-avoidance. We used a government-installed food pole to hang our food, and from our campfire we could hear mooing and an occasional shout from the creek. On my way back from fetching water I stopped and took some of my only photographs of the day: huge piles of cow shit, guttered with maggot holes, drying on the scuffed and denuded earth.

◊◊◊

In the morning we said goodbye to Tammy. As her trip was drawing to a close—she'd be back in Montana that night—I tried to wrap my head around 59 more days to Bozeman, and failed. Sam, who worked long shifts on a fishing boat on Yellowstone Lake, had twelve days off that coincidentally lined up with our day one. The three of us proceeded up hill.

---

[*] In most wilderness areas, camping setbacks from riparian areas are intended to protect that most fragile biome from excessive trampling. Here, the intent of the regulation was thwarted by the far greater impacts of grazing cattle—animals that have a destructive attachment to stream banks.

There is a nasty pitch of trail that climbs out of Three Forks Park. Five years earlier, I worked on it for an entire eight-day hitch. It was discouraging to see much of our labor had fallen into disrepair. Time had loosened the slope-shouldered blocks of granite we'd manipulated to form steps in the sandy canyon wall, while snowmelt washed away fill that once evened the trail bed. Although I'd hiked through many times since that project, even those trips were years ago, and it started to feel like everything that day belonged definitively in the past.

To keep it alive I started telling one of my favorite trail crew stories—one that Jen had surely heard several times before. Basically, we used a lot of explosives during that workweek in 2010. I enjoyed the company of three coworkers all born a century too late—the mule packer, especially, who was leading our project, embodied the term "outlaw country" to me. When I tried to clarify one thing or another about preparing the bombs, he liked to quip, "Y'all take this job way-too-fucking seriously." After one shot, as I headed back up the trail to fetch more detonation cord, I found where a spark had started burning along a downed log and into a green lodgepole. The lower branches were already on fire. So I took off running, clumping in my work boots, a quarter-mile each way to our explosives cache to get one of the water bag backpacks that firefighters call piss pumps. Then I fought the flames single handedly until my crewmate Barry, smelling the smoke, came and joined me. All he had was a shovel. After running out of water, I'd skid down to the creek to refill the pump, only to find the fire gaining on Barry by the time I got back. It took four loads of water to finish it off. Returning to the blasting site, Barry and I found that our coworkers already had another shot lined up. Then I noticed, almost in surprise, that I'd managed to make it back with the det cord in my hand. "Find a smoke?" our lead muttered, taking the roll from me, to which I replied in the affirmative. "Put it out?" I said yes a second time, and it was back to blasting. What I often neglect to mention is that, on that same day, the fire crew was working nearby, mopping up a fire that the blasting crew had started the week before.

It was one of those experiences I'll never forget. Partly because I can't seem to talk about it without bragging a little. But also because it captures the scrappy and exciting feeling of Forest Service work that I love, an aspect that officially doesn't exist but is pretty inevitable whenever a group of people put iron hand tools to big rocks in remote places. That part will always hold immense appeal to me. But on days when a job seems impossible, and the list of backlogged work feels infinite, those same experiences can feel discouraging and ill-fated. As we continued walking, I regarded many other little trail projects through the lens of old memories, some of them holding up much better than others. So many memories enrich and deepen a scene. They also conjure nostalgia, and speak to the heaviness of time.

The feeling only got stronger when we passed a couple rangers on horseback. I knew them both, but not well. One didn't appear to recognize me, although I know that he did, and it piqued a little deserter's guilt I've had since moving back to Montana. They had a long day of work ahead of them, and while the words we exchanged were friendly, they felt distant and impersonal. Both men were about to retire, and when they did, they took entire histories of the backwoods with them.

◊◊◊

It's worth saying that, at this point in our walk, the scenery was phenomenal. An introduction to the Winds is probably in order.

On any map of the Greater Yellowstone Ecosystem (which is shaped something like a top-heavy "R", with Yellowstone National Park sitting in the hole), the Wind River Range sticks out like a sore thumb (the diagonal leg of the "R"). If the map color-codes land designations, then that range of mountains—clad in the ranger green that denotes national forest—diverges southeast, deep into a stark BLM empire called the Red Desert. A map highlighting elevation will depict the Winds as a great white pill, arctic over its surroundings, a reflection of the fact its real estate over 12,000 feet exceeds the rest of the ecosystem combined. And if the map's emphasis is geology, the Winds again light up with exceptionalism: like a great gobstopper, granitic beds over three billion years old erupt from the retracting lips of limestone and sandstone we saw on the way in. Most importantly to us, these graphical distinctions, however incidental, translate into real attractions for the visitor.

The great guidebook author Joe Kelsey ascribes the Winds a "mysterious allure." Another, Thomas Turiano, mentions "a magical quality." Naturalist and long-time wildlife biologist John Mionczynski deems them superlative Bigfoot habitat—which itself is an interesting corollary to regional Native American stories about resident "little people" (*Nimerigar*, in Shoshone). All of these impressions strike toward a wide consensus—one that I would elaborate in this way.

A friend once paraphrased this quote from an unknown hiker: "I love the Winds because you can walk anywhere you want and it's just as easy as walking on a trail." While it doesn't take long to prove this theory dangerously misleading, the range frequently gives such an impression. By fortune of elevation and climatic trends, the high Winds abound in subalpine forests of mature whitebark pine. These trees have a distinctively asymmetrical profile—muscular, brooming arms that lend easily to personification. In a typical old-growth stand of whitebark (individual trees can live over a millennium) there is little downfall. Rather, a few white boulders crop out of a dense understory of grouse whortleberry—a relative of the huckleberry that grows tiny but tasty red berries from an anemone of stems and tiny leaves—and the combined effect of these elements is pure fantasy book. The trees are old souls, the ground is soft and green and encourages wandering (if not somersaults), the view is enticingly obscured but always full of promise. "Where man becomes lost in the midst of his dreams," Finis Mitchell wrote, in the original, 1975 Wind River guidebook. When one indulges the forest's invitation to cut loose, a decision that might depend on the size of one's blisters, great cliff faces sail above the canopy. Glittering lakes materialize through branches—and if pursued uphill, the forest thins quickly into a timeless realm I've christened "Holy Highcountry;" rolling expanses of alpine tundra. The effect is, as hinted at by the hiker quoted above, enchanting and liberating: a platonic ideal of the mountained landscape. I'm inclined to read something into the fact that the Japanese term *feng shui*—"harmonious ambience"—translates as wind-water: primary elements in which this range singularly abounds.

As a result, the Winds invite off-trail exploration like few other sub-ranges of the Rocky Mountains do. And they feel bigger than they already are because of this: where every cranny is worth a look, and every lake worth a night's camp, wilderness feels endlessly alluring, always leading you on.

◊◊◊

As we headed west, we took time to climb a couple of the more prominent peaks in the Popo Agie Wilderness. The atmosphere was sharp and clear, and we identified summits dozens of miles north that we'd scale the following week. But we didn't really depart from the trail until the Cirque of the Towers, where we turned toward Texas Pass.

For all the great things there are to say about the Winds, make no mistake: in no way are they "undiscovered." Their attractions have been hyped and hyped again; they are mainstays on Backpacker Magazine-type top-ten lists and claim a following of diehards that is limited to neither the American West nor the Western Hemisphere. Working there, I never ceased to be amazed by the number of backpackers I ran into who, despite having lived in Pennsylvania or Tampa or Morocco all their lives, spoke proudly of 35-year backpacking careers in the Wind River Range. This cultish reputation is deserved. But the devious part is that so many new visitors keep being sold, headline style, on the Winds as a "best-kept secret." Certainly it seems like this mountain range should be: located in a rural part of our country's least populous state… ploughed from edges of emptiness… *not* a national park. But if that's what you've been taught to expect, you're all set up for a strange surprise.

The way to Texas Pass begins at Lonesome Lake—an obsolete name if there ever was one. Lonesome Lake serves as the base camp for dozens of climbing routes in the Cirque of the Towers. Shortly after two of these routes were included in a famous coffee-table rock climbing book (*Fifty Classic Climbs of North America*, 1979), the brilliant waters of Lonesome Lake tested high for *E. coli* (stuff that presumably leached out of human feces), and a camping restriction was imposed for a quarter mile around the lake. Since this safeguard has been put in place it has been roundly ignored: of seventy-four campsites I monitored in the Cirque in 2012, the majority fell within that perimeter.

Jen and I scrambled up a nearby peak while Sam fished Lonesome Lake; over dinner the three of us shared stories. When Sam mentioned speaking to a father and son, "flustered" because the trail down from Texas Pass wasn't better marked, I felt dumbfounded for a moment. Texas Pass isn't on a trail. It's not supposed to be marked at all. Why did they think it would be? And a connection formed in my mind: other groups I've talked to, many groups over many years, wandering in unusual places, who've mentioned following itineraries they'd found online. It was an unmistakable trend, I'd thought that more than once, and the use patterns and impacts of the backcountry were visibly changing in turn. For one thing, social media is dialing up the "*Fifty Classic Climbs*" effect. First an iconic picture inspires copycats. Then it becomes a must-have. By the time a backdrop like the Cirque of the Towers reaches meme-status, the momentum can't be stopped—popularity begets more popularity, life reduces to an assemblage of collectibles. I also knew, from my time with the Forest Service, that this pattern wasn't being tracked or accommodated for in any meaningful way—not by an agency that expects workers to backpack in green jeans, carrying radios with the dimensions of bricks.

In the moment, such thoughts ride surges of emotion, an emotion increasingly categorized as "elitism." I felt that excitement over the Wind River Range's charms—and the cachet of *off-trail*—was carrying all too well; that it was being parroted by those drumming up attention for cyberspace monikers, and sold to people who, without bothering to learn what suits them, have already decided that they want it all.* Blame commercial interests, sure, but don't forget the hikers and every-men and writers like myself, everyone who doesn't do something just to do it, but goes to work processing intangibles until the mainstream starts reaching for their checkbooks. Yes, I was overly invested in the issue,

---

* I speak from the perspective of one who knows the northern Rockies well, and the Colorado Rockies and Sierra Nevada—let alone the Adirondacks—not at all. I will, however, share one comment I found online: "The Winds may be the Times Square of the backpacking world, lack of lounge chairs notwithstanding. ...Even as a Coloradan I can say that." And Orville E. Bach Jr., who has worked as a park ranger in Yellowstone for over forty years, describes the *laissez-faire* management of Wind River backcountry as "horrendous," emblematic of a failing system.

but I'd also spent a lot of summer months trying to clean up the place, and made a lot of unpleasant surprises in the process. An eye professionally trained for impacts carries a permanent tint of pessimism.

This less-than-wild effect of the Winds is exacerbated by their perplexing deficiency of large game. Famous herds of bighorns, once the largest in North America, were decimated by diseases introduced by hundreds of thousands domestic sheep unleashed each summer of the early twentieth century. While the domestics are mostly a thing of the past, the natives still haven't recovered beyond the extreme northern portion of the range. Mountain goats, meanwhile, haven't yet immigrated from nearby introduction points, elk are not nearly as common as one would imagine (this is, after all, northwest Wyoming), and I completed more than two whole seasons of ranger work there before I ever saw a bear. By the time our sixteen days in the Winds ended, Jen and I would estimate that we'd seen more horses, llamas, and cows *apiece* than all wild ungulates combined.

Even when they're not managed as cattle pastures, wilderness areas have carrying capacities: thresholds beyond which essential qualities diminish. In fact they have several. *Biological* carrying capacity refers to how humans influence the flora and fauna, *physical* carrying capacity how soil types degrade under human and livestock traffic, and *psychological* carrying capacity how the wilderness atmosphere disappears when it is as crowded as a mall. When it gets bad, the three tend to snowball together in my head, making me a little hysterical, a little irrational. The next day I told Jen I was renaming Texas Pass "Perforated Pass" because that's how stabbed the tundra looked from trekking poles—being hardened to the Winds' popularity also made it easier for me to make light of it. But as we continued to run into one group after another, a day's travel and better from the nearest trailhead, I thought of Sam, who had never visited the Winds and, a month earlier, gone a week without seeing a soul in the Absaroka-Beartooth Wilderness. Borrowing his perspective (shock), I decided to start a tally of the people we encountered. We saw fifty-seven people that day, almost all of them off-trail (that is, not following a trail created or maintained by the Forest Service). After passing a NOLS course of ten—half of them enacting a medical scenario, the other half taking notes—I felt the old sarcasm bubbling up.

"Here we are, off-trailing in the Winds," I announced to Jen and Sam. The user trail I followed was beaten in harder than many system trails I know: edged as crisply as those incised by pick and beveled adze.

Continuing north, making decisions on the fly and trying to be creative, I fell into trails, nevertheless. Over one divide I found turf worn like hopscotch: each foot placement defined. Step here, around the rock, two little steps for a big leg up. The Wind River mainstream is hounding out "the last blank places on the map" at a fever pitch. Other times, after inadvertently falling into lines of cairns, I'd realize there were cairns leading in almost every direction I could see; impotently, I'd kick a few of them over. Isn't the assumption of risk the precondition to reward? Why this insistence on depriving the next person of fresh canvas?

Popularity is a loaded status in any arena, be it the music industry or high-school lunchroom, but nowhere is it more conflicted than in the wilderness. Here reverberates the din that drives so many of us to seek wilderness in the first place: premonitions of an overpopulated doom, a planet swarming with human flesh. But is this complaint legitimate, or a lot of snobbery soaking through? Perhaps my griping belongs to a broader refrain, one described well by the historian Patricia Limerick:

> In [Western] resource rushes, people hoping for exclusive opportunity often arrived to find a crowd already in place, blanketing the region with prior claims, constricting individual opportunity, and producing all the problems of food supply, housing, sanitation, and social order that one would expect in a growing city, but not in a wilderness* ...Contrary to all of the West's associations with self-reliance and individual responsibility, misfortune has usually caused white Westerners to cast themselves in the role of the innocent victim.

The resource, in this case, is wildness—the autonomy of the non-human world—and complaining about a crowd remains as futile as it is inevitable. We can't rationally fault each other for doing what we ourselves are doing, and shared values are insurance, affirmation. Old-timers can long for the good old days, when what was good was also obscure, but they can't blame newcomers for following their lead.

---

* Here, Limerick uses the word "wilderness" as a synonym for the frontier.

It's very easy to kill conversations about human carrying capacities with cries of elitism, because it is unconscionable to bully people away from these places. As a society, we need places like Texas Pass to be explored, known, and talked about; we need these places to take their deserved roles in our cultural definition of wonder. How many times I've had the thought: ninety-nine out of a hundred people must not believe places like this exist—if they did, their lives would change. So on the one hand, the elitism of solitude really is something we have to learn to get over. Pity the backpacker whose day is ruined by a salutation from his peer. Or as Tina Deines writes, "At a time when too many people are being told they don't belong in the United States, I hope the outdoor community will say there's still a place for everyone on America's public lands."

On the other hand, if we make impartial acceptance our goal—if we follow Tina Deines' suggestion, and treat hobbyists like other races or religions, affording them the sovereignty to regulate themselves—we fall into other flimsy assumptions. We either blindly take for granted that sufficient protections are in place for wild lands to retain their integrity indefinitely, or, upon awakening to a forever-degrading environmental baseline, we wave it off as the price of social cohesion. As for the first position, there's no shortage of evidence indicating otherwise (unless you politically dismiss all evidence that could be considered scientific). And with regard to the second, we can't afford to shutter sustainability questions in the name of cultural sensitivity—especially when that culture is a doltish one, blazing forth to the power of exponents on an obsolete civilizing impulse. Social cohesion and environmental quality are not mutually exclusive: in fact, one is not possible without the other. When the two are placed at odds—and we shutter the debates so as to not offend anyone, like Deines recommends—quality of life goes first, and it is going fast, now; quantity of life soon follows. We need to celebrate places, yes, we need to encourage sustainable habits, *and* we need to be unflagging critics of our own culture, never downplaying the collateral impacts of our own choices.

There are no hard rules to help us distinguish destructive trends from constructive ones—least of all when both originate from the same places within ourselves. Keep that in mind and every footfall on the tundra makes you flinch a little.

2

It's possible the Winds harbor so much explorer's intrigue today for some of the same reasons that they were a rallying point for other early westerners. For now I'll skip over the earliest and most compelling Wind River explorers—those evidenced by lichen-encrusted visionary figures, incised in boulders, that are scattered around the foothills of the range—and let it suffice to say nine of the sixteen Rocky Mountain Rendezvous, between 1825 and 1840, were held in the shadow of the Winds. One on the Popo Agie, two on the Wind River, and six on the upper Green River. That's when the earliest wave of Rocky Mountain trappers (or "mountain men," those paragons of the will toward exploration,) gathered to sell furs, buy trade goods, tell the tallest tale, and debauch for a month or two. Since the Winds were not only the highest mountains around but also looming the closest, it's inevitable they'd inspire their share of legend.

On dry west winds those legends carried. After Benjamin Bonneville crossed the plains in 1832, with an entourage of 110 hunters and trappers, he headed straight for the western slope of the Wind River Range and built a fort—"Fort Nonsense," because it was never used for trading. The next year he attempted a shortcut across the burly topography, east to west, and as far as shortcuts go, his was classic: "He soon found that he had undertaken a tremendous task; but the pride of man is never more obstinate than when climbing mountains." Bonneville and his three companions reached the top of the first "gentle acclivity" all right, the only one they could see from below, but from there the horizon eluded them, appearing ever higher, more treacherous, and further away. Along a chain of false summits the team laboriously soldiered, scrambling up and skidding down. At one point, a number of their loaded pack animals trundled ass-over-teakettle down a granite slab. Before abandoning the route completely, the four scrambled to the top of what had appeared to them the highest peak in North America. After returning to civilization, Bonneville left this possibility open—actually, his summit is just high enough to reveal that the mountains grow unmistakably taller going north. Regardless, Bonneville's written account of climbing what was most likely Wind River Peak is momentous for being the earliest in the ecosystem. (Coincidentally, that's the first mountain we climbed on our trip, as well.)

In 1842, for the first time since Lewis and Clark, a government survey struck west from St. Louis. John C. Frémont's commission mentioned only grassland and prairie—that is, lands east of the Rocky Mountains—but Wind River tall tales exerted their sway. Bonneville's mountaineering episode was too riveting—and the ring of "highest peak in North America" too glamorous—for Frémont to pass up a side trip to the Winds. "A great part of the interest of the journey for me was in the exploration of these mountains, of which much had been said that was doubtful and contradictory," Frémont admitted afterward. The zenith of his equally colorful adventure now bears his name—it's but the second highest in the range (13,745'), to say nothing of North America as a whole.

The greatest explorers tend to fixate on their own misjudgments; society is often all too willing to overlook them. Posterity was generous to Frémont: he returned to the nickname "The Great Pathfinder," and any Tom Sawyer looking for a hero at the time could find one in him. One such young easterner was Gustavus Cheyney Doane, who'd grow to be quite the pathfinder himself, guiding top brass around the recently designated Yellowstone Park. His name would stick to a strikingly conical mountain on the east side of Yellowstone Lake, and another summit in the northern Tetons. Frémont's off-task foray into mountaineering imparted an important—if strangely economical—life lesson to Doane, one by which he set his life:

> Explorations furnish a source of reputation wherein the rewards are, and ever have been, more than commensurate with the efforts put forth… A poor subaltern, yet unknown, while traversing with weary steps the barren wilderness or scaling the mighty summits from which the waters part and flow, may stumble, under fortune's favor, upon some new discovery, the merit of which will secure to him all that history vouchsafes to greatness—a paragraph in the encyclopedia of the human race.

And so mountains—sized somewhere between a man and a planet, conceivable enough to bear our own names yet no more knowable than gods—acquaint us with the eternal. They are the lanterns and we are the moths.

◊◊◊

In the predawn starlight of our fifth day Jen and I set off to climb Mount Bonneville. Benjamin Bonneville never climbed Bonneville Peak, and there's no reason he should have—it's neither inviting nor prominent. Although it would ultimately be the lowest of the dozen or so named summits that Jen and I ascended during our pass through the Winds, Bonneville was also the most technical. Descriptions of our chosen route, the easiest way to the top, give a climber's rating of 5.2. To me, that means a rope is advisable, but experienced climbers might choose to go without. And since a rope would've worn out its welcome on all our days spent walking and not climbing, we decided to approach the mountain conservatively and see how it went—knowing full well that we might get turned around.

Our first look at the route was less than encouraging. In the hard light of sunrise, an arête split upwards between a black chimney and an impervious white headwall. That was a fine line we'd need to balance. No matter how easy the climbing, we could see that the exposure would be absolutely dramatic: unlike some fifth-class routes, which take their rating from a single move on a fifteen-foot cliff band, this one sustained for hundreds of feet. Even a flood of apprehension couldn't drown the spell to summit, though, and the going started to make more sense once we got into it. Before long we passed a rappel station. These motley collections of slings and cords and metal wedges are abandoned by climbers descending their ropes. They are, by their very nature, impossible to retrieve by whoever uses one, and many people who don't spend time in vertical environments would be shocked to see how they accumulate over the years. Although the Forest Service would classify this as illegal abandoned property, and the bolts that climbers drill in wilderness are illegal on other levels,* leaving them is common practice, and climber ethics turns a blind eye.** In magazines and on websites, first ascent parties still volunteer information about all the new fixtures they've stamped on wilderness walls.

I usually take as much as I can out with me. Part of it is out of principle—but to be fair there's plenty of trash (spoiled socks, toilet paper, food waste) I let be unless I'm working. I mostly take climbing gear out of the packrat's conviction that it could be useful for something around the house. That day, however, I was thinking about our descent,

---

* Bolts are not specifically prohibited by the Wilderness Act, though "permanent improvements" and "installations" are. The issue has been addressed differently by different agencies. In national park wilderness, Director's Order #41, in 2013, made allowance for "rare" climbing bolts, if they received prior authorization. In national forest wilderness, bolts were explicitly banned in 1998 by a statement that was intended only to clarify the language of the Wilderness Act. But that statement was rescinded, and bolts once again reside in a grey area.

** Indeed, rappelling cannot be avoided in many situations, and the possible complications of attempting only clean descents are far out of proportion to the environmental impacts of rappel anchors.

and I raided the anchors for all they were worth. I even pulled out two "fixed" pitons with my bare hands, which isn't usually possible. Climbing down is scarier than climbing up—you can't plan out your footholds, the friction of an out-sloped ledge is harder to employ—and so, like a cat in a tree, it's not especially difficult to get yourself stranded. In a worst-case scenario I imagined myself rigging up some knotted mess, jailbreak style, as a hand line to get Jen and me down through a tricky spot. But the climb went without hang-ups, and Jen—who has much less climbing experience than me—impressed me with her calm problem solving. No hand line necessary, thank goodness, and ten oxidized carabiners, along with pounds of other junk, were now my cross to bear. As I stood watching Jen negotiate one spooky spot, I noticed a manmade something cached in the narrow "V" between Bonneville's main and north summits. Definitely worth a closer look. A short scramble revealed a backpack with a tube of deteriorating USGS quads lying at its side.

The fabric of the pack was bleached and frayed. Opening it for more clues, I was chilled to find all the essentials you'd bring for a day in the mountains. There were water bottles (one filled with water, the other an orange solution), a bulging Ziploc of Tootsie Rolls and bags of other snacks, a recreation map, rain gear, warm layers, a headlamp, flashlight, extra batteries, GPS... things you wouldn't want to lose. I didn't question the owner got into a desperate situation. And on a mountain like Bonneville, that could only really mean a bad fall. For the remainder of our descent, as we gingerly down-climbed short vertical sections with awful exposure, I couldn't stop looking down, waiting to see a body.

After letting the banalities of recreational patterns distract me for a few days, that old backpack brought me back to a harsher dimension of the landscape. Everyone was out there to engage something real—despite my cynicism—and for all the Winds have been tracked up, rappelled down, and canoed across, they've also hosted their share of tragedies: realities that no one can possibly prepare for. It wasn't until I got home that I established beyond doubt that the backpack belonged to someone who didn't survive his climb.* On September 14, 2006, a man's body was recovered from the base of our route. The journal in his tent breathlessly described aborted attempts on Bonneville from September fourth and fifth; it stands to reason that his third attempt in as many days was what did him in.

The article reporting the recovery paints an endearing image of a family man—a passionate and principled public defender. It also gives insight into how our strongest and most admirable qualities can occasion our demise. His family "said Ken loved Mount Bonneville because he said it was the one he always wanted to conquer." And from an earlier entry in his journal: "Quitting is NEVER an option!" A lyric from M. Ward popped into my mind: "He summoned all of his strength in the climb/ he suffered all of his strength in the fall."

The relationship between modern humans and mountains is symbolic—there's nothing we need on top. At the same time, our senses tell us that nothing is more real than the mountain; nothing more substantial than the heft of a chunk broken from its face, nothing so boundless as the living minutiae that inhabit its uncountable facets, nothing so unimpeachable as the silhouette standing between our feet and the arc of the sun. Within this paradox we taste a life beyond our years, an intimation of something greater—until, at some point, the mountain's physicality comes crushing back down. Stone that rasps, gravity that much stronger.

◊◊◊

That afternoon, as our route diverged from Sam's, Jen and I continued north into an easy tramping mid-section of the range that is popularly overshadowed by its famous bookends. The people thinned out—we only saw a party or two a day—and it seemed ironic that the forces making that section of high country relatively hospitable to life (that is, slightly less rugged, retaining a bit more topsoil) also make it less

---

* In a briefing for rescuers, the missing person's daughter listed things she knew her dad always carried. From "a huge military poncho" and "green wool pants," right down to the bag of Tootsie Rolls, it hit almost every item I found up there.

desirable to destination backpackers, myself of summers-past included. We found it more than worthwhile. In fact, at the time I called it among the most majestic places I'd ever seen.

Ancient fault lines are responsible for the unique character of the place. For millions of years shattered planes of bedrock, just off parallel to the divide, have channeled streams and glaciers to erode along corrugations. Since the faults direct water and ice *across*—rather than *down*—the prevailing topography, gravity goes easy, and the resultant valleys turned out shallow and traveler-friendly. This creates a strong distinction from the east side of the divide—which not only lacks such faults, but also receives more snow. Over there, lateral motion along the range entails a succession of climbs and descents in and out of major canyons, carved by much larger glaciers, that lie perpendicular to the divide.

A lot of places make this claim, but the rock we passed near Medina Mountain legitimately ranks among the oldest in the world. Parts have been solidly dated to 3.4 billion years ago, and estimates for other parts approach the record-holding 3.8 billion years of Greenland granite. It's hard to measure that far back—especially because that specific blend of Wind River granite and gneiss, called migmatite, has been chopped, melted, twisted, and dunked in baths of magma several times since the date of origin scientists are looking for.

As we walked, the ageless character of the rock rippled outward through my perception of sky and water and life. That was a world of scant timber, broad lakes, scrims of willow in powder green, grasses curing into browns and yellows, tumbles of white boulders, pikas chirping, and always the severe and naked mountainsides. We felt suspended in sublime exile. When we weren't moving we carried out a routine that bordered on ritual: we would bathe in clear water, rinse our clothes, spark a cooking fire (we never had trouble finding an existing ring), then sit out and read as the temperature started to fall, drinking cup after cup of tea. I love what Anatoli Bourkeev said: "Mountains are not stadiums where I satisfy my ambition to achieve, they are the cathedrals where I practice my religion." This was no test of endurance: it was healthy and sustainable and we were game to go that way forever.

At the same time, we couldn't simply ignore our lifelines to the industrial nation that claimed us, and seven days into our hike we already had to think about getting more food. Eight days' worth awaited us in the back of Sam's car at the Elkhart Trailhead (Sam's route departed from ours' after five days—he had fishing spots to check out), and getting it required descending from the divide and trudging out and back from the busiest parking area in the range. I could tell how spoiled I'd already become by just how unappealing this errand struck me. Before we knew it we were back on trail, passing one party after another. Nobody seemed inclined to talk. They looked the way I must've looked—a little too serious and driven for forested terrain that, though usually written off as intermediary to more picturesque destinations, still held a lot of charm. Before punching out to Elkhart, Jen and I camped above Elklund Lake. There were many other groups camped on the lake, including, when I went down to fetch some water, six fly fishermen spaced evenly around the perimeter. Three of them were yelling back and forth about how bad the fishing was. I found a broken arrowhead, took a picture, then pushed it further into the moss. The next morning was an early one. We started down the well-worn trail just after dawn, and we were all business. After dropping six miles to the trailhead and retrieving our food, we planned to retrace our tracks, then go an additional nine miles with our eight days of supplies.

The lousy state of the Elkhart trail, which was trashed after a couple recent rains and a lot of horse parties, got me thinking about trails in general. One to over-complicate things, I considered it as a record of foot placement, and more than that, a document of collective decision-making. In a perfect system (where the trail offers a path of least resistance, a durable surface, and has all the obstacles removed), a well-used trail would reveal little more than its original design. The Elkhart trail is anything but perfect. It is braided throughout—walked on as much as off—and stricken with mud holes, busted turnpikes, and water bars in ruinous dysfunction so as to become obstacles in themselves. You can see how hikers in running shoes, distrusting the first signs of dampness in the soil, take to the woods—and just like that, a strip of slow-growing, woody-stemmed whortleberry is annihilated. You can see how a trail with loose rocks on it, or eroded more than five inches, is shunned by horses. Rather than alter their gait, the animals will move over two feet, and another strip of wildflowers is wiped out. One trail becomes two—and two may, believe it or not, turn into twelve. The cumulative effect of so many unconscious decisions of personal convenience can manifest into an ecologically wasted corridor wider than a state highway.

Combating these tendencies are demonstrations of government control: paths blocked, water bars installed, switchbacks dug. That's been a big part of my job for the last eight years. Such efforts reduce erosion—and work toward an ideal of form and function that many people, their decisions recorded by "impacts," either do not recognize or agree with. Perhaps they see government trails as a form of manipulation—an overbearing nanny state—because they will go out of their way to lift an obstruction from an area closed for revegetation when effort- and time-wise it doesn't matter one way or the other.[*] Some hikers cut switchbacks with a tenacity that suggests a sustainable trail grade is the only thing standing between where they are and that most vital expression of self. Mountain bikers rip out water bars and bank turns on trails that previously shed water, thereby accelerating erosion and shortening the trail's functional life (which should be infinite), all in pursuit of indulgent rates of speed. Horsemen will cut down five young, healthy, whitebarks—I've counted—rather than a larger tree that has fallen in their way, and otherwise reroute at will, blazing trails across loose duff that quickly erodes into gullies worse than what came before, all because it's hard to cross a wilderness on a timetable when you're hauling hundreds of pounds of freight for well-heeled clients. At such times, our best efforts at conservation fail us: they succeed only in multiplying costs. Even worse, sides are outlined, the power struggle is on.

That's how a tired mind reads a tired trail. Becoming invested in "making a difference" breeds many a despairing hour, just as, back at home, I can become overwhelmed by an inventory of our used plastic bags. When I find myself staring at the trail a little too intensely, I know

---

[*] Some of the many merits of walking off-trail are considered in Part Four.

that my line of work is getting the best of me—that it's time to let go and think about trees for a while. And they were majestic that afternoon.

◇◇◇

Several days later we camped north of Mount Helen, one of the higher mountains in the range. Back at home I'd tried and failed to find any ascent routes described from that direction. I didn't make much of the fact—we were in an obscure area, isolated from the nearest trails by high passes. But I knew the omission could be significant, too: the best maps withhold crucial details, and these mountains were cliffy and loose, the glaciers rotting. Rock fall took out two NOLS students on the Helen Glacier the last time I was working in that area, and two separate helicopter flights were required to rescue them.

Not that I was looking for reasons to walk away from the mountain. Jen and I couldn't wait to finally put to use the crampons and axes we'd been carrying. In the pale light of dawn we discovered that, unlike the dangerously loose moraine of Knifepoint Glacier that we crossed the day before, it was smooth walking right up to the toe of Helen. When we got on the ice it only got better. My knowledge of glacier travel may be limited to my own intuition, but that one made for uncomplicated and efficient traveling. The aprons of Turret and Warren, derelict temples of nameless gods, met at our feet. After half a mile we left our axes at the base of a bedrock ridge and transitioned into a glorious scramble that brought us to the top of the mountain. Dense smoke, drifted in overnight, obscured everything beyond a dozen miles, but we were close enough to study all ten of the highest summits of the range. It turned out to be the loveliest summit of the leg. The air was so still that, after studying the map, I let it lie open on top of a boulder—something you just don't do in those aptly named mountains.

"It's the kind of day we could get away with anything," I said to Jen with a laugh, as I tried to take it all in. She looked at me skeptically. What did I mean by that? I don't know. I just felt good. Earlier that morning, hyperaware of all the things that could turn us around short of the top, a magazine article came to mind. It was a monthly column that detailed real-life rescue situations. In a narrative of the hiker's ordeal, green type highlighted smart decisions and directed the reader to a side bar elaborating survival techniques: *remove wet clothing. Build a shelter with tree boughs.* Bad decisions like *hiking off-trail* and *not carrying emergency flares* showed up in red, of course, and were similarly expounded upon. I thought of it because Jen and I are always doing things "wrong" and we know it: by the time we got to the summit of Helen our entire day could have shown up in red. But it also went smoothly. The ice, the weather, the gravity—all those things behaved more or less according to my understanding of them.

Despite the authority of such articles, I think they fail to find a science that can begin to make up for first-hand experience. Methodologies don't accommodate the number of variables that engaged minds assimilate on their own. One problematic consequence of trying is that, by describing the wild like a set of rules, readers are distanced from the lessons of their own experience—the most sophisticated information of all.*

If you spend a lot of time outside, and try to go into each day with a naturalist's desire to learn rather than the sportsman's imperative to conquer, you don't need to import the authority of specialists and professionals into your experience. You can just do what makes sense because, on a basic anatomical level, that's what you're made to do. It also feels better. But there's a pretty major catch that makes this harder than it sounds. In order to do so we have to make peace with risk. Because I believe in natural consequences and learning the hard way, I try to accept that anything I do out there can still bite me in the ass: that I might *die*. Society, meanwhile, teaches us that this is unacceptable.

---

* In 1945, psychologist Gilbert Ryle influentially divided knowledge into two types: cerebrally "knowing that," and experientially "knowing how." To assume that the former leads to the latter, he believed, was fallacious. "Rules, like birds, must live before they can be stuffed," he warned.

Our time on Helen was to be one of two days we didn't encounter other hikers in the Winds and we were enjoying the solitude immensely.* But as Jack Turner wrote, solitude, no longer a de facto byproduct of remoteness, "is marked by an awareness of how much care and thoughtfulness are required to find qualities that should, one thinks, be normal... in designated wilderness." I find his use of the word *marked* significant: society is such a pervasive reality it leaves traces even in its absence.

While climbing down, Jen and I talked about our experience two days earlier when we walked out to resupply from Sam's car. That long, hot day was a disorientating one. Because we hiked it two ways before ten o'clock, then broke camp before bumping up the trail for lunch, we had many opportunities for people watching. In case you didn't know, there's no better talking fodder for people living in isolation than the superficial habits of others.

There was the group of six Europeans we leap-frogged three times. Dressed in tight and impractical clothes, they were lively, fun, and stubborn about letting us pass. They preferred to try and match our pace until they were sucking wind and tripping over their own feet. Then there was the group of three college kids talking rapidly about video games in between nervous shouts of *"HEY bear!"*—On one pass, when I was gaining from about twenty feet behind, the young guy in back heard my boot scuff, and cried wildly as he spun around: "WHOA BEAR!" I should've thanked him for not carrying a gun, I told Jen. Then Jen mentioned something I hadn't noticed. At least three of the hikers we passed wore SPOT devices attached to their shoulder straps. SPOTs are the most popular brand of satellite emergency notification device (SEND)—gadgets that can, with the push of a button, alert the preprogrammed search and rescue outfit of your choice. That people are now fixing them to their chests suggested to me a rather paranoid view of the mountains.

---

* We did bear audience to a small prop plane repeatedly shooting a gap between our summit and the next one to the south. Maybe they were taking pictures of the mountaineers—assuming the lost-and-loving-it would be more likely to smile and wave than flip the bird.

Of course, who am I to judge—it's whatever makes you comfortable, right? On the other hand, rampant misuse has won SENDs enough infamy to make you wonder. I remember when a Colorado man visiting my ranger district in the southern Winds played an unconscionable trick on his wife ("HELP!!! I AM ALIVE SOMETHING IS TERRIBLY WRONG SEND HELP IMMEDIATELY," she read on her cell phone one night. Ha ha, joke's on her; a tax-payer-funded helicopter called his bluff)—of course, that's just straightforward abuse. More telling was the group of fathers and sons in the Grand Canyon, who ordered search and rescue helicopters three separate times because their water kept tasting funny. (The third time, they were removed by helicopter, whether they liked it or not.) In 2012, after two Australian National Parks began providing SENDs free of charge to backcountry users, their rescue units predictably got a lot busier. Authorities received over 1,700 distress signals that year, and each one of those initiated a legally mandated emergency response—even though only about six percent proved to be "genuine emergencies." That's nearly 1,600 pointless, costly, dispatches. One sour moral: if, in times of strength, we make ourselves available to save people from their uncertainties, the response will be crippling.

From movies to campfire yarns, one unfortunate side effect of storytelling is that it makes worst-case scenarios all too easy to imagine. You're doing something utterly mundane—fetching water, going to pee behind a tree—when disaster strikes. Be it a landslide, allergic reaction, or psychopath, loss of consciousness is imminent, but one push of the big red button and this nightmare segues into a happy-ending helicopter rescue; it's all just another day on the Elkhart trail, that exceedingly well-packed strip of mud. What we forget, in seeing the world this way, is that our stories distill a pool of human experience astronomically larger than was conceivable even ten years ago, from which the overwhelmingly ho-hum median of human experience has been evaporated. Wild lands are places of uncertainty: that's not disputed. But we must learn to see this as one of many benefits, not a side effect to be neutralized. Jen and I have never been in the practice of carrying any communication devices into the backcountry, phones included. (We did carry a phone on this trip in order to coordinate with friends in towns we visited along the way.) It's an omission that seems gratuitous and irresponsible to many. It's also a decision that we see as ours to make; a decision that we can be intentional about and appreciate for its complexity. As I said to Jen that day, there might come a time when we'd give up everything for a SPOT—that's just a fact. I also want to know what it means to accept that fact.

3

How the grizzly bear makes wilderness more real. This topic is an all-time greatest hit among GYE visitors;* within the minds of millions of others, people who will never visit grizzly habitat, shadows of our ancestral predators toss and turn in instinctual dormancy. The first lesson and perhaps greatest gift of our multi-millennial relationship with the great bear is that, when barriers fall between humans and nature—

---

* It's been a convention at least since 1935, when Aldo Leopold speculated on its origins: "I think it was Stewart Edward White who said that the existence of one grizzly conferred a flavor to a whole county..."

when we find ourselves embroiled back in the food chain, as it were—things start to look differently. And not necessarily for the worse. The senses sharpen and, consequently, there's more to be sensed. Details to the landscape—the groundcover, the voice of a bird, a cloud crossing the sun—suddenly, if inexplicably, matter. Modern ennui dissolves. In short, simple awareness of the grizzly bear makes it easier to engage with the natural phenomena we set out to engage; it's a feat that can't be faked.

While it's good to experience this around grizzlies, it's even better to cultivate this feeling of "realness" in more general ways, so it's not contingent on factors beyond our control. (Grizzlies have long been absent from the majority of the Wind Rivers, not to mention over 95% of their historic range in the rest of the lower 48.) A more generalized way of describing the psychological function of grizzlies is to say they require that we care. And caring is pivotal to how we see the world around us; to whether we see it at all. When you size up a handhold because you're going to hang your weight off of it, or take the time to key out a new type of moss, or generally just feel invested in planet Earth because it's the only planet you're going to get, caring creates meaning. And meaning might be the most endangered resource of them all.

Nobody wants to be scared all the time. But paying attention requires energy, a lot of it, and long after our receptors go numb, the perception of danger remains a useful shortcut. Danger taps the self-preservation instinct, mobilizes self-interest, and, for a moment at least, gives you no choice but to pay attention. In a particularly tense moment that might look like the fight or flight response—one of the most untamable reflexes we carry within us. Meanwhile *survival*, a more general state of keenness (and a way of life for every non-domesticated animal) that regards ever-present dangers, rarely penetrates our risk-adverse society. But when it does, it fascinates, by creating a minimum-level of functional engagement with our surroundings—the kind adventurers rave about for making them feel alive. Absent the inclination or willpower required for the practice of ongoing awareness, many people need the possibility, at least, of danger to stay involved. And again, by involved I don't mean fearful, but conscious and interested. Caring. That, as far as I can tell, is why comfortable people crave risk.

Full-on danger carries other layers of intrigue. We get to see how we do with it—how the subliminal and the rational parts of ourselves interact. After the fact, it serves a reminder that we are no exception from the natural laws that shape our surroundings.[*] Personally, I learn greater empathy for other people and life forms—I imagine other types of pain, broader standards of value. It is another, more loaded question to ask what level of risk is "appropriate," and for that matter, whether or not any level of risk can ever truly be accepted. From the position of comfort and health, who can really appreciate what suffering consists of? It's the sort of talk that makes a hypocrite out of a person. When we feel desperate we are also in the moment, but it's not a moment we want to stay in.

The impasse here may be the fault of the question. So often we focus on the decision-making side of accepting risk, as though life is a sequence of yes-or-no questions. I see accepting risk as a state of mind, and for that matter, an end in itself. Given that we seek the unknown in order to find things in ourselves we can't otherwise, which at heart is a matter of broadening our perspective, the covenant of natural consequences is a beautifully efficient means. It's not recklessly dangerous, either, despite the sensational stories you'll hear. Even in remote wilderness the baseline risk of mortal danger is extremely low[**]—but you can choose to increase it if you want. If any and every risk is too much, if a person finds the very premise of natural consequences objectionable, it is only appropriate that they stick to the main road.

What I do not agree with is seeking out risks that you find unacceptably high because you carry the trump card of high technology.

---

[*] This is equally true in "controlled" environments—we're never exempted from natural laws—it just doesn't feel true. Most of the human endeavor has served to separate cause and effect by layers of abstractions.

[**] Less true in winter. Still, there is great bias in which risks we engage warlike and which ones we accept unthinkingly. How many people will read a book on defensive driving techniques before visiting Yellowstone, versus a book on bear attacks, when the actual dangers are a thousand to one?

That's what the rest of the world is about. And while there is a lot of positive social reinforcement right now to wear cameras and pull stunts in the last corners of the globe, those places are diminished for it. It's all very inspired, of course, but self-importance is the value that's ultimately communicated and reinforced, and endangered values like quietude and awareness get further marginalized. Wilderness is a place to teach ourselves about natural order and to practice relinquishing control—not the place to assert our shortsighted domineering impulses by beating the dead horse of naturalness into further submission. *But*, you ask, *what if my ability to care isn't affected by my carrying a SPOT? What if the security it offers frees me up to appreciate my surroundings more?* Then reconsider the forest, I say—the realm where life and death are made inseparable. Perhaps the "nature" you crave is nothing more than this unity.

Consider that the immaculate safety net of civilization might be robbing not only your life of meaning (you're over twenty-seven times more likely to kill yourself than succumb to some wild contingency), but vitality from the planet. Humankind's version of safety comes at the expense of a very sick biosphere. Your assumption of risk, your peace with mortality, is capable of restoring balance—but it's not going to work if you remain aloof from the founding principle of natural selection; the founding principle of life. So go to the wilderness if you're interested. But if it turns out you're going to die, don't act like it's not fair. Don't assume you can just start cueing up helicopters. All kinds of organisms will be dying all around you, that's what makes it beautiful, and to have a human die in the midst of it all—even you, who cares—is the fairest thing in the world.

◊◊◊

Jen and I returned to our ice tools on the saddle between the unnamed forks of the North Fork of Bull Lake Creek. This obscure watercourse drains several of the largest glaciers in the Northern Rockies. Deep in the southern Fitzpatrick Wilderness, its reaches have been nicknamed "the Forbidden Zone" by Forest Service employees for its lack of both radio coverage and developed trails. We were interested in dropping south—opposite from the way we came up—to check out the Sacajawea Glacier. Before deciding whether we'd take the plunge, we stopped for an early lunch.

While we ate we gazed over the lifeless-seeming landscape below. There might not have been a single vascular plant in that thousand-acre basin. The Sacajawea Glacier looked sickly, with boulders strewn across its surface and a lake of gravy-grey water pooled at its toe. The moraine holding it in marks the extent of the Gannett Advance, the most recent global cooling period that ended just a hundred and fifty years ago.[*] Though the air remained still, the smoke suffusing our vista steadily thickened. For all the rhetoric I could muster, death in the high alpine was by no means a comforting thought. By the time we finished eating no question remained. We were checking out this new fork. Was it smart or stupid? As can be said for every trip in the mountains, which in itself is an unnecessary risk, chance would have the answer. At the time, beholden only to our curiosities, we felt free enough to know it was worth it. We walked among rocks the size of Slugbugs, each one sitting on a banded pedestal of ice. Small icebergs, with the poise of glass swans, bobbed in the murky lake. A field of enormous boulders fooled us into thinking we'd left the glacier behind. Then, suddenly, the rocks fell away and we stood on a twenty-foot tall toe of ice, its bowels gutted by a rapid of melt water.

As Jen scouted a way down I noticed a bone lying out on the lip, and I gingerly crab-walked down to retrieve it. It was the lower leg of a very small quadruped—a bighorn lamb, more likely than not. The flesh and tendons were mummified, a thick lock of hair held on between the lobes of the hoof. Except for the shattered bones severing it from the lost body, it was in excellent condition. Raising the leg in my hand, before a backdrop of indifferent stone and ice, I wondered if it was a decade or a millennium old.

---

[*] The Gannett Advance is named for Gannett Peak, the highest in Wyoming, only a few miles northwest of Mount Helen.

We descended into Dinwoody Creek on the eleventh day of our trip, and followed the trail down to Gannett Creek. Beside this noisy torrent braiding through the trees, Jen found a comfortable spot to wait with our packs while I went to find Max. Max is my closest friend from Wyoming. If he could have, Max would've walked all summer with us. He couldn't, of course, but he did make time to walk with us for five days from Gannett Creek back to his place in Dubois.* Now the day had come, and we had a vague window of space and time to find one another.

Scattered over a mile of that remote stretch of trail—over twenty trail miles from any vehicle—I greeted students and teachers from Central Wyoming College. They were hauling armloads of research equipment from a horse packer's drop to their base camp: laptop computers and solar panels, buckets, tubing, and who knows. It's not what most people go in there expecting to see (we were only a couple miles from what is mathematically the eighth most remote spot in the lower 48), but at that point, it really was just another day in the Winds. I gathered from one group of six that Max was on his way, so I sat with them as they rested in a bright clearing, and peppered them with questions about their work. Bearing witness to the retreat of the glaciers, basically. Two other parties passed us during this time, both of them set on climbing Gannett Peak from the head of Dinwoody Creek. Inexplicably, a bat flew around us in full sun.

When Max showed, I was delighted to see he brought along a friend of ours from Dubois—Callie, who I worked with five years earlier. (Neil Young's "Unknown Legend": Callie deserves a song like that.) Soon there were four of us thrashing our way through the brush up Gannett Creek. We took the first and last good camp at the edge of tree line. It featured a view of Gannett Peak, softened in the smoky orange light of late afternoon, and currant bushes heavy with luminous red berries. We

---

* Since both of us work in the woods and never have our phones turned on, our planning was limited to a couple postcards traded throughout the summer. But we were able to firm it up during a chance run-in at a Jackson coffee shop the day before Jen and I started hiking. Max was warming up from a rainy night spent emergency-bivouacked with a female friend in a shallow cave on Symmetry Spire, we were waiting to meet Sam before dropping his car at Elkhart. To my great delight, Wyoming wasn't such a stranger.

picked handfuls. I found extraordinary peace in front of the fire that night, and not just because Max carried a flask. When all your needs are met under sublime scenery, when you're bone-tired and well-fed and talkative, when old friends materialize from the spruce and boulders: then the world has embraced you.

◊◊◊

That wilderness has any social function may seem paradoxical—it is so often celebrated as something opposed to society. But wilderness is nothing if not a place to be reminded of simple pleasures, and human company can top that list. Wilderness is not anti-human, "all natural." Instead, the human and non-human come together in wilderness to form a complicated relationship. In his classic guidebook, *Wind River Mountains*, Joe Kelsey writes:

> Many of us automatically express a desire for solitude and fewer "trail encounters" and "campsite encounters," but we belie our responses by pausing to chat with passersby on the trail and inviting neighboring campers for tea. I suspect that most of us enjoy encountering people who seem to belong in the backcountry and dislike meeting people who don't. I never think of the wilderness as crowded when I pass hikers who smile and exchange pleasantries, but when I pass hikers who stare sullenly ahead, pretending I don't exist, the land seems overrun.

Kelsey's suspicion is supported by the fact that plenty of people who value solitude never even consider backpacking by themselves, and very few begrudge the company of good friends. Solitude, then, is not a simple extension of the word solo, which my dictionary calls "an action or feat carried out by one person alone, for example, a flight in an aircraft or a climb up a mountain"—solitude makes exceptions for quality.

Although I try to minimize encounters in general, I wouldn't hesitate to say that even the most random people can complement not only my experience of wilderness, but even my sense of solitude. For example, an "Old Man Winter" and his conspiracy theories at Roberts Lake comes to mind; a young couple at the limit of exhaustion, whose despair brought back childhood fears of forests full of beasts and ill-will;

and all those talented and anonymous travelers who, by spinning a story out of afternoon sun and a subtle observation, have helped me bring the landscape into tighter focus. For me, solitude in the wilderness is reinforced by whatever doesn't remind me of hyper-socially-conscious hell. Natural history and authentic human interactions both do that.

◊◊◊

What people meant by solitude hardly mattered until a little over half a century ago. When Congress passed the Wilderness Act in 1964, it officially recognized a value that at the time lacked standing in mainstream culture. Along with the qualities of "naturalness" and "untrammeledness," which relate to specific management priorities, the act is just as much a commitment to preserving the public's "opportunities for solitude." Like the other two wilderness values, solitude is essentially fragile and can't be improved by the simple application of capital or labor. But its subjectivity is unusual in that it exists exclusively in terms of personal perception. The Act's inclusion of this word meant that federal land managers (people trained to calculate forage quality and board feet of lumber) were now also responsible for managing a resource that exists only in the mind. In order to do so, they needed to figure out what, exactly, it consisted of. Their attempts call to mind Justice Potter Stewart's professed inability to define obscenity: solitude is something that each of us knows when we feel it, but the conditions that preclude that feeling are stubbornly inconsistent and indistinct.

It is easiest, and most logical, to start by assuming solitude is fundamentally a function of minimizing how many people are around you. Quality and quantity often seem to have an inverse relationship in human encounters. The smile or nod requisite in a small town may be treated with suspicion in the city; I live in a community where all the vehicles wave to each other on county roads but not on Main Street. Insofar as this negative correlation is true, it is inevitable. Taking comfort in the presence of other people requires seeing them as individuals, not as representatives of an impersonal culture. It takes creativity and effort, abilities that can be quickly exhausted.

Regulating for human density is possible but problematic. For one, it limits human access to wilderness, jeopardizing another value described in the Wilderness Act as the opportunity for "unconfined recreation." Secondly, short of curating itineraries, it can guarantee nothing. People miss or encounter one another by chance. Even if you curtail use to just two groups, luck has it they'll end up vying for the same tent pad on their first night out.* But most importantly, even if a permit system was perfectly implemented, it might be unnecessary. Studies have shown that a larger number of encounters with other people doesn't necessarily result in a loss of solitude. In one experiment, 61% of wilderness visitors, after stating the maximum number of people that their sense of solitude could accommodate, didn't report any actual loss when that number was exceeded. As summarized by one academic,

> Anthropocentric wilderness inventories can only establish a wilderness threshold by an essentially arbitrary decision because the perception of wilderness quality by recreationists differs widely among individuals and is influenced by such a variety of personal factors as to defy logical analysis.

In deference to illogicalness, two alternate versions of the preconditions for solitude have been framed: in one, *encounter norms* refer to human density. Simplistic, but containing some truth. In the other, *social norms* describe how people share or don't share core values. (If we were managing for Joe Kelsey's norms, "sullen starers" would count as detracting from solitude, but not those who "exchange pleasantries.") This second concept was inspired by studies into a broader psychological inquiry: the nature of privacy.

Privacy, and its media-speak counterpart "the right to be left alone," are big buzzwords nowadays. They are championed like endangered species. They are politicized. As might be expected, they have come to refer to other things, things that can be bought and sold. A keyed-up appetite for privacy is a keyed-up demand for products and services, for

---

* In his book *The Deepest Yellowstone*, Philip R. Knight recounts just such an instance in the Gallatin Range. Two hikers catch up to Knight and his girlfriend by taking advantage of the steps he post-holed through deep July snow. They pass the two of them, and then manage to stay ahead long enough to score the only snow-free campsite on the only lake around. "Amazing how a huge range like this gets crowded with just two parties," he laments.

comforts and distractions. We seclude and insulate ourselves in larger-than-necessary homes and personal entertainment systems; we work in cubicles rather than on crews or assembly lines; we shop online. Those of means surround themselves with great tracts of land, then take up the pet cause of property rights. As Jonathon Franzen says, "Far from disappearing, (the right to be left alone is) exploding. It's the essence of modern American architecture, landscape, transportation, communication, and mainstream political philosophy." Privacy means more stuff, more attachments rather than fewer, less time alone in our heads. While Americans demand all the online privacy they can get, they simultaneously volunteer more personal information about themselves than others would dare (or care) to ask.

In 1967, the sociologist Alan Westin defined privacy as "the claim of individuals, groups, or institutions to determine for themselves when, how, and to what extent information about them is communicated to others." I think he nailed it. In the over-connected realm of modern psychology, the battle for privacy is a battle for control over self-image. It's a matter of projecting oneself, not a disappearing act. As much as I'd like to believe that privacy in the wilderness remains something very different—say, the necessarily uncalculated act of being yourself—other people will still challenge you on that. But at least they give you space to breathe in the meantime.

◊◊◊

I can't say that wilderness functions as a social lubricator without admitting it can also do the opposite.* Some people read more into recreation than just merry-making, because here, in proxy, we see the dysfunctional relationship between the human and non-human playing out in real time. I'm one of those people. Sometimes, oftentimes, I struggle to keep my charity. The part of me wounded from perceiving a thousand and one abuses of the natural resource (not to mention the planet as a whole) wants to recognize the person who's going to carve their name into a granddaddy whitebark before they do it, or the group

---

* Maybe we're best off just calling it an amplifier: fertilizer for any sentiment.

that's going to leave a four-foot fire ring piled with scorched cans before they jet out. To do so, my brain grapples for "types."

It's a bad habit. Yet stereotyping user groups on national forest land should not be compared to other, more insidious types of stereotyping. Walker, runner, rider: these are fluid identities for recreationalists to try on and play with. Everyone who partakes in one partakes in others at other times. The four of us at the campfire on Gannett Creek were typical examples: sometimes-peak baggers, pinheads, partiers, squares, or government stooges. Talking about user groups is a way to talk about different drives and tendencies within us; it is also a way to leaven the self-importance of it all. Inevitably our conversation veered toward Gannett Peak, up there in the smoke and starlight, which Max climbed a month earlier. His experience was colored by a guided group that created a large, noisy, and unavoidable presence. That got the two of us rolling on a favorite rant.

For being the highest peak in Wyoming, Gannett draws a lot of people into the Winds who otherwise wouldn't be there. (My first boss in Dubois joked we need to build a thirty-five foot cairn on the Grand Teton, to make it number one.) Highpoints attract a group of people that have a very specific goal. That's why they're called "highpointers." Some literally belong to the Highpointers Club and receive newsletters with that name, others function independently, and would resent the term—the important part is that, by definition, on some level all are motivated by the trophy, and clawing to the top of the heap is their pivotal reason for being there. It's not just mountaintops they're after but the crowns of all political boundaries; frontrunners share tick-lists thousands of items long, which disclose, among other things, hundreds of miles spent driving to bag the loftiest elevations of eight East Kansas counties in a single day. It is wrong to think that highpointers are an obvious type, that they can be identified by appearance or attitude. But sometimes you can't help but guess.

To fully indulge the caricature, highpointers demand information that will increase their chances of success. They seem nervous. They seem desperate to prove themselves. They don't seem comfortable with the mountains; rather, they seem adversarial. The successful highpointer downplays the difficulty of his ascent by speaking derisively of the mountain as though it didn't prove worthy of his ability; the unsuccessful highpointer sounds wronged, because some weatherman or guidebook author or boot manufacturer is to blame. I don't know what role social media has come to play in highpointing, but I can imagine.*

One obstacle on Gannett Peak's easiest route to the top is especially notorious among climbers. Where a steep finger of the Gooseneck Glacier meets the larger, dish-shaped body, a deep crack forms in the ice. This crack, or bergshrund, is often passable on a bridge of the previous winter's snows. But the snow bridge shrinks and sags in late summer. and some years it nearly disappears. At such times, seasoned mountaineers can avoid the obstacle by scrambling around on dry rock or trying a different route. But few highpointers come with such pluck: instead, they pack detailed maps and annotated descriptions and a black-and-white understanding of the minimum they have to do in order to "bag" the peak. It's been said that stereotypes are only ever right by coincidence—but a final anecdote will illustrate what I'm getting at. I'll never forget one trailhead register entry I saw. Six people from out of state drove (many hours) to the Glacier Trailhead. They wrote down their two license plates, their destination as Gannett Peak, and their length of trip five days. But after recording those outgoing hopes and aspirations, they'd come back, crossed out the "5", and wrote a "1". Indignantly scrawled in the margin one of them had added, "Got to Arrow Pass [six miles in] before anyone told us the SNOWBRIDGE IS OUT." The story implied by this quick little note almost floored me. Seconds passed before I caught myself standing there, staring into space, imagining the return trip this group now had to endure—backpacks still packed, trail food untouched, and a story of an adventure aborted before

---

* This sounds petty because it is. After our hike, when I got home and read my journal, I chastised myself: *that's what you were thinking about? When you were out there?* Yet I force these sentiments to the surface—to cut the syrup of romance, to admit that I was struggling with ways of seeing more than a backpack or a mountain. The goal is not to codify a type; types don't exist. Rather, it's to illustrate a problematic tendency, one that pops up in every sphere, and to which I feel terribly vulnerable. That is, motivated experience. Highpointers, unhappily for them, can be used to illustrate this universal tendency on only the most superficial level. I have more than a little highpointer in me, myself.

it even began by extreme tunnel-vision toward their goal. It just so happened that the weather that week was heavenly.

I don't hold anything against anybody who doesn't get to the top of anything. But I couldn't forgive that snow bridge group for not even wanting to see the mountains for themselves.* "Beauty... comes unsought, and comes because it is unsought," Emerson wrote. Of all the things to see out there, surprises are greater than any of them. We lose everything when we lose our curiosity.

---

* By chance, I climbed Gannett a week later and found the bergshrund abundantly negotiable, by ice and rock both. But that's neither here nor there.

4

For the next five days, the three of us (Callie had to head back first thing in the morning) wandered along the high divide. Our first view of Grasshopper Glacier—one of my highest-anticipated attractions in the range—revealed a large group of people standing on its surface, wearing orange helmets. A training group of NOLS instructors: Max recognized them from his hike in, and it exasperated him to see them again. All summer long, he said, he couldn't go anywhere without running into a group from NOLS. He orated a list for me.

Much of the popularity of the Winds can be traced to a historic moment. In 1965 an inaugural group of students from the locally formed National Outdoor Leadership School headed into the Popo Agie

Wilderness. They were led by founder Paul Petzoldt, a mountaineer with a dream of developing a benchmark program in wilderness education. It wasn't long before he accomplished just that. Exactly half a century later, when Jen and I walked into the same wilderness, as many as fifty different NOLS groups (averaging around twelve people each) were wandering the Winds at the same time. While the guiding service has diversified to five other continents and several other modes of recreation, the Winds mountaineering course is the NOLS trademark.

I find the presence of commercial activity in the wilderness to be jarring. It trips up my "social norms"—my concept of who, I think, "should" be there. Dangerous mental terrain, to be sure. But it hangs me that the clients pick the place out of a catalogue and the guides are there because that's how they get paid.* I like to think of wilderness as a place of self-determination. I refer to the Wilderness Act, which states, "Except as specifically provided for in this Act, and subject to existing private rights, there shall be no commercial enterprise... within any wilderness area." And Aldo Leopold, who wrote "the wilderness and economics are, in every ordinary sense, mutually exclusive." In summary, the market influence is to be cut out as much as possible; it's against the spirit of things. I don't know what's "possible" and what isn't, but in the Winds the standards have gone out the window. For receiving tens of thousands of user days in the Winds each year (one user day equals the presence of one person for one day), NOLS is a buzz-kill, plain and simple. Consider that the frontier closed when a territory reached two people per square mile: this one guiding service alone just about has the place settled.

I can't disagree with their basic mission: students receive instruction in the best techniques and highest ethics for wilderness travel currently known. Still it runs foul. You have to weigh this claim against the very real environmental impacts brought by spiking traffic in incredibly fragile ecosystems (they're not training a preexisting user group so much as creating one), and you have to factor in the more ephemeral taint that a concessionaire brings into church. I believe that what NOLS teaches, people can—and should—teach themselves. But people won't teach

---

* Disclosure: I've led commercial groups in the wilderness.

themselves, you point out. But does that change the fact that they *should*? There's no need to pay five thousand dollars to camp for a couple weeks on national forest, and the industry's assertion that you do is being leveraged as one of the strongest arguments for privatizing the public domain.

If you really want to get out there, enough to research what you're going to need, you will be amazed at just how little is required. Three teenagers heading up the Middle Fork trail, Coleman sleeping bags swinging from their book bags, one carrying a frying pan in his hand, come to mind. Those kids make me happier with every remembrance. What NOLS really does is sanction backcountry recreation by giving it an elite price, a social scene, a corporate polish, and some perfunctory college credit. Yes, it's the recipe for a fabulously profitable product. But it doesn't answer the question: does this have anything to do with wilderness?

There are some pretty good answers to that one, too. NOLS indoctrinates the young, urban, and wealthy in the value of public land. They also have scholarship and adult programs for people who don't meet all the criteria. In this sense, the existence of the company addresses a political reality: as much as wilderness needs to be left alone, sometimes it needs invested constituents even more. I'm slow to warm to this reasoning because I don't understand why wilderness should be any more political than it was in 1964, when 434 out of 435 members of the House voted it into being. I wish that it wasn't political. And even though it is, divisively so (21st century Americans haven't awarded the right-to-be-left-alone to anything on this planet except themselves, and where they have, other people are challenging it), I don't think the impacts of these realities should be as evident in the furthest nooks and crannies as they are. But as Max would cheerfully remind me, wish in one hand and shit in the other…

Whatever the determination, I believe we all still need to be asking: Is the outfitter thing working? (It's not a leading question. There are good ones, of course, people with a lot to share.) Is it worth it? How can we prove it's working, and that business isn't just having its way? I have a bias against NOLS that I obviously can't hide. It's based on interactions I've had, inevitable for an organization of its scale, with those who do not practice what they preach.* At such times, the noble claims of the company seem like a ruse. It starts looking like a very conceited summer camp that has gotten its way one too many times with their permit officers. I start thinking: NOLS is exactly what the ultimate corporate infiltration of wilderness *would* look like: sexy. Rich. Progressive.

It is of particular irony to pilgrims of solitude, then, that despite the astronomical user-days allotted to NOLS in the Winds each year, they are able to orchestrate their itineraries to isolate themselves from one another. It's an illusion maintained in consideration of their students, who get to feel like they're the only ones out there, and not getting marched to the rhythm of a well-oiled machine. Meanwhile, the public user, the one that seeks out obscure backcountry by their own research and means, risks bumping into one NOLS group after another in a regular procession. These unwelcome rubs with the tourist industry are augmented by all the other guided parties: nation-wide church groups and Boy Scouts and summer camps, a nearby Catholic college that runs every single one of its freshman through their own thirty-day courses. It is a land of self-sufficiency, all right: American self-sufficiency, where you have the freedom to pay for your choice of a dozen different services that will take care of you. After some trips, the range doesn't seem well-loved so much as well-marketed; the more time you spend out there, the phonier its illusions begin to seem. As C.L. Rawlins has said of the high Winds in a different context (acid rain), "only the self-deluding could find Eden up here, knowing what we know."

As we drew closer to Grasshopper Glacier I fixated on a pond pooled against its uphill side. Six feet above the water's surface an overhang projected into the air: craggy and wizened above, glassy and blue underneath. That, along with icebergs the size of sofas beached around the pond's perimeter, suggested a significant, recent drop in water level, consistent with glacial lake outburst floods Jen and I

---

*Okay, one example. After calling my job a boondoggle, and sharing an aggressive litany of complaints, a couple off-duty, self-declared instructors directed me to ignore an illegal cache of canoes (which itself is widely rumored to be the work of NOLS). "Not many people know about it," he explained. "And those of us that do, really enjoy it."

witnessed years earlier, which traced to the Grasshopper. Above the outlet of the lake—which punched directly under the middle of the glacier—the high-water mark sculpted an ice cave. Obviously, we had to go inside. Grabbing headlamps from our backpacks, we noted, happily, an absence of boot tracks in the mud. NOLS hadn't been in there; ice caves must not have any safety protocols yet.

The ceiling of the cave, smoothed by the lapping water that created it, was as polished as an upside-down skating rink. Its semi-transparent depths drew the eyes into a dizzy mirror-world of black ghosts and fleeting shadows. Vertical plunge holes interrupted the sheet, bored from the surface by crashing columns of water. This water, the uppermost reach of Grasshopper creek, ran out of sight down the constricting tunnel. The violence of its course cast a blind of vapor that reflected our headlamps back in our eyes. We explored a side chamber of fractalate ice crystals, our lights scattering into static on gemmed walls; elsewhere, an ambient translucency tricked the vision into depths that called for telescopes. On the way out I removed one crystal—a nine-inch turkey tail—so that I could take its picture. But like the plunder from a dissolving dream, I realized that the treasure of this cave could not journey back into the world with me. After a while I felt the way I always feel in caves—unsettled, out of my element—and it was a relief to return to the light.

◊◊◊

One evening, as I was setting up the tent in terrific wind, I heard voices coming from Max's spot. I didn't assume that Max was talking to other people—I assumed that he was cursing at his tent, because that's what I was doing. But after sitting down with us for dinner he recounted a strange interaction. As he was tightening his tent fly, three guys suddenly appeared behind him.

"Are you doing the High Route?" one asked.

"No—what?"

"Oh. Are you doing Gannett?"

"No," Max replied again.

"What are you doing?"

"Uh—" inconveniently, it didn't have a name. "Our own thing."

Without encouragement, the men proceeded to educate Max on this "High Route." Pioneered by so-and-so, first completed in this style on this date—they were trying what's-his-butt's variation, which entailed this and that and this. They wanted to know where they could camp, how were the passes, and how fast did we do whatever it was that we did. Max felt blind-sided by a scene he wanted nothing to do with. "I thought he was going to offer me a bowl," Max said sadly, "but he was just getting out the map to ask more questions." When the man asked if we'd mind sharing our camping area, forever-cordial Max thought he was being clear when he replied, "You know, there's a lot of room up here, and this is a pretty small spot." But soon the three were staking shelters a couple dozen feet away. (This solitudinal killshot seems to befall Max far more than most people. I guess he should take it as a compliment.)

Relieved as I was to dodge the exchange, I nevertheless prodded Max for details. His account gave support to my theory that what most people want out of trail-less areas is the chance to establish their own; purists about it being pristine when they get there, if it's developed by the time they leave, they pat themselves on the back. There's an obvious analogy to human sexuality: the virgin is only worshipped in order to precipitate her fall. Joe Kelsey calls this drive to leave a mark "humanity's irrepressible desire," and it's true that many of us leave a mark without wanting to, or knowing we want to. Even the NOLS group we saw, purveyors of leave-no-trace, camped on a moraine groomed into tent pads, the rocks piled and rolled into neat rings. Groups that follow will doubtlessly add on, building the wind breaks higher, deconstructing the wild. We took the time to cave a few back in: a token gesture.

Though there are illicit rock and wood and tarp shelters to be found throughout the Winds, most of the civilizing work done today is intellectual. Numerous books compete for the backcountry-guide market of that range alone—like this wilderness is Louisiana Territory, and all of humanity demands a pioneer to tame it. I've never read these books, but I've heard them referenced more than I've cared to. Authors name the unnamed, publicize routes, and scribble in the blank spots.* To my mind it's an obvious disservice to everyone that follows. To others, it's a question of convenience, and information worth paying good money for.

As should be expected, the digital age has allowed this tendency to explode beyond the limits of logic and into absurdity. I might've forgotten about Max's encounter, but when I got back a coworker emailed me a link to one of these "high router's" web pages. It featured, among other things, a "store." The creator, Andrew Skurka, was, I discovered, something of a celebrity for hiking very far very fast, and while we were putzing through those first weeks of our trip, several groups were racing to be the first to complete what he deemed "THE ULTIMATE Wind River High Route."

A couple things stuck out to me from his website. First, the number of ways a trip of this transcendental sort can be quantified. Apparently, the ultimate wilderness experience can be reduced to replicable data, advertised, sold. Techie trailblazers (Skurka lists four other bloggers that devised competing high routes) break down their routes into distance, vertical, and hike time, then break the hike time down further into calories required and weight carried (and, on another level, training regimens). They provide extensively inventoried lists and boost brands of everything from sweatbands to apps to gym memberships. Needless to say, they GPS every step, and by sharing this data they funnel impacts into places where little to none existed before. And they do it all for the consumer—the consumer of wilderness—who wants nothing so much as to put down what's wild. This mentality has created a paradoxical demand for wilderness areas that can be precisely defined, prepared-for, and then dominated definitively in accordance with set rules. By completing all the steps, consumer victories over the wild contingency are comprehensive and all but guaranteed. Skurka's route claims to be a best-of-the-best of the range—by selling it as such, he removes

---

* Wendell Berry drew a parallel between such literary trends and other extractive industries. "Industrialist[s] of letters," he called the information-developer types, mining "one's province for whatever can be got out of it in the way of 'raw material'…"

something that, to me, may be the only truly essential component to the whole experience. It's called "exploring."

Another surprise: the number of value judgments in his writing. Alternatives to his route are "boring," "unaesthetic," and "fail to fulfill the range's true potential." It's as though physical reality isn't nearly as impressive as his interpretation of it.* Skurka's appropriation of wildness for his products and services should be contrasted to other writers who have penned tributes to the Winds—the ones that fell in love with the place decades before they started writing about it. Even as they published books they knew there was little point in glorifying their accomplishments—that appealing to the masses or provoking the competitive edge does nothing to further the causes of the places that inspire them.

Americans need more opportunities to confront what's wild, not more strategies for dismantling it. In *Sky's Witness*, Cheyenne writer C.L. Rawlins' surprisingly personal portrait of his time in the Winds, the author bluntly states "We don't want to make history up here." Terry Tempest Williams writes, "These places of pilgrimage matter …to me because in the long view, I do not." And Joe Kelsey, once again, does everything he can to encourage people to pursue their own experience. For leaving his route descriptions purposely vague, his *Wind River Mountains* could almost be considered an anti-guidebook. He explains:

> I've tried to minimize imposing myself… by adapting my writing to what I perceive to be the Wind Rivers and their traditions. Wind River climbers have traditionally taken pride in self-reliance. Most prefer the pleasures of solving route-finding dilemmas to the efficiency of guidebook recipes. The book's primary purpose is to help you enjoy the Wind Rivers; keeping you on-route is secondary.

Little did he know how far these micro-managing recipes would go. Later, he states, "First-ascent data is relegated to the back of this book… dispelling the notion that Wind River accomplishments lead to fame." All of these writerly asides constitute invaluable gifts to attentive readers:

---

* I couldn't help but take issue here because some of these adjectives were applied to options that Jen and I had taken. So I indulged myself, and rather pathetically, compared pictures from our "unaesthetic" route to his until I was consoled.

they are reminders that the mountains come first. Only then can you too enjoy Emerson's "original relation to the universe"—the highest attainment of the wilderness experience.

But when I first studied the high route web page, one thing disappointed me more than anything else: how similar it was to our route. I could specifically bring to mind those lost-feeling pockets of terrain and know that they now had the attention of the fast and furious destination recreationalist—people like the commentator on Skurka's website who praised the determination of an "absolute best-of-the-best route… for those of us who work for a living." Jen and I felt fortunate to take our time and soak it in, doing what seemed interesting, and make on-the-fly decisions. We were able to do so, *and* work for a living, because we structured our entire lives in a way that gave us more time than it did money. We saw this dedication to the wild not unlike the mendicant's vow of poverty. By contrast, the speed hiking culture is a metropolitan force. It allows capitalism's most frenetic to have their cake and eat it too. If the high routes catch on like their creators hope, future visitors to these places will have to choose whether or not they want to expose themselves—or concede these places—to another arm of the rat race. I remembered our days up there differently after learning that, at the same time, ultraliters were trying to turn it into the next big thing. Somewhere in there, Skurka blitzed back and forth past us (we never saw him, but we did see two of the other three groups he mentioned contending for it at the same time). After giving himself nine days for the trip, he found he only needed "4.25," so he turned around and hurried across the range again. Two times is better than one, right?[*] "In the to-be-released Wind River High Route Guide, there are turn-by-turn directions, both in narrative form and in annotations on the maps…" *Okay. Credit card in hand, I'll start holding my breath.*

I shouldn't act so scandalized. It could be that what he's doing and what I'm doing are only different by degrees. Everyone wants to be a trailblazer, groundbreaker, Great Pathfinder. Everyone wants to exist at the precise boundary between what is wild and the onrushing tide of

---

[*] Ernst Jünger wrote, "Increasing haste is a symptom of the transmutation of the world into numbers." And transmuting the world into numbers, of course, encourages haste.

civilization. It hardly matters if they love wilderness, or think they do—they still want to lead the charge. In a field of pink elephantheads I talked to one woman so eager to direct me through the details of an upcoming pass she never bothered to figure out that wasn't where I was going. She was friendly; she was excited. I couldn't hold it against her.

In fact, I don't hold it against anybody I meet face-to-face. It's toxic to preach intolerance—I believe that—and I have no interest in banning certain people from the landscape, or even asking them to slow down if they don't want to. But if you think we've lost our priorities, as I do, it's equally dangerous to hold your tongue. Our culture is such that it has to be forced to look at itself. The glorification of speed is everywhere, already, and that's not a message we got from listening to these ancient mountains.*

We already miss so much.

◊◊◊

We had a couple more days in the Winds, a few more serene moments in the presence of glaciers. These visits had a bittersweet aspect to me, like holding hands with a dying relative. The glaciers continued to emanate power. But I knew they were in fast decline.** And not knowing when or if I'd ever get back, I was challenged to rue and celebrate them at the same time. We made sure to visit some melted-out deposits of *Melanoplus spretus*, extinct Rocky Mountain locusts, which Jen and I found years earlier. Still impressive—but that much more deteriorated.

How did this species that swarmed in the tens or hundreds of billions crash to extinction within just a couple decades? The naturalist Bernd Heinrich offers a compelling answer: when "the crowd itself becomes the dominant environment, and so it (like money for art)

---

* It seems I'm channeling Mary Oliver. In "The Poet Dreams of the Mountain" she writes, with rare emphasis, "All that urgency! Not what the earth is about!"

** "A corpse," Jack Turner exclaimed in the high Winds, comparing a twenty-first century Knifepoint Glacier to his memories from thirty years earlier. That one's volume is in free-fall: it has been receding thirty feet a year, and deflating six.

becomes a new stimulus," it leads to "extreme examples of animals homing to each other rather than to place, [and] the ultimate of maladaptiveness—extinction…" In other words, the Rocky Mountain locust was so successful at reproducing that the survival of every individual came to depend upon the survival of the mob. Then, with the proliferation of the mid-Western farm, the species lost important breeding grounds. Despite all the remaining habitat, their populations couldn't adjust. One can imagine how this moral may apply to modern humans: our current survival technique relies on a division of labor on the global level. Locally sustaining populations are nowhere to be found: it's a way of life that no longer exists. Like the locusts, no one knows from experience how to survive independently. When things crash, they're bound to crash hard.

In between bodies of ice, our slow progress across choppy boulder fields (evocatively known as *felsenmeers*—German for "sea of rock") offered Jen and me time to catch up with Max on two years of stories. We talked about recent trips and earlier trips and what was coming next, and then we'd let the wind take over, the sky drift over us. One day I almost stepped on a ram skull melting out of a glacier. It had full, bulky curls and deeply worn teeth. The three of us gathered around it in awe; as sacred as anything I've managed to perceive. Finally it was time to come down. After a very high camp at 13,000 feet, the ridge began to descend. Plants appeared between rocks. Down, down. They stitched into a threadbare turf, and that thickened into a cushion. There were flowers again; we could see trees. I felt relieved. Below Three Waters Mountain—the triple divide of the Mississippi, Columbia, and Colorado headwaters—we kicked our boots off in yellow grass, snacked, and pointed to every lake we could name.

Our last camp on Simpson Lake was so calm it untethered from time. Max told us he wouldn't be back in Dubois the next year, and I believed him, and now I know he was right. I looked around with the understanding it was our last best chance to enjoy this place together— the end of the Wyoming years. And that every day is your last best chance to do what you've never done before. Grey mountains rose off shores of placid water, the dusky timber drowned my pupils, there was the sunset to consider. I told a bear story of mine that took place nearby—they'd heard it enough times to tell it to me. When I went down to wash some clothes I had one of those ridiculous discoveries that make you feel like everything is meant to be. Two Budweiser Clamatos bobbed in a corral of cool lake water. When I came walking back it was a good trick to tell Max I'd been carrying them fifteen days just so that we could share them now; he only believed me for a second. We popped them open one at a time and passed them around the fire. Jen said she'll never drink a Clamato again, because there's no way they taste as good as that memory.

◊◊◊

The first leg of our trip ended with a plummeting jeep trail off Windy Mountain. From great grassy slopes three thousand feet above the Wind River, Dubois, Wyoming, our first pit stop, was clearly visible. Without the aid of highway signs counting down the miles, and no businesses anticipating our arrival in all caps, Dubois laid exposed in purely geographical context. A few pixels of metallic disruption in the center of a gigantic dusty red and yellow vista; fields of irrigated green streaking north. It looked miniscule and fragile, at the mercy of the land, and I found that heartening.

Part Two. ON RUNNING AWAY

Hikers, like Midwestern drivers, are bent on telling you how 'far' they've hiked. "I did twenty-three miles carrying fifty-one pounds." I usually advise more lateral or circular movement.

–Jim Harrison

1

At Togwotee Pass—a lightly forested saddle where Highway 287 crosses the Continental Divide—two great mountain ranges converge. The contrasts between these two ranges are profound enough to inspire parables, but the pass itself presents a lopsided comparison. The furthest reach of the Wind River Range, reaching Togwotee from the south, is unrecognizable as such. Since it rafted during the Laramide Orogeny 60 million years ago, the northernmost of its famous granites have been buried by volcanic debris, furred with lodgepole pine. The result is an undulating, nondescript ridge, dozens of miles long, which dips down to another roaded pass before rising to the first of the Winds' characteristic plateaus called Union Peak.

North of Highway 287 is the Absaroka Range—the source of those volcanics. Though unknown and unvisited in comparison to their southern neighbors, the Absarokas erupt from Togwotee with a roar. Brooks Lake Mountain (who names such heights after a water-filled depression?) looms behind a glowering thousand-foot cliff that wraps the mountain's flanks for miles, and Pinnacle Buttes, just to the east, features colorful banding, even greater verticality, and a series of fierce pinnacles trailing away to one side. These gatekeepers don't just feign to guard rugged and mysterious expanses. They actually do.

Moving southeast down Togwotee Pass, the Winds and Absarokas pull apart across willow bottoms and gridded ranchland of the widening Wind River Valley. By the time one reaches the town of Dubois, thirty miles out and 6,900' elevation, the river corridor has narrowed into a fertile slot through arid steppe. A twenty-mile wedge of desert separates the ranges. Dubois' northern horizon culminates in an icon called the Ramshorn, slender and severe at 11,635'; east of the Ramshorn, layered ramparts of the Cougar Plateau magnetize storm clouds and flaunt the icings of unseasonable snows. The glory of the Winds, meanwhile, lies obscured behind an unremarkable screen of "foothills"—one of which hosted the last few miles of our trek into town. As we braked our knees hard down Windy Mountain I gazed north toward the captivating realm we'd be entering next. Smoke from Oregon wildfires had drawn a blurry cloak across the valley (that fire season set a record in our country: more acres burned than any before), so I summoned the Absaroka skyline from memory and a few shadows in filmy blue. Just knowing it was there entranced me all over again. I wasn't over the Winds—I was remembering how much else is out there.

Five years previous, it was the Winds that drew me to Dubois. I found them boundless, spectacular, everything I hoped. But I never succeeded in making them my own. Over the following three years, as I returned to Dubois each May through November, I felt like it was the Absarokas that were bringing me back. While each range holds a lifetime of exploration, and comparisons are odious, there was something about the Absaroka's labyrinthine canyons of black timber and friable brown cliffs that got inside of me and never let up. When that's the case there's no asking why—there's only the matter of submitting oneself to the greatest conceivable power.

◊◊◊

In a town of one thousand everybody can say they live on the edge of town. Dubois, Wyoming especially feels that way. Humans fit to the land rather than vice versa. Property lines hug promontories of candy-striped shale; the waterways chatter cool behind buffers of willow. Although vanity ranches do spill over into some of the surrounding hills, nobody is (or was) calling it "the next Jackson Hole:" it was two years before I noticed that the trailer park downtown was called the Whistling Wind and not the Whistling Wino, which until then I'd accepted without a second thought.

Downtown Dubois is one mile of Highway 287—right on your way, if you're driving from Beaumont, Texas, to Choteau, Montana. Garish competition for the attention of drivers identifies it as a tourist gateway to Grand Teton and Yellowstone National Parks. Most of these efforts are hokey, 1950s style yee-haw and chuck wagon, transparent to the point of innocence. The Rustic Pine Tavern confoundingly claims to be "The Most Unique Bar in the World" (having been inside, I have less of an idea why this would be than you do). Until a fire burned half a block of Main Street on New Years Eve, 2014, the tavern faced off with a boardwalk, pillared with burlwood—its most visible storefront featured the antiquated advertisement INDIAN CURIOS spelled in "summer kamp" log segments embedded in its façade, while a storeowner there (real estate, or western gifts?) surprised gob smacked vacationers by playing unannounced ditties on an upright piano that sat on the boardwalk out front, while wearing a Doc Holiday vest. Go west a couple blocks and an enormous black pig-bear, frozen mid-roar in front of a motel, vies with a saddled and mountable fiberglass jackalope in front of the Exxon "Cowboy Store" to be the "daddy-stop-the-car" photo opportunity that will rule them all. Other contenders include a fifteen-foot tall fiberglass bison skull that forms a portal-like entrance to the laundromat, an elk statue at the KOA, a bighorn at the Discovery Center, a drugstore Indian. Dubois is surrounded by space and these weird efforts to command it make the space seem indomitable.

Most people live in a residential grid that hugs the converging waterways of Horse Creek and the Wind River. Gravel backstreets reveal this to be a town where people still work with their feet on the ground: leave the river and the trees disappear. Rabbitbrush reinforces fence lines. Horses are corralled in backyards. Garages double as autobody repair or game processing shops. Trailers beached in mineral soil impart an air of desperation. Sheds, shops, carports, and outbuildings crowd lots without design—everything plays defense against the openness of the air.

The town's online motto is "Where real cowboys work and play"— and there really is a rodeo every week of the summer. Chief Washakie called the site "warm valley," and this sentiment lives on in the town's other slogan: Valley of the Warm Wind. Nobody will argue the wind, but plenty of times the adjective "warm" seems like part of a joke. On the hottest days, however, when you catch an even hotter anabatic rising out of the Bighorn Basin, it is memorable.*

For all these reasons, Dubois feels like a town with few pretensions, and I was happy as always to get there. We walked in on a hot Monday afternoon, all of us out of water, and it felt like the desert it is: just seven inches of precipitation a year. Max was renting half a duplex across town with three other seasonal workers. It sat two blocks from the barbed-wire fence separating houses from hayfields in the small, flat, valley formed by Horse Creek. When we got there, we were locked out—the first and longest leg of our journey officially ended when our host crawled through a side window to open the door.

There, Jen and I laid over for a day. We mailed our crampons and ice axes home, along with books we'd finished, and a Rocky Mountain locust cushioned between the taped-up bubbles of an egg carton. It may be hundreds of years old. We bought groceries, greased our boots, attempted to eat a whole box of ice cream, and had dinner at the house of an old friend and coworker. I'd envisioned the day as one of glorious

---

*This effect is additionally memorialized in the town's original name, Neversweat, a reference to the way this summer wind can evaporate perspiration before it gets the chance to run. In a classic conflict of rural and urban sensibilities, Neversweat was rejected by the post office as uncouth, and replaced by the current name—homage to Fred Dubois, an Idaho Senator who already had one town named after him on the western edge of the ecosystem. Noted for his vindictiveness toward Indians and Mormons, residents took revenge by purposefully mispronouncing his name. Forget your French, it's DOO-boyz.

relaxation, but instead, the town—small as it was—over-stimulated me. It was a reminder of what I've always known: I'm far more relaxed walking than trying to relax. Mindlessly, I flipped through all the magazines on Max's coffee table. During a brief stint at a library computer, I forgot my password and was locked out of my email due to "suspicious activity," then wasted that idle corner of the day on the phone trying to get back in. At night, I tossed and turned in our too-hot bedroll on the basement floor—the lawn would've been great but for automatic sprinklers. After a second night of awful sleep, we made a valiant effort to finish the pile of groceries we'd impulsively bought before finally getting out the door at 8:30. Even though we were leaving free lodging and generous acquaintances behind, it was a relief.

Our path started along the gravel streets of Dubois. We cut through the parking lot of the Forest Service warehouse where three guys I hadn't seen in years stood around the tailgate of a pick-up. I was struck with a sheepish feeling: half the truant flaunting it in front of his teachers, half the entitlement of the footloose before the wage earners of the world. None of them actually gave us a hard time, not even jokingly. Instead, we exchanged greetings, Jen and I banked a few words of encouragement, and we kept it short, never removing our packs. As I walked away, this reminder of the workaday made my degree of freedom freshly poignant. I was reminded why the two of us prefer the luxury of time over the luxury of material—why we only stayed any place long enough to leave again, by dusty trails.

That Forest Service compound, where I lived for two summers, abuts a horse corral, and on the other side we followed ATV ruts that run between the hayfield and the Dubois Badlands. When I lived in Dubois, the Badlands exerted a strong and constant presence. I used to wander them after work, and they are more than large enough—about thirty miles long, with generous tracts of state and BLM land—to absorb an entire day here and there. Considering they also host the town's dump and cemetery, the Badlands feel surprisingly out there; when you are alone in them you feel very alone. Fire-colored shales belong to the

Willwood Formation and date from the Eocene. In an interpretive brochure for the Dubois Badlands Wilderness Study Area, Hannah Hinchman wrote, "Sometimes a lucky hiker will find an old—very old—bison skull sticking right out of the wall. If she's very observant, she might find a fossil tooth from an eohippus." Locals do still pull charms from its mealy soils. The last spring I worked in town, an immaculate chert knife went on display at the drive-through liquor store.

While Jen and I walked out the base of a bluff, a rancher, cruising around the hayfield on a dirtbike and knocking on sprinklers with a wrench, gave us a wave. We were about a mile out. Then I realized I forgot my water bottle. Just a flimsy, disposable 20-ouncer, it was a completely integral part of my system. I'll be back, I told Jen, as morosely as possible. I felt incredibly dumb. It was embarrassing enough to go past the Forest Service shop again, and my old shop-mates, fifteen minutes after our proud departure; the shame of the privileged vacationer came flooding back. And it sucked to make Jen wait in the dirt. On top of it all, I just hate forgetting things, how absent-minded I can get. My initial, optimistic jog devolved into a power walk. By the time I got back to Jen I was flustered and overly anxious to make up for lost time. The sun had gotten hot.

We climbed out of the Badlands to a county road that rolled away into powder blue sage. The way my stiff boots played on the flat ground was irritating my feet, but I ignored them as a sort of penance—I was trying to find the walker's peace again, pulling my brain apart, putting out thought fires. When the reverie of the road becomes as elusive as sleep to the insomniac, physical exhaustion appears a useful surrogate. It's silly. What was wrong? I don't know. Town had bewildered me again. When you're worked up, it makes visceral sense to keep pushing on ahead—marching the legs—whether it's improving the situation or not.[*] We aimed for the mountainous horizon. The only map we had for the next two days was one I'd drawn by hand. We'd have to leave the road soon, ford a creek, flow toward the high ground. Slowly, eventually, I reentered the refuge called simplicity of motion. By afternoon we were

---

[*] As Robert Macfarlane puts it, "Sometimes walking can be the mind's subtle accomplice; at other times its brutal antagonist."

back in our element, bushwhacking through a short canyon of the Wiggins Fork that dragged a line of tall cool spruce across blinding gold prairie. We stopped when we found a good camp under big trees, and that's where I had to face the fact I now had blisters on my feet. Five of them total, on our seventeenth day of walking, when I'd hardly gotten a blister in years.

I called the blisters psychosomatic: as my mind wrestled conflicting feelings, my body, unable to help yet insistent on trying, made the tension manifest. Counterproductive feedback loops are a side effect of modern minds occupying ancient bodies. Even though our problems can no longer be addressed with a thumping pulse and clenched fists, still the body insists on doing something. So why not dump out sweat, strip you of your reason? As the doctor Lee Goldman writes, "Four traits specifically helped our ancestors survive as they tried to avoid starvation, dehydration, violence, and bleeding... [today, they] are directly responsible for more than six times the number of deaths they prevent." My misfiring traits were apparently designed to both help me avoid some unseen violence and gear me up for it. In the days to come, as I struggled to bring my blisters under control, they grew to the size of quarters. It's never too late to feel like an amateur.

Grateful to be out of the sun, we both took our only naps of the trip and woke to rain on the tent. When it stopped, I stepped out in the sweet smelling forest and started a cooking fire in damp sand. Still, there was peace out there. Still I was stumbling into it.

◊◊◊

As the landscape emptied out and my blisters nagged on, I regarded the rubbing sores as reminders of how, despite the purity of my surroundings, my thoughts belonged to humanity. (My preoccupation with user trends, as we passed through the Winds, was all the more evidence I needed.) From this acknowledgment, other realizations followed: civilization is my inherited mode. It provides the terms by which I think. If I don't want to spend so much time hung up on social norms, if I really want my world to be one of sandstone and hawks and the respiration of winds, I need to be intentional about it.

Modern science is just now confirming what so many have long intuited: experiencing nature has quantifiable therapeutic tendencies. We can even cut out the word therapy, loaded as it is, and say that spending time outside is good for you, in the most general sort of way. It is preventative medicine for some of the greatest health epidemics of modern, first world countries like our own. But few people will go outside because they've been told it's good for them. They will go because it feels nice. So let us enjoy the knowledge that three days of wilderness backpacking might give us fifty-percent improvement on creative problem-solving tasks, but let us pay attention to our instincts even more—which often have the answers all along, even when they can't provide proof.

I've always felt overly sensitive to social contexts. Throughout my childhood this manifested in excruciating shyness, an unstoppable blush, mild phobias, a loner streak, and a haunting call to the forest. My history of accommodating this tendency is also the story of my life: plunges in and out of peer groups, confrontations with the great lonely. Today, I have a fuller appreciation for the delicacy of the balance between culture and greater creation that's right for me. I underestimate the complexity less often, now.

Time in tranquil scenery promises tranquility of mind. Yet finding oneself helplessly fixated on the single most distasteful detail in a place of magic and wonder appears to be more common than not. Lynx, a Washington woman who founded the Stone Age Living Project, shared this representative story from a student: "I'm walking through the wilderness wearing deer skins and carrying all my food in a tump strap, yet Britney Spears is still pumping in my head!" Soon your only company is the ordeal you tried to escape, and Sartre's "Hell is other people" reveals its cruel corollary: hell is your inability to deal with other people. Running away has made it worse.

Another affront to inner tranquility unfolds from a famous quote by the historian William Cronon: "'Nature' is not nearly so natural as it seems." On planet *Eaarth* (Bill McKibben's name for a "post-natural" Earth, in which environmental systems respond to human-caused disruptions, rather than vice versa), wilderness doesn't just *happen*—cultural trends and the decisions of land managers allow for localized expression of some human idea of wilderness. In this sense, the words "nature" and "wilderness" may still have meaning, but they no longer encompass what we wish they did. "An idea, a relationship, can go extinct, just like an animal or a planet. The idea in this case is nature, the separate and wild province, the world apart from man to which he adapted, under whose rules he was born and died...[and] the meaning has changed." So our world's topsoil is washed away, the weather is haywire, the animals and plants are out of sorts. By design, a discarded Kit-Kat wrapper remains more eye-catching than our most elegant wildflowers. Refuge is nowhere.

I feel this at times. Yet I also believe that we, the inheritors of millennia of written history, must speak the world as we know it. The loss of a "perfect" nature or wilderness becomes irrelevant;* the question of how we ourselves can know and value nature remains. Answers to this question run the gamut. Some say it's impossible to know nature: the level of understanding we seek was voided by the self-knowledge that literally or figuratively evicted us from Eden. Others believe such knowledge is not only inevitable, but all encompassing: the same patterns shaping the modern environment shaped the primitive one (as Wallace Stegner pointed out, "Nobody ever tamed or domesticated or scientifically bred us"), hence we *are* nature. But the only interesting answers that I can see are the ones that relate to actual choices we make.

Although the word nature is mired in a house of mirrors, I feel loyal to it. For the same reason, say, that Thomas Mann celebrated the word love:

> Is it not well done that our language has but one word for all kinds of love, from the holiest to the lust of the flesh? All ambiguity is therein resolved: love cannot but be physical at its most holy; it cannot be impious at its most physical... The meaning of love then varies? In God's name, then, let it vary. That it does so makes it living.

For encompassing all kinds of nuances and grey areas, the word "nature" is not alone. What word doesn't? Specifically, I support the current, overly loaded, even flawed connotations of nature that are

---

* How such relativism blinds us to the further slippage of standards is another, more serious topic.

currently in use. People know what you're talking about—you have to give them some context, of course—but the gist is non-human. Or if it is human, unconsciously so. Making peace with this ambiguity beats running circles around the tiresome fact that the line between human and non-human has not been completely settled, because it never will be. Such distinctions remain useful. For one thing, they help illustrate how the present informs the future.

Insisting upon the naturalness of humans (and thereby making the word "nature" so general as to be meaningless) downplays the role of human accountability. Being all-natural is a free pass to do whatever we want. It means this planet's sixth mass extinction*—which is going on as a specific result of our way of doing business—is as natural as anything else. It means that DDT is as natural as bald eagle eggs. Meanwhile the basic, third-grader version of the word nature holds that the proceeding evolution of almost the entire suite of existent species is natural, whereas the disappearance of thousands of forms of life each year is not. "Natural" differentiates between what is because it evolved that way and what is resultant of choices we make. It doesn't matter that we'll never fully grasp the degree to which this is the case—only that we acknowledge the obvious examples, let them inform our future decisions, and keep looking closer. And yes, maybe the inexorable human drive toward self-destruction is the most natural thing imaginable: we might then ask if that's a dimension of nature we might still overcome.

Everywhere Jen and I walked were human traces, and everywhere those traces were tangled through with autonomous nature. Everywhere I faced the choice—an anthropocentric or biocentric reading of my surroundings. Both were engrossing and valid. While I was finding that my mind tended toward the anthropocentric, and it was good to admit this, for reasons of sanity I realized that I also needed time with the older story. The one about planet *Earth*, with only one "a."

It might be just as well to say that the nature I was seeking a relationship with was my own—that finding an internal place where I

---

* Between one and ten thousand species go extinct each year, perhaps one thousand times a "normal background rate."

could be present and inhabit my senses and my own physical potential, where I wasn't distracted by thinking errors and guilt, required an immersion in a lot of other places, first. Non-human nature is a place where abstractions, placed in the sharp light of day, find their true places in the order of things. A spray of red fir needles is better fire starter than a hundred dollar bill, and therefore more likely to save your life. Walking on, I never stopped getting pop songs stuck in my head—but at the same time, the wealth of organic form and wild agency became steadily realer to me. It helped that, as our immersion in mountain living grew longer and deeper, the people we saw and the impressions they make became fewer and further between. My tally from sixteen days in the Winds was 235 first-hand human encounters in about ninety different groups—and that would end up accounting for almost ninety percent of our backcountry human encounters for the entire trip. Hallelujah.

2

The Absaroka summits that are prominent from Togwotee and the Wind River Valley, stunning Pilot Peak in the northeast corner of the range: these are the exceptions. Ultimately, the range is withholding. It guards its secrets well. Day hikes don't scratch the surface, and even the trailheads may require long approaches on road surfaces that deteriorate into miles of committing 4x4 or ATV ruts. So you have to want them. And it's not immediately evident why you should. There are few of the destination-type features that backpackers like to shoot for before turning around—most glaringly, a paucity of lakes compared to neighboring ranges. Perhaps a couple dozen named bodies of water are sprinkled throughout the entire Absaroka Range, Wyoming to Montana, while 1,300 stud the (smaller in area) Winds, while the Beartooths, on the other side, boast a similar density.* While Absaroka peaks are exceptional in their way, most require nasty bushwhacking followed by nastier scrambling. More than anything else, there's just country in there—country that goes and keeps going, the kind that ducks analysis and sheds plans. Dangerous creek crossings. And bears—some locals won't go in there for the bears.

As befits a land of little use, abundant wildlife, and incredibly remote and inaccessible tracts, the Absarokas elude concise definition, and that even goes for their macrocosmic footprint. Unlike most mountains ranges, which consist of a linear backbone, the Absarokas hook and divide and plateau, then taper off into expanses something less than mountainous, all factors that make their exact parameters a matter of confusion. Efforts have been made to distinguish among these parts: the author and geologist Burton Harris refers to distinct Wapiti, Hoodoo, and Ishawooa Ranges, while Thomas Turiano recounts a long, dynamic history of Absaroka aliases that includes Snake Mountains, Snow Mountains, Great Yellowstone Range, Sierra Shoshone, and Stinkingwater Mountains. The confusion is still with us today. The name "Absaroka Range" is variously applied to a mountainous area in Montana, a much larger one in Wyoming, parts of both or each, or all of it together. Depending on how they're defined, the Absarokas might even be the largest subrange of the Rockies—but that's just one more imprecise label that only alludes to their psychic vastness. It might do just as well to say that the second highest peak in the range is not marked, let alone named, on any Forest Service map.**

---

* Absaroka breccia is soft and very erosive. A disproportionate number of former Absaroka lakes, scooped out much like lakes in bordering ranges during the last glacial advance, have already filled with sediment.

** I would be remiss not to quote consummate mountaineer Lorraine G. Bonney's description, from her book *Wyoming Mountain Ranges*:

> The Absarokas: Wyoming's mysterious, least known and most misunderstood range of mountains. The Absarokas: a vast confusion of crumbly snowy peaks, deep canyons, disoriented streams and haunting tales... How is it that this vast mountain wilderness called the Absarokas can still be described, in the words of Aldo Leopold, as "a blank spot on the map" even though it is as well-mapped as the rest of Wyoming? It is because this

For many, natural devotion is based less on rational understanding than an aura of mystery. In this resource the Absarokas abound. But devotion grows with the application of knowledge, and when it does, it grows in layers of complexity that can't be conceived by one imagination alone. To understand what the Absarokas are really about, it is good to start with what they are made *of.* No mountains can be discussed independent of their geology (as Annie Dillard says, "It is all, god help us, a matter of rocks"); over this framework, ecological and hydrological attributes drape like sheets.

Like Yellowstone itself, the plateau over which these mountains tower yet always defer the spotlight to, the Absarokas are volcanic in character. It would be logical to assume that their history is related to the Yellowstone Hotspot—that material ejected during the excavation of the Yellowstone calderas piled into mountains south and east. It would also be incorrect. The pre-history of Yellowstone can be traced in an arc of volcanic plains that swing to the southwest through Idaho and Oregon, while the Absarokas have their own volcanoes—vents that plod in a northwest-to-southeast diagonal for about one hundred and forty miles, and predate Yellowstone geology by tens of millions of years. When Absaroka volcanoes were active over 40 million years ago, the Yellowstone Hotspot appears to have been located somewhere between its oldest definite caldera, the 19 million-year-old McDermitt on the Nevada-Oregon line, and 70 million-year-old volcaniclastic piles in the Yukon that bear a similar chemical fingerprint. Or maybe it didn't exist yet.

The latest expression of the Yellowstone Hotspot has blown three holes into what would've otherwise been the western Absarokas, between 2.1 million and 640,000 years old. (A fourth, diminutive explosion created the West Thumb of Yellowstone Lake, just 174,000 years ago.) By obliterating over nine hundred cubic miles of continental crust, these blasts prepared ground for the relatively mountainless but biologically fertile hub of the ecosystem we now know as the world's first national park.

---

awesome region is perhaps the least known, the least understood, and certainly the least appreciated mountain area in the state.

The origin of the Yellowstone Hotspot goes deep. It is a plume boiling up through the eighteen hundred-mile thick mantle from the earth's incomprehensibly remote core. The Absaroka origin story, on the other hand, is more superficial but no less dramatic. Beginning about 125 million years ago, an oceanic plate called the Farallon collided with the west coast. Over dozens of millions of years, its islands scraped off to create exotic terranes of the Pacific coast's Insular Belt, while the rest plunged down into the hot mantle. Portions of the plate melted into superheated plumes and ballooned upward.* Unlike most subranges of the Rocky Mountains which, like the Winds, rose during the Laramide Orogeny about ten million years before the Absarokas, these plumes didn't just hoist the earth's crust. They burst through it.

As the North American Plate drifted about one-and-a-half inches a year across Absaroka vents, a line of volcanoes formed. Their expansive floods of ejecta define the Absaroka Volcanic Field of today. In a setting uncomplicated by preexisting topography, this field would be synonymous with the Absaroka Range, but the volcanoes happened into a scene already crowded with other mountains. That's why Two Ocean Mountain, the northernmost and least characteristic peak in the Wind River Range, is a castle of striated conglomerates: it is a foster child of the Absarokas. It also explains why the Wyoming Absarokas looked so familiar to me the first time I saw them. That pastiche of welded, coffee-colored cobbles streaked in rust, lavender, and silver isn't much different from parts of the northern Gallatin Range visible from the streets of my hometown. Other affected ranges include the Owl Creeks, the Eastern and Western Beartooths, and the Madisons. The grand total is a sprawling "volcanic province"—or as John McPhee wonderfully puts it, "a spinning pinwheel of geology, with highlights flashing from every vane."

One of these preexisting mountain ranges was hit more directly than the others—with Absaroka lava and debris flows "filling valleys on the north side of the range and spilling over the top of the range to the south" until it was completely subsumed. The great Wyoming geologist

---

* NASA has modeled the current shape and position of Farallon's remains, twisted and stretched like ghostly viscera beneath America's east coast.

David Love uncovered this story during research for his master's thesis in the 1930s. He suggested renaming the southern flank of the Absarokas the "Washakie Range," where a surge of sedimentary layers—similar in character to Wyoming's Overthrust Belt, which includes the southernmost ranges of the GYE—remains entombed.

Considering the fact that the Washakie Range is topped off and interwoven with Absaroka volcanics, and the present topography offers no clues as to where one begins and the other ends, his proposal has added to the confusion of the place. Various maps take up the name in various ways—sometimes, the entire Washakie Wilderness is labeled the Washakie Range; other times, just a ribbon along its southeastern front. It could be that, by serving as a reminder of what's unique here, the title is worth the added confusion; that names should slip on the landscape and not fit too neatly. I just haven't personally taken that moniker up in conversation. But I will say the lost range can be seen most colorfully exhumed in the vicinity of the Absaroka Trail, which connects the Wiggins Fork of the Wind River with the East Fork. There, plum, cream, and ochre slopes break away from their backdrop of brown, atop which Wiggins Peak sails like a giant peach.

All told, the Absarokas were active for several million years. During that time they laid a bed of debris that approaches two miles thick. In the nearly fifty million years since they went cold, the great volcanoes have been completely dismantled, dissected by glaciers and dissolved by thaw, but nine thousand square miles remain covered in volcanic debris—enough to cover the entire planet two inches thick—along with the unique floral arrangements that take to their potassium-rich soils.

◊◊◊

The next day I stopped consulting my map. A landscape bereft of names is full of integrity, and we faced it silently, two passing mortals.

I was starting to sense some of the objective rewards of long, contiguous walking. One of the most obvious advantages is that, as opposed to walking the same distance in parts, it cuts a few car trips out of the equation. Millions treat the Yellowstone road tour as an end in itself, but for the hiker desperate to get his or her feet on the ground, every hour in the car is but a necessary evil. Road travel can be excruciatingly slow in Yellowstone traffic, so much so that it can influence one's experience away from the road, as well. Suspense builds expectations and a demand for results. Weekend warriors justify lost time by seeking reliably exciting experiences. It gets to the point where only the most highly reputed, conventionally beautiful, or novel attractions will do. You've probably heard it referred to as, "getting the most bang for my buck."

If we had to drive hours each time we hiked in the Greater Yellowstone, or if we only had a couple days at a time, Jen and I never would've walked the couple of dozen cattle-stomped, beer-can-littered, and sun-bleached miles that we did between Dubois and our trailhead. But after setting ourselves up to do so out of necessity, we found it more than worthwhile. As Alfred Barron wrote in *Footnotes, or Walking as a Fine Art*, in 1885, "If we are reverent and receptive enough, one place is as good for a walk as another." And of all those equally good places, our setting was occasionally quite spectacular. We passed a log cabin, sod roof collapsing, eaves insulated with blue jeans. Then a limber pine that had died back to a single arm, and that arm became a new tree, flexing hard muscles into the direction of wind. And we saw more birds of prey than I thought possible—as stern and silent as spirits, they oversaw our passage with noble postures and unblinking stares. Such territory melts the line between wilderness and civilization, and illustrates how both work together—or clash, as things may be. Whatever its classification, everything was equally *there*, couched in the order of things.

We hadn't gone a hundred yards up the East Fork Trail before I deviated onto a small rise. My gaze wandered southeast to a scene I knew well. Three other years I'd taken nearly the exact same picture from that spot and, in the process, formed some illustration of time. A group of lodgepole saplings in the first image, taken during a cold May drizzle, succumbs to bark beetles and flames red in the second; the creek jumps from an east to a west braid in its wide gravel channel. In the third picture, the dead trees are grey, the sun glares hard, and a shrunken river slithers down the middle. Meanwhile, the surviving trees grow—it's a picture of survival as much as mortality, a collaborative cycle. As I framed the scene for the fourth time, I realized a reference tree in the foreground had disappeared over the cutbank. Years had passed since I'd last stood there; all the pictures I hadn't taken weighed like regret. Sometimes it seems like there's nothing more important I could do with my life than bear witness to the way that time washes the land.

This is an age of consumptive movement, transportation cheap and fast. It's not likely to last long. Everything urges us toward knowledge of a plurality of trivia rather than the relationship between place and time—our larger predicament reflects that. I often play these two value systems off one another in my head: quantity comes at the sacrifice of depth, while isolation can breed ignorance. In the search for a balance, I find places I never want to leave—but when I do, I find more. And there are times traveling when I would trade the whole world for a dandelion's sense of home: its terminal grip on one handful of earth no less than the contract of life.

The balance we seek is personal, but I suspect my generation errs on the side of motion. At least, I know that I have: it's fashionable and exciting. During hungry times, driven by the assumption I can assimilate substance and redemption from mere novelty, it's the dimension of time I take for granted. When I neglect it in my worldview, things catch up, sadness comes in. In planning our days, Jen and I didn't avoid places we'd been before as a matter of principle. Some places we were eager to explore, others we couldn't wait to get back to. Passing a remembered campsite or creek crossing can touch off cascades of memory, and then it seems that every place worth visiting is worth visiting twice—while each investment of time and energy beyond that pays off in additional richness and depth. But we didn't get far up the trail before a ridge to the east caught our eye and we knew it was something we had to try. Our previous experiences in the area emboldened us to spend the next couple days wandering off-trail.

As we climbed out of the creek bottom, our view opened up to the west. Over Steamboat Ridge I could see the upper walls of Bear Creek, torched in the twenty-some-thousand acre Norton Point Fire of 2011, and I considered how not a single thing out there was simply the way I remembered it. It was all somewhat how I remembered, and also somewhat different, an intermingling of imperfect memories and unforeseen changes. Memory may provide a useful foundation for looking at the land, but every fresh look will challenge it with a revision. (I'll also say that, for providing false confidence, half-baked memories can be worse than nothing.) I felt grateful the Absarokas weren't too new to me—that there wasn't such a glut of alien novelty to numb my attention span. Instead, memories dwelled behind every ridge, memories with lives of their own—shifting, spatially adjusting in a finely tuning mental map, then fractalling into finer details.

◊◊◊

From the top of Crow Ridge, our view emptied ocean-like to the east. We neared the eastern edge of the Absarokas, where the skin of the earth softens into high rolling prairies of the Owl Creek Range. There, dual treelines—one, low, defined by temperature and aridity, and the other, high, defined by coldness and desiccating winter winds—nearly converge. It created the illusion that, rather than edging out of the alpine, we were still rising into some atmospheric desert.

A pair of dark, harsh summits studded the center of our fresh vista. Dome Mountain and Washakie Needles are the southeastern-most volcanic vents of the Absaroka formation; compared to the surrounding topography they look raw and superimposed. Although their names suggest a study in contrasts, their profiles make them twins, and indeed, they are the offspring of a single dissected volcano. Washakie Needles, the higher of the two by just sixty-eight feet, does have a sharper, truncated summit, but knife-edge ridges scouring the west and south faces of both mountains are the strongest defining feature of each.

Washakie Needles is sometimes said to be the site where Chief Washakie, leader of the Eastern Shoshone for sixty years, went on a three-day vision quest in 1850. As illustrated by his son Charlie on an elk hide eighty-two years later, the quest provided Washakie with insight into the future, much of which can be considered prophetic. Though only a handful of trappers and explorers had visited the Northern Rockies at that time, in his vision, "Washakie could see the Iron Horse, carriages without horses, and men flying"—suggestions of the trains, automobiles, and planes that would soon disfigure the western environment almost beyond recognition. Baffling changes, ambiguous power, dark magic—these nightmarish images demanded, if not admiration, some other sort of humility or respect. A spiritual guide helped Washakie to an interpretation. It was agreed, "The Great Spirit [was telling] Washakie he could not fight the white man but instead the Shoshone would have to live peacefully with them." Faith in his vision equipped Washakie with an unequivocal answer to one of the most consequential decisions of his time: whether the tide of white immigration should be fought to the death, or accepted diplomatically. As Washakie modeled for his people what such acceptance could look like, a procession of equally impossible decisions began to unfold.

Despite little or no direct evidence indicating Washakie Needles was the site of this historic vision quest, one glance at its otherworldly grandeur says it *should* be the spot. Rugged and isolated, it seems logical that from a place of such expansive panoramas the powers of insight, clairvoyance, and revelation are sure to follow. Before we could approach the base of the mountain, Jen and I had thousands of feet to lose and regain. The first leg of the process, descending into Owl Creek, was a tedious affair. While we gained Crow Ridge by one of the features that the high Absarokas are most beloved for—an expanse of rolling alpine tundra—we now had to pick down through the attribute for which they are most dreaded—an anarchic mountainside of layered volcanic rubble.* It's been called kitty litter for its skittery instability; I call it Absaroka ball bearings. It feels like a mountain of bonded gravel, in which each crumb is designed to blow under one hundred pounds of pressure. Even when eroded to an unassumingly low angle, the rock remains unpredictable: bad footing salted with loose debris. When you go down, you go down hard, and it's especially miserable with a heavy backpack.

When we reached the safety of the alpine basin below, we couldn't help but notice the tremendous amount of elk scat fertilizing the turf. Then we saw a group of fourteen of them: big chestnut bodies milling on a ridge. After those took off, another group appeared in a different

---

* The degree to which tiered bedrock typifies the Washakie Wilderness is indicated by its original name: the Stratified Primitive Area.

direction, and the next two hours, walking down through fir and spruce, remain the elkiest of my memory. Bulls sequestered with cows in isolated glades came charging out to investigate our footsteps; cows with calves dozed along florid strips of spring-fed forbs; unseen herds rumbled behind blinds of timber while issuing their peculiar mews and barks. It was a welcome inversion of our time in the Winds, where every animal sighting was worth writing home about and human encounters were a dime a dozen. Here was the headspace I yearned for: a world where what was "real" was millions of years of natural selection and geologic phenomena, not the whims and furies of people impatient with one another.

◊◊◊

At 38.8 million years old, Dome Mountain and Washakie Needles are the youngest mountains in the Absarokas. After they were brought into creation, the Absaroka volcanic plume cooled, never to break the surface again—and the two monuments were left standing in shared isolation on the edge of the expansive Wind River Basin, the last in a long line. In this sense, Washakie Needles is a surprisingly appropriate memorial to the last traditional chief of the Eastern Shoshones, who died in the valley below. Chief Washakie's death on February 20, 1900, aged somewhere between 98 and 104, was the end of an era. His friend Reverend John Roberts, awfully down-to-business, wrote in a memorial,

> I am greatly grieved to report the death of an indian churchman, Washakie. With Washakie the chieftainship of the Shoshones has passed away. No successor will be appointed to his office. The present policy of the government in dealing with indians is to break up the tribal relations and to deal with indians as individuals and to prepare them for citizenship.*

---

* Though Chief Washakie's son Charlie Washakie also came to be known as Chief, the title was hollow. When Charlie sought to make his chieftainship official he was bluntly informed by Captain H.G. Nickerson, "The indian wars are all over, and there is no need of indian chiefs." Decisions affecting the tribe were handed to a six-man council. It's possible the intuitive guidance of a warrior chief really wasn't suited to the decades of soul-crushing political battles that lay ahead of the tribe—but then, it's hard to imagine what was.

It deserves repeating that Chief Washakie led his people—variously referred to as the Eastern, Wind River, or Washakie Shoshone—for a solid sixty years. In that time, they changed—from an autonomous group of buffalo hunters, centered on the Black Fork of the Green River, to a deeply disrupted culture, confined to a compromised rectangle of land with the Northern Arapahos, their historic enemies. Throughout these transitions, Washakie's dedication to coexistence was evident. The Eastern Shoshone accommodated the demands of the US military and white settlers as well as any native culture could.* This may appear the inglorious path to all who will never be tested in their recitation of the all-American maxim, "Live free or die." Rather than complacency, however, Washakie exemplified a disciplined survival strategy, one that was appropriate to a community that held precious few options. Diplomacy spared the Eastern Shoshone the worst violence of the Indian Wars and left them with what today is the seventh largest Indian Reservation in the country.

It's important to remember that, in the decades preceding the first white immigration, most of Shoshone homeland was already in turmoil. Feral horses had migrated from the southwest only a few generations earlier. They brought with them great hunting advantages, long-distance transportation, and an influx of intertribal conflict and warfare—basically, earth-rattling upsets to an age-old way of life. It's known as the equestrian revolution. While the Eastern Shoshones adopted some of the nascent Plains culture, they didn't exemplify it to the degree of their enemies—the Sioux, Cheyenne, and Arapaho—who ranged widely in a powerful alliance, and constantly tested the fortitude of neighboring tribes. For Washakie's tribe, small and hemmed-in compared to their adversaries on the plains, the utility of powerful new allies was too obvious to ignore.**

---

* The chief of the Crows, Plenty Coups, had a premonition similar to Washakie's, which was also interpreted to mean that an alliance with the whites was the only way his people could remain on the land they loved. Meanwhile, neighboring plains tribes such as the Arapaho, Cheyenne, Lakota, and Sioux declared war on the invaders, and in turn were among the most violently persecuted tribes in America.

** Which is not to say that the Shoshone lacked in warrior spirit. One of Chief Washakie's best-known exploits is battling a Crow chief one-on-one on present Crowheart Butte. It is

It also helped that a precedent for negotiating with whites came from within Washakie's own culture. Sacajawea, who is buried in the tribal headquarters town of Fort Washakie,* mediated not only the first encounter between whites (the Lewis and Clark expedition) and a Shoshone tribe (the Lemhis of Eastern Idaho), but a mutually beneficial encounter, at that. It was dumb luck for Lewis and Clark that the long lost-sister of Cameahwait, once abducted into servitude by the Hidatsas, lost in a game of chance, and then married to the trapper Toussaint Charbonneau, was to become their sharp and cooperative guide starting in North Dakota. It was luck again when, passing through Lemhi territory, they ran into Cameahwait, who was by then a chief: the explorers got to play the role of "rescuers" (even though they were the ones being guided), and were rewarded with horses. Shoshone-white relations remained more or less amiable after that.

Chief Washakie commanded the bearing and respect to achieve remarkable solidarity among his tribe. When he forbade armed conflicts and retaliation against trespassing miners, hunters, and wagon trains, it worked. Unfortunately, the whites weren't as predictable, and Washakie had to walk a precipitously fine line between compliance with capricious U.S. military orders and negligence as a guard of his people's interests. By 1867, a gold boom sprouted the towns of South Pass and Atlantic City in the middle of Shoshone country. While the Shoshone leader's patience and civility was widely recognized and praised in official reports ("...like George Washington in bronze," said Lieutenant Colonel E.E. Hardin), one suspects these qualities were less appreciated than taken

---

general consensus that he cut out his opponent's heart and held it aloft. Some versions go on to say that he then ate the raw organ—which wouldn't be unheard of. Frank Linderman wrote, "I knew an old warrior who told me that he had once eaten a small portion of a human heart, the heart of an especially brave enemy, and that he had seen this done more than once when he was a young man." Another time, when Washakie was over seventy, he responded to taunts from his hotheaded warriors by disappearing for days, and not returning until he carried seven fresh enemy scalps.

* It is not known whether the Shoshone woman, who died in Fort Washakie at the age of ninety-five and whose gravestone reads "Sacajawea," was the same one who guided Lewis and Clark. Journals and adoption records suggest that the better-known Sacajawea died sixty-nine years earlier, in South Dakota.

advantage of by many military officers and reservation agents who, even when not outright hostile to the interests of Native Americans, ultimately answered to the impossible expectations of the American public and the firebrand politicians they elected.

In one sense, the designation of the Wind River Reservation was a great success for Chief Washakie, the end that justified his means. It secured a coveted hunting ground for the Eastern Shoshone (the same one for which Washakie had once slain a Crow chief in single-handed combat), while other tribes that utilized the area were removed to reservations in other states, or otherwise driven to the margins. But if it is to be considered a success, it is only a relative one. It wasn't nearly enough land to support the tribe's traditional way of life, especially as whites methodically slaughtered the buffalo toward extinction, and the reservation's area was reduced by 665,120 acres within twenty-eight years of its creation. (Other losses followed, some were restored. Today it's about 2.2 million acres.) Little to none of the promised restitutions for these reductions actually came through, and while the Eastern Shoshone grew hungry and destitute, Washakie strained to remain compliant. The introduction of an enemy tribe to his impoverished nation was a final indignity to Chief Washakie.

Today, the Wind River Reservation is home to about twice as many Arapaho as Shoshone.[*] A sort of bureaucratic shotgun marriage hitched the two together. On November 29, 1864, Colonel John M. Chivington's Colorado Volunteers massacred 105 women and children, plus twenty-eight men, in a Cheyenne and Arapaho camp on Sand Creek in eastern Colorado. The deliberate planning of the incident, and the ghastly executions and mutilations that ensued, are certainly among the most disturbing on record. It drove the involved tribes into a wide scatter north and south. By 1872, with the Arapahos fragmented into numerous bands, the government sought a place to isolate those still willing to consider their terms of "peace." One cooperative group was shuffled to the four-year-old Wind River Reservation for the winter.

---

[*] Many other Shoshone people from the Greater Yellowstone, including most of the Sheepeaters, ended up on the Fort Hall Reservation along Idaho's Snake River Plain. They share Fort Hall with members of the Bannock Tribe.

From there, it was out to the Pine Ridge Reservation with the Sioux, and in 1877 back to the Wind River Reservation, with Chief Washakie's consent, to spend another winter. But come spring, the government didn't provide anywhere else for them to go—and with Washington working to dismantle the existing reservations, a new one was out of the question.

Chief Washakie never stopped insisting on the terms of his agreement: that the Arapaho presence be temporary. The broken promise rankled him; it compromised his legacy as protector of his people's interests. He never offered an Arapaho his entire hand to shake but two of his fingers, a sign of distrust. (The traditional Shoshone word for Arapaho was *sa:'idïka*, which translates to "[he]-eats-dog.") And he continued to plead with visiting politicians, winning their admiration, bringing tears to their eyes, but never improving his lot. When the Shoshone Reservation Agent James Patten justified lumping the antagonistic cultures together, he unapologetically explained, "Washakie and the head men, though they dislike bitterly to divide their property with other bands, have too great hearts to say no." Whenever Washakie met with another diplomat, everyone knew who was the bigger man.

In his last years, Washakie's foil was an Arapaho chief named Sharp Nose. These two leaders, never to befriend one another, shared a common fate in the impoverished Wind River Basin. Never again to ride wild and free, clash in combat, or stir the plains into storms of color, the chiefs of the respective tribes struggled to reimagine life in boxes, the way demanded by whites, as they watched a thousand generations of traditional wisdom bleed away. After living through greater cultural eviscerations than we dare to imagine, many "took the other road home" with some sense of relief. Sharp Nose, the last traditional chief of the Arapahos, passed away just fifteen months after the last traditional chief of the Shoshones.

Washakie's historic position and willingness to compromise immortalized his name across the Wyoming landscape. Before reaching Washakie Needles, Jen and I traversed the Washakie Ranger District and we rock-hopped Washakie Creek, we walked through the shadow of Washakie Peak and were swallowed by the Washakie Wilderness. The list of related place names goes on and on. There's recognizable truth in poet Marc Beaudin's words, "In all our histories, the true heroes have no monuments"—at the same time, Washakie's plethora of monuments doesn't exempt him from "true hero" status. Rather, we should keep in mind that only one quality of Washakie is being recognized, one that was useful to whites, and the ubiquity of his name doesn't correspond to some exceptionality that justifies all the names omitted. So little is known about the Arapaho leaders Sharp Nose, Dull Knife, Little Wolf—let alone their forgotten comrades. It shouldn't be so easy to escape their equal truths.

It occurs to me that Sharp Nose would be a more appropriate name for Dome Mountain.[*] Though overshadowed by Washakie Needles from the Wind River Basin below, it is as powerful as its twin, and Dome offers even deeper views into the wild heart of the Absarokas.

The summits stand only half a mile apart; a gulf yawning fifteen hundred feet deep divides them.

---

[*] Not that this would be preferable to reinstituting traditional Native American names. For example, the Shoshone called Washakie Needles *I'sawë*, or "coyote penis." Variously described by anthropologists as "an inchoate being of undetermined proportions" (Paul Radin), an "erotomaniac" (Robert Lowie), and "Trickster, Imitator, First Born, Old Man, First Creator, Transformer, and Changing Person… conjoined good and evil" (Lopez), enigmatic Coyote was equally celebrated and joked about across many native cultures, his virility truly the stuff of legend. As one Western Shoshone creation myth concludes, "Coyote was the father of everyone"—and this reading suggests additional layers of significance for I'sawë/Washakie Needles.

3

An ascent of Washakie Needles' sharp summit cap begins on a sloughing skin of rubble, and culminates with a steep climb up a block of treacherously fractured dacite. "Fifth class," as climbers say: you're using your hands as much as your feet. Dacite has a high percentage of silica and very little iron, which makes it lighter in color than better-known volcanic lavas, and flashy with large crystals. It is formed from molten oceanic crust—easier to find in the Southern Cascades than west-central Wyoming—and offers a telltale clue to the origin of the range. Most importantly to us, it's far more stable than it looks, especially when compared to the ubiquitous Absaroka breccia.

The mountain remains obscure despite its prominence. The first time I drove from Lander to Dubois, returning from a Forest Service training in the back of a crowded crew-cab, my eyes latched to the great pyramid lurking back of the horizon. "What's *that?*" I exhaled—and nobody could say. I couldn't believe it: these people had worked there for years. That said, the logical access to the mountain is across the Wind River Reservation by roads that aren't open to the public, so few end up anywhere near there by accident. The day that Jen and I stood on top, I was surprised to find that, in the three years since I'd last been up, only one other group had signed the summit register.

Back down at our packs we took an early lunch. Hunched below the ridge against a strong west wind, a sudden clatter of rocks put me on the alarm. About a hundred feet away, directly behind us, a sow grizzly with three cubs pawed through the broken rubble of the mountain's north slope.

A few decades ago this behavior would've taken bear researchers completely off-guard, like it first did Jen and me. Here was a family of enormous omnivores hanging out, just under 12,000 feet, in some of the most barren-looking moonscape imaginable. There were absolutely no visual clues to suggest these bears were hot on the trail of one of their favorite food sources—one that is, gram for gram, more nutritiously rewarding than the 260-some others that have been documented. (Tactfully, humans have been left off this list.)

Army cutworm moths hatch on Wyoming plains. In late June they migrate west, as many as three hundred miles, to pollinate the spectacular array of alpine wildflowers along the Rocky Mountain Front. After drinking nectar all night they spend their days sheltered from ever-present winds in fields of rock. By mid- to late-summer the moths are living nutrition tablets—the closest thing to an ideal nutrient ratio as a bear can find. At seventy-two percent fat, twenty-eight percent protein, and one percent carbohydrate, these diminutive, dust-winged lepidopterons, licked from mountainsides, build fat stores that carry grizzlies through months of winter hibernation. That doesn't, of course, mean that finding one moth is as rewarding as finding one dead bison. But when conditions are right, the insects can be found clustered in the thousands—sometimes comatose from the cold—and a single bear will eat 60,000 in a day (each averaging one half of a calorie) when given the chance. In one month, an expert moth-eater can obtain *half* of her yearly calories.

Because this behavior went unobserved through many years of intensive grizzly research, it has been suggested that mothing became something of a lost art during the "dump era" of Yellowstone bears. If that's the case, it's enjoying a wildly popular comeback. Ever since a sow was tracked by a radio transmitter to "one hell-of-a-spot to get to" in 1985, alpine sightings of grizzlies—and the occasional black bear—have become more and more common. The most grizzlies Jen and I have seen on a summit is fifteen; I talked with a Wyoming Game and Fish employee who'd counted fifty-nine. As has been noted at other such food bonanzas, grizzlies eating moths are relatively non-competitive. It is family-friendly: especially popular for sows with cubs. In the coming week, Jen and I would see an additional eight grizzlies feeding in the high alpine of three different Absaroka peaks.

Two days later, prior to noticing a sow with two cubs digging in the talus near the summit of a 12,400' peak, we inspected fresh pits dug in the tundra. Piles of bear scat near the holes were variously composed of plant fiber, insect parts, or both—apparently the omnivores were complementing protein courses with starches and greens, the Cous biscuitroot being especially plentiful. While it's nice to think the grizzlies were getting everything they needed up there, it's just as likely that some were driven by desperation. Many of their other food sources were crashing in widespread ecological turmoil: it was another bad berry year, a bad pine nut year, a bad year for cutthroat trout. Bears would be hit by cars, trapped and relocated, and shot by gun-toters "in self-defense" in record numbers all throughout the ecosystem that year. I couldn't know it at the time, but in less than two years they'd be stripped of the protection of the Endangered Species Act.

◊◊◊

Years ago, a hunter—from the only group we encountered on a six-day Absaroka walk—asked Jen and I if we'd seen any bears. It's a common conversation starter. After I unthinkingly shared the when and where of a very recent black bear sighting, he stared over my head with a twisted smile and said, "We wanna shoot it!" Ever since then I've resisted such questions, figuring I'd rather lie than turn my wandering into reconnaissance for what are usually guided hunts.[*]

A couple miles out the ridge from Washakie Needles, Jen and I were shocked to see a human figure suddenly break the skyline. In the final approach we could see that he was set up with a Therma-Rest and a spotting scope. Finally we noticed a horse camp below, a pack-string on the way—all things unimaginable a couple of minutes earlier. But this was bighorn season, and big trophies and big dollars are the two most predictable draws for those venturing the Absarokas. We couldn't avoid walking right through this hunter's scoping spot. When we did, he was astonished to find that we—that anybody—would be up there if not to hunt.

"Well, have you seen any sheep?" he asked.

"Just a few ewes on Washakie Needles," I replied. Nobody hunts ewes because they don't have status symbols on their heads; we saw nine rams about twenty minutes earlier.

"Really? You didn't see any rams along that ridge you just walked?"

"No. No, we were just—watching our feet!" I said, caught in my lie. I guess he'd been over there earlier, then left when he saw us coming, our progress scaring the rams away. He leaned back on his pad with a smile.

"All right. It was nice to meet you two." He was gentlemanly. I told him the same, and we walked on. I guess my fib didn't cost him anything one way or the other; the question that remains is why he even bothered to ask.

◊◊◊

As we skirted the eastern edge of the Washakie Wilderness, rising and falling thousands of feet in canyon after canyon, we entered an

---

[*] Hunter banter, after all, is rarely intended at face value. A poker face and a good deal of skepticism are only prudent.

utterly unique environment of colorfully mineralized mountainsides and scarcely a tree to be seen in any direction. We were in the Wood River Mining District, once headquartered in the ghost town of Kirwin at an elevation of 9200', and now mostly de facto wilderness. Even among boomtowns Kirwin was quick to bust. (An especially high "metabolic rate," as Wallace Stegner would say.) Hunters first discovered gold there in 1890—but their difficult-to-access find languished for twelve years, while funding and logistics were worked out, before finally catching a wave of enthusiasm. Kirwin climaxed as a town of 200 in 1904.[*] By the winter of 1907, only one company was still working the valley's three-thousand-foot mountainsides when a deadly avalanche swept through the settlement, destroying company buildings and killing several workers. The survivors packed up and vacated. Standing there, it's all too easy to imagine. You can also tell that something special stayed in the ground just by looking at it. The colors are what I remember first and best, colors of flames, sulfur, ash.

From the head of the Wood River, it's your choice of three passes into the upper Greybull River: a living gallery of western history and myth. Sheepherder cabins rot in folds and hollers, Sheepeater hunting blinds crumble on ridges with forgotten names. The river hosts the most significant population of genetically pure Yellowstone Cutthroat Trout, a sub-species of the Wyoming state fish threatened throughout much of its historic range by introduced non-natives. And the black-footed ferret, two years after it was officially declared extinct, was rediscovered on the lower Greybull near the town of Meeteetse in 1981. Today, there are four populations of this mustelid all descended from the Meeteetse

---

[*] This sentence could've read a lot differently. In Rick Reese's *The Greater Yellowstone: The National Park and Adjacent Wildlands,* he describes how, in 1984, over 2300 claims existed in the Washakie and North Absaroka wildernesses—many of them staked in a regular gold rush as the window for new patents in federal wilderness approached its twenty-year deadline after the passage of the Wilderness Act. At that time the Forest Service was giving American Metals Climax (AMC) the green light on an open-pit copper mine just above Kirwin. The mine planned, among other things, to decapitate 12,012' Bald Mountain. AMC's P.R. proffered an imaginative consolation to outdoorspeople: removing Bald was in everybody's best interest, they said, because it would create "a better view of the more impressive Spar Mountain." Ultimately, it was market prices that made the mine less than viable.

group, and the Greybull area keeps doing what we need it to be doing: expressing the function of all its irreplaceable parts, in a reservoir of the type of wildness that used to be everywhere.

It's only fitting that Ernest Thompson Seton chose the Greybull as the rearing ground for Wahb, the protagonist of his classic 1899 children's book, *The Biography of a Grizzly*. Here is evidence the Craigheads were not the first to appreciate the permeability of park boundaries to wildlife: two of Seton's characters hash out the surprisingly far rovings of grizzlies while watching Wahb feed at Yellowstone's Fountain Hotel dump.

> "That! If that is not Meteetsee Wahb, I never saw a Bear in my life! Why, that is the worst Grizzly that ever rolled a log in the Big Horn Basin."
> "It ain't possible, for he's here every summer, July and August, an' I reckon he don't live so far away."

"The wildest part of the wild West," Seton calls the Greybull—which wasn't to say it was the most isolated from settlement, but hosted some of the most viscious scrapes between civilizers, their quarry, and everything that stood in their way. Seton's character is modeled on an actual bear given that name by ranchers; a "cattle-killer," Wahb is shot five times throughout Seton's story, trapped three (narrowly escaping a fourth), and kills two men. Most notably, *The Biography of a Grizzly* fictionalizes one "ripped from the headlines" incident, ascribed to the real Wahb, which took place along the banks of the Greybull. Varying newspaper accounts from 1892 describe a mortally mauled trapper named Phil Vetter, who crawled back to his cabin to pen a goodbye note to his friends and family… a note punctuated with spatters of blood. The note's legibility deteriorates as the man succumbs to his wounds, before finally breaking off mid-sentence.

Seton's imaginative personifications of animal characters landed him at the center of a literary controversy in the early 20th century. A new breed of writers, believing that nature writing should educate as well as entertain, branded him a "nature faker." Birds in his stories set their own broken bones with mud compacts; Wahb outwits the ranchers by teaching himself how to release leg-hold traps. But it's Seton's willingness to extrapolate Wahb's feelings that makes *The Biography of a*

Grizzly an enduring illustration of the Greybull today: "No one meets a friend in the woods" is the motto his ruggedly-individualist protagonist adopts early on. And so Wahb grows into a cantankerous old bachelor, settling scores against bobcats and black bears, echoing the same sensibilities of the reclusive miners and range hands whose log cabins he plunders from the upper Wiggins Fork to Little Piney Creek. More than a couple of these expressive ruins can still be visited today—meanwhile, the politics of isolationism and dog-eat-dog competition flood outward from such symbolically traditional strongholds as Wyoming: the Cowboy State, and reddest of them all.

◊◊◊

Weather reaches the upper Greybull after wringing itself out over a hundred miles of westward ridge and plateau. The basin rain shadow starts there, even though Francs Peak—by far the highest in the Absarokas—is further yet to the east. When we entered the Greybull via Yellow Creek, we saw sagebrush growing at 11,000'. The high-desert feeling was exaggerated by the fact that several of the largest upper tributaries of the Greybull held no surface water. Instead they rumbled, faint and Stygian, from within deep beds of gravel. Only scattered stands of trees clothed the canyon bottom, segregated into whitebark on the east side and Engelmann spruce on the west, and one species was decimated by bark beetles as much as the other. By the time we descended to what would be a productive tree line, the forest was scorched out by the Venus Creek Fire, which ripped nearly 30,000 acres up the canyon's dusty walls in 2006.

We never would've imagined it at the time, but the small bull moose that Jen and I saw browsing brushy cottonwood saplings in a Greybull canyon would be the only moose we'd see on our entire trip.[*] This, in contrast to a trip of comparable length that Gary Ferguson wrote about in the early nineties: "Over the five hundred miles that I walked through

---

[*] Needless to say, our sampling was anything but scientific. On a two night trip into an area along our route the following January, Jen and I saw ten moose. But that was even more unusual.

the Yellowstone Rockies, the moose became an extremely important animal to me, a creature that I saw on nearly every leg of my journey." Go back another fifty years, and in 1938, one Eugene Young counted seventy-six in a single day along the Yellowstone River.

The simplest explanation for our lack of moose is that there really aren't as many as there used to be. A theory put forth by Dr. Dan Tyers, then a biologist for the Forest Service, blamed the profusion of recent forest fires in the ecosystem. Consider subalpine fir: a staple of the moose's winter diet. While almost every other animal moves down in elevation during the winter, some moose move up. Subalpine fir is slow to recover from a burn. It is a late-successional species that must wait for pioneers like lodgepole pine to provide them with shade, so well-developed fir forests around Yellowstone are often hundreds of years old. Beginning with the 1988 fires, an exceptional percentage of this type of forest has recently burned in the GYE.*

Subalpine fir isn't a moose's first choice for food, but it became especially important in the twentieth century, when preferred forage species were decimated by a gross overabundance of elk in the ecosystem. Many of those plants are rebounding with the return of the wolve—at the same time, more moose are getting eaten. Look at moose throughout the rest of the country and the picture gets increasingly dire. In western Montana, *Elaeophora schneideri*, "the arterial worm," is carried by horseflies that thrive in the increasing number of hot and dry days every summer. The worm blocks blood flow in the heads of moose, and it can lead to blindness and the loss of extremities. In New England, the same warming trend is encouraging an explosion in ticks. The parasites colonize a single animal in the tens of thousands, and the local expression *ghost moose* refers to animals so anemic they're going white, and scraping off their coats in agitation. In some areas, less than one-third of the moose calves survive their first year.

---

* This doesn't make fires "bad," or out-of-the-ordinary. Before 1988, moose numbers may have been unnaturally high from generations of thorough fire suppression and predator control—a theory supported by trapper journals. A natural regime of regular, un-fought fires would also have reduced the likelihood of cataclysmic "super fires," and thereby supported more moose with a larger diversity of vegetation.

Even if moose numbers do stabilize, however, they still serve as a reminder that, even on land afforded the greatest levels of protection, the natural equilibrium has been upset many times and in many ways within our lifetimes. Even greater fluctuations are to be expected as the ecosystem oscillates toward a theoretical "new normal." We can be sure only that it won't look normal to us.

◊◊◊

For four, long, physical days, Jen and I unknowingly fell into step with one of the largest elk migrations in the ecosystem. In doing so, we missed bumping into a small film crew who, earlier that season, documented on foot and film the biannually trodden paths of the Cody Herd. This diffuse collection of several thousand animals winters on the high plains of the Rocky Mountain Front, east and southeast of Cody, then migrates west for fifty exceptionally rugged raven miles into Thorofare country. Elegantly prepared data from the Wyoming Migration Initiative leads me to suspect that there might not be a more transcendent expression of the GYE's function as a living system than such migrations. The tangled runners of pathways the Initiative has mapped, connecting high to low, desert to forest, show "how [the ecosystem] breathes," as Arthur Middleton says, the biologist who led field research on the Cody Herd. Indeed: their paths resemble capillaries. Another migration biologist, Joel Berger, compares such spatial knowledge, passed between generations of ungulates, to "human language." By that, he means it is both fluid through deep time, and terribly vulnerable to even a short interruption.

Days on the trail proceed with a satisfying logic. That your labors are getting you somewhere is self-evident. Even if the ultimate destination is an impossible distance away, even when the forest is deep and devoid of landmarks, each step carries tangible progress. It's not just about progress toward a goal, but tiny ends in themselves, because every step is also an opportunity to see something new: another possibility of discovery.

The logic is so intuitive because walking worked in step with language to become one of our oldest and most persistent metaphors for the greater human experience. (Take a look at how many self-help books riff on foot journeys in their titles.) As Peter Matthiessen summarized Taoism, "To become one with whatever one does is a true realization of the Way"—and how beautifully this applies to moving up a trail. Because the trail—a record of linear movement draped over three dimensions of land—is nothing less than a description of how land-dwellers seek and find in the world. It is a documentation of impetus and desire, a trajectory of curiosity. It links things according to their relative value to us, even if what is sought after is as general as distance, or as evasive as the horizon.

The symbolic potency of trails can partially be explained by the sheer bulk of our genetic history that has been spent negotiating them—whether in transit between points, or seeking along their continuums. Everyone knows that trail building is not unique to our species, but it is also easy to forget. On one outing, after I identified a muddy rut as an elk trail, my friend refused to believe me. It must have looked too familiar, too human. Yet even ants create trails, and commendable ones at that, logging corridors of grass stems and removing debris until their routes look swept and paved. Maybe it says something that, after humans, cows do the business best of all—stomping in trenches that override our own, with the capacity to terrace entire hillsides. Trail making is a transcendent expression of life on earth: it is the way that mortal entities, patterned after the landscape, pattern the landscape in return. If this claim seems outmoded, consider the extent to which the trail's modern equivalents—roads, sidewalks, and hallways—pattern your physical existence, and the extent to which our business of making them changes the face of the world.

After we left the Greybull River Trail we found and lost others. I lost the Piney Creek Trail in an uncleared, overgrown burn—then in no time picked up a braid of cow trails, and there were the wild, reckless cattle that made them. Higher ran elk trails, trails that cut to the chase, gobbling elevation in the least number of steps, and when I had enough of that it was time to make my own. It wasn't a good one (my blisters were bothering me)—just a thread of disturbance, rippled through the dimensions, the grass slowly rebounding behind us. It need not be repeated. We walked to see what was possible, walked to see what it was that we wanted. When the scenery floods your pupils and there isn't a thing you'd change if you could, a passage writ in disappearing ink is all the legacy you'll ever need.

◊◊◊

Boulder Ridge is a ribbon of dry grass that dangles between projecting knobs of volcanic rubble. Jen and I followed it down for miles, and thousands of vertical feet; somewhere along the way, we encountered a conspicuous line on the ground. Composed of rocks, mostly, grown into the alpine tundra, it diagonaled across the ridge for a couple hundred feet before terminating in a pile of heavily weathered logs and root wads.

This unassuming structure once served as a bighorn sheep driveline—a trap. More than a dozen others have been described in the area, and they correspond to what remains excellent sheep habitat today: Jen and I counted twenty-six bighorns in the hours preceding our discovery. The best-preserved drivelines tell their own stories. One ruin consists of converging walls near tree line, five feet high with a bit of an overhang, that funnel toward a corral where concentrations of sheep bones still lie. The structure we saw on Boulder ridge isn't nearly so elaborate, probably because it didn't need to be. One hunter could've stampeded sheep along the ridge, as the wall forced them out onto the steep and crumbling mountainside. Other hunters could've hidden behind a small outcrop at the end, catching them off balance.

In the summer of 2003, a research team led by Chris Finley traveled up Boulder Ridge to document the little-known site. Finley's team soon found a second sheep trap along Boulder Ridge, as well as a deteriorating wickiup in the nearby forest. They also inventoried a few small artifacts before heading home. Lawrence Loendorf and Nancy Stone, in their excellent book on regional alpine archaeology called *Mountain Spirit*, record what happened next. In a perfect demonstration of the fragility of the archaeological record, just ten days after Finley and his crew left their discoveries on Boulder Ridge, the site was swept by wildfire. Anxious to see the damage done, the crew revisited the site as soon as they could the following spring. They found both destruction and revelation. The wickiup and a wooden portion of a driveline were incinerated, while thousands of additional artifacts were laid bare in the ashes of the former forest floor. Most of these artifacts were tiny flakes of non-native stone, created during the manufacture of tools. Others were more unusual: the team found pieces of pottery and soapstone vessels, bone scatters, and a wide inventory of tools—including metal that originated with European traders, indicating that the trap was used into historic times. A beaver mandible suggested at least one visitor might have been enlisted in the fur trade. All in all, the site became one of the most significant in understanding the unique, mountain-based culture of the Sheepeaters.

The name *Sheepeater* may sound derogatory, but it is translated from a traditional method of identification. Sheepeaters are a subgroup of a large family of Shoshone Indians who speak Numic languages that trace to a common ancestral population in eastern California. Over thousands of years, Numic speakers moved north and east in a series of migrations to become the Northern Paiutes in Oregon, the Comanches in Texas, and many groups in between. Shoshone groups settled in the northeastern parts of this "Numic Spread"—some in Idaho, some in the mountainous parts of Greater Yellowstone, and others on the western edge of the Great Plains. The primary protein sources they found in these places said a lot about who they were: the area they settled, their primary industry, the kinds of tools and resources they might have to trade. In a word, preferred foods summarized distinct human cultures as well as anything could. In the canyon country of Idaho, Shoshone that learned to take advantage of the great salmon runs became the *Agaidika*—or "salmon" (agai) "eaters-of" (dika). Groups that adopted the bison-oriented Plains Culture, such as the Eastern Shoshone, were known as *Kukundika*. *Tukudika* was the name given to high-elevation dwellers, from the GYE to central-Idaho, and it literally means something closer to "meat eaters." But Tukudika suggested—and was sometimes elaborated as—"(bighorn) sheep eaters."

There is no doubt the Sheepeaters made extensive use of the bighorn. Bighorn range described their homeland—a rugged spectrum from deep canyons to high mountains, precariousness being the common theme. Bighorn hides provided them with one of the strongest and lightest available forms of clothing, and ram horns were key to constructing sophisticated hunting bows—bows that excel by modern standards. At the most thoroughly studied Sheepeater site—Mummy Cave, on the North Fork of the Shoshone—researchers found ten times more bones from bighorns than from mule deer, and few from any other ungulate.

Like so many other animals, bighorn numbers crashed from overhunting and disease during the Euro-American conquest of the west. By the 1890s, fewer than 300 were estimated to remain in the lower 48, and at least one subspecies went extinct. Meanwhile the Sheepeaters, an innovative group widely respected for their superior trade goods and spiritual connections to powerful landscapes, became not only impoverished but the targets of derision from so many champions of Manifest Destiny. Well into the 20th century, there were historians that dismissed the tribe as fictional.

◊◊◊

Somewhere along the western Absaroka front, not far from where we walked, is what is so often referred to as "the most remote place in the lower 48." No impregnable fastness of topography, it's part of an area known as the Thorofare. For native people and trappers traveling into that complex region south of Yellowstone Lake,[*] the Thorofare comprised the central artery of a straightforward migration corridor, one favored by trout, beaver, bears, elk, and wolves alike. In other words, it was not remote to them—that's why its name is an unconventionally spelled synonym for "primary road." And despite its modern claim to fame, one could make the case that it isn't remote today, either.

The Montana author Gary Ferguson spent a summer volunteering there with a friend in 2001, which he documented in a book, *Hawks Rest*.

---

[*] Today, the Thorofare is split between Yellowstone National Park and the Teton Wilderness—which is adjacent to Grand Teton National Park, but does not include any of the Teton mountain range. In his farewell tribute to the area, *A Week in Yellowstone's Thorofare*, Michael Yochim uses the name Thorofare to encompass all contiguous protected roadless areas around the Thorofare itself, including the Washakie Wilderness, Teton Wilderness, and southeast Yellowstone Park.

As for solitude, he writes: "Beautiful as it may be, this most remote region in the lower 48 is by far the busiest slice of backcountry either of us have ever seen." A "cowboy version of Burning Man," he says elsewhere, with slight hyperbole. Ferguson then offers a short history of the surprising reputation of the Yellowstone River's uppermost valley. "By the early 1960s... There was a nearly unbroken line of camps" lining its inviting central meadow. A decade later, "Ranger Gordon Reese was contacting on average a hundred people every week and spotting close to 400 horses and mules. 'Almost without exception,' [Reese] writes in the logbook in July 1979, 'everyone I talked to this summer brings up that there are a lot of people around.'" (Since the 1980s, some recreational uses have exploded, others have diminished. Visitation to the Thorofare seems to be significantly lower today.)

Hawk's Rest may be far from any trailheads, twenty-five miles or so, but the miles are easy ones, and a routine commute for outfitters. Pack strings set out in the morning along paths beaten so hard they could walk them with their eyes closed (just stick to the smell of horseshit, the suck of mud on the feet), and reach camp with a fresh supply of beer, batteries, and propane by that evening. The nickname for the approach from Turpin Meadows says it all: "The Giddy-Up Highway;" the approach from Deer Creek goes by "I-90." The epicenter of the Thorofare is a confluence of valleys called Hawk's Rest, after a forlorn-looking promontory splitting the uppermost Yellowstone from Thorofare Creek, which carries a comparable volume of water. On top of Hawk's Rest sits a permanent radio repeater installation. A large Forest Service cabin, a Park Service Ranger Station, and a Fish and Game cabin, all with their associated outbuildings, are connected by a triangular grid of trails. Conventionally, all or some are occupied by rangers or volunteers throughout the summer and fall, and may also play host to trail crews and biological surveys camped outside. Grassy meadows ensure efficient helicopter service during medical emergencies, because Yellowstone National Park—where the nexus of supreme remoteness is located—is not managed to wilderness standards, despite its recommendation for that status. Yellowstone Lake and its Southeast Arm eat up about 15 miles of the Thorofare's isolation, and boats motor around most of that—including the last bit, when it's considered necessary for "administration."

In what sense, then, *is* the Thorofare remote? If you got out a map of the lower 48 states,* and wanted to draw a circle that didn't include any roads, the biggest circle you could draw would be centered there. The Thorofare maximizes this single variable. Intuitive as that variable may be, and surely indicative of one thing or other, it tells us amazingly little about what remoteness consists of. Why would remoteness be affected by motorized land travel and not motorized water travel?** Or an abandoned logging grade on the other side of an impassable ridge, more than an administrative outpost of corrals and cabins? It's no surprise, then, that the Thorofare's claim to "most remote" is contested. But none of the other candidates find consensus on a basic definition of terms. I read a report arguing that the most remote place in the lower 48 is Hinsdale County, Colorado. Hinsdale's qualification hinges on an algorithm that compares the population densities of counties. In other words, the most remote *place* is used as a synonym for the most remote *county*—a sketchy deduction if there ever was one. Although Hinsdale County is less than a third of the area of either Park or Teton counties—the two that meet in the Thorofare—it was calculated to be more remote because its county seat, Lake City, has fewer people than Cody or Jackson. The article reporting this discovery also announced the most remote spot in Hinsdale County: Rock Lake Basin, in the 488,210 acre Weimenuche Wilderness, about seven miles as the crow flies from the nearest Forest Service road. In directing readers there, the article makes reference to passing "loads of peakbaggers," as this spot is trail-served, and close to a base camp for several of Colorado's crowd-ravaged fourteeners.

Upon reading this article, my first impulse was to take up Hinsdale's challenge: compare it, really, to other places in the southern Absaroka block, which is guarded by approximately 2.5 million acres of contiguous roadless land, including the Teton (585,000 acres) and Washakie

---

* Alaskans must read these debates and laugh. Their numbers blow ours out of the water.

** Actually, the Thorofare is such an outlier that it retains its number one position even if the circle is shifted to exclude the large, motorized portion of Yellowstone Lake.

(704,274) Wildernesses, two Wilderness Study Areas with pristine character, plus the undeveloped southeast corner of Yellowstone National Park. Entire realms, seven miles from roads and double that—triple that—is what the place is made of.

But the more important take-away is that a determination of "most remote" is so subjective that dozens of places could make the same claim, by tailoring their own criteria. And it goes without saying that all of them would also have their asterisks. Alaskan wildernesses, huge on an entirely different level (Wrangell-St. Elias Wilderness, 9,078,675 acres, would be the 42nd largest state), provide exceptions for snowmobiles, chainsaws, and even the construction of new cabins if their use is associated with subsistence hunting—plus airplanes and helicopters for other reasons. Death Valley Wilderness, which holds the title of largest in the lower 48, is actually shattered into dozens of smaller wildernesses with dirt roads, highways, visitor centers, and parking lots sitting between them.* The Frank Church-River of No Return, the second largest, has over two dozen landing strips within its borders. Many are on private ranches, while those on public land make no attempt to regulate the small private planes that treat them like RV parks; meanwhile, jet boats lap up and down the main Salmon—"River-of-No-Return" no more. And number three, the Selway-Bitterroot, like the Frank, has a steady stream of raft parties (parties: in both senses of the word) parading through from an upstream, road-accessible launch, in addition to landing strips of its own. In all of these places, getting deeper doesn't necessarily mean getting more isolated. Jen and I learned this lesson when we passed an outfitted group of bear hunters twenty miles up the Selway, who flew in on a helicopter a couple days earlier. One motioned us toward a water trough, fed by a piped spring, in which dozens of beer cans were bobbing.

"Now, *how* did you two get in here?"

---

* Finer measurements of wildness avoid such confusion by focusing on complexes of roadless land, regardless of designation, rather than wilderness boundaries. This criterion illuminates the fact that, in the Sierra Nevada, abutting management units without roads separating them comprise a roadless area of over 3,700 square miles. Larger than any other in our area of focus, it is spindly and skewered by "cherry-stems" when compared to that which includes the Thorofare.

"We walked up the Selway," I said, as I popped the top of a Coors Light—like, you know, the river with a major pack trail, only a couple hundred yards away.

"And where's *that?*" he asked, knotting up his brow like he'd never heard the name in his life.

When we talk about remoteness, it's usually assumed that we're talking about a characteristic of the physical world. Yet our reliance on computer calculations to find it for us suggests it might exist less in nature than in our language—that it's an idea we have, not a dimension of place. I suspect that's the only reason we would try so hard to substantiate it with information. The weird part, then, is how our yearning for nature in its purest form morphs into going where the computer tells us to go. The irony struck me as I watched a documentary called *Into the Cold*. As the adventurer Sebastian Copeland reaches the North Pole, a spot that looks exactly like everywhere else for hundreds of miles, he is staring at the screen of his GPS. When he looks up his eyes go directly to the lens of the rolling video camera, and he recites some rehearsed facts with utterly unconvincing enthusiasm: "No matter what direction I go, I'm going south. And here's the other thing... in doing this, right now [he removes his chest harness and walks in a small circle], I've gone through every single time zone on the planet." When he's done, he and his partner sit back and wait for the helicopter that will return them to the great indoors.

Remoteness becomes valuable as a statistic precisely when it fails us as a feeling. We bring mental baggage into wild places and the wildness eludes us, so we ask for a souvenir or a bragging right instead. It allows us to believe that rare and glorious things were felt, even if we don't remember what they were like, or weren't receptive to them at the time. The calculation of remoteness is an attempt to legitimize experience in a language that does not recognize or value such experiences.

Meanwhile, the hardships we endure in pursuit of remoteness speak to the depth of a need. The depth can hardly be overstated: it's both an outgrowth of our meritocracy and a reaction against it.

Popular knowledge teaches us that hard work is rewarded with wealth and recognition. A simple extension of this logic tells us that a journey to the ends of the earth will result in something almost inconceivably distinguished: hence the unflinchingly self-destructive polar races, with their death-wish drives and anti-climactic goals. Ironically, those who are skeptical of such patriotic morals—and aim to physically escape their nonsense in the company of greater forces—might find themselves in the very same places as these "heroism-for-heroism's-sake" types, the ones who are there to plant flags.

If getting away is really what we want, there are other ways besides calculating the most remote spot. We can ask: what do we want out of remoteness? What are we trying to measure—*can* it be measured? And if it can, why would we want to? While the impetus toward remoteness may be real, the way we pursue it may be counterproductive. If we discover it's a feeling we're after, rather than a characteristic of place, it might change the ways we search. We might turn inward rather than outward.

Gordon Hempton, self-described "acoustic ecologist," said a particularly wonderful thing: "Silence is not the absence of something but the presence of everything." I think the same could be said of remoteness. It is a distance from chatter. From tired thought processes. From acquisitiveness and boredom. When these distractions leave, the rest of the world pours in to take their place, and whichever world that is is as valuable as any other. Remoteness is the urgency of an autonomous moment.

Remoteness is knowing: this is your life.

◊◊◊

If holding the title of "most remote" has started to sound like a popularity contest, believe me, it is. And the contest has less to do with getting away from society than bringing it in. Holding the title is a kiss of death. Like the subatomic particle that can't be observed without coming under the influence of the observer, the most remote spot cannot be preserved and recognized at the same time. As Hinsdale County reveled in its brief spotlight, a newspaper reported the County Clerk's telling reaction: "Well, that might be a selling point for tourism, which we really need." When the Nevada Commission of Tourism designated US 50 "The Loneliest Road," they did so with the professed aim of making it *less* lonely. Remoteness requires anonymity; recognition is its anathema.

I thought about these things as we walked Absaroka ridges. What we were seeing seemed incredibly important to me. I wanted to praise, but I didn't want to publicize. I wanted to pay tribute without selling out. Was I being naïve? Years earlier I chanced upon a *National Geographic* article that described grizzlies eating cutworm moths on an Absaroka peak.[*] From the first words of that article, my mind started racing. I felt blood rise in my face. It affected me so strongly because a year earlier, on the same peak, I'd stumbled onto the same phenomenon with three good friends. None of us had any idea of what we were in for, and we were awarded with an exceedingly personal experience in return. Remembering that day while I read the article, I thought about how much the beauty that I perceived was related to fragility. I suspected these gatherings of bears were protected from the meddling masses only by the greater obscurity of the place. I told myself that I would never write about such a tenuous phenomenon (in fact, I posted a heated comment to the author), because some forms of wildness only survive by remaining secrets.[**] Now, here I am, touting the secrets of my favorite mountain range. Undoubtedly, there are dangers. Says the Colorado writer, Damon Falke:

> The trouble with giving away a place name is that then we can guarantee someone else will go there… If the fellow in the cowboy hat who drank his coffee at the morning café didn't want to inform me exactly where a certain creek was, then that was his business. If I was patient enough then I could find the same creek, and likely a good deal more, when I went looking for it. That too is a kind of ritual. A kind of effort, and an invocation…

Falke makes a case for withholding place names. This makes a kind of sense to me. And at the same time, it doesn't. While I agree that the integrity of places is mortally threatened by advertising, I believe this is

---

[*] In fact, I referenced the article for this book.

[**] In 2016, another friend visited this spot and confirmed my fear. He watched a group of seven people, one of them carrying a shotgun (for "self defense?"), sneak up among the feeding bears. Then, in unison, they began screaming, just to watch those families of endangered souls flee in terror across the treacherously unstable mountainside. Of course, they probably didn't learn about the phenomenon because they read *National Geographic*.

more an issue of *how* we talk than what we talk *about*. The message communicated by a place name needn't reduce to an exploitational sales pitch. It may just as well be reverential, bringing that place to life: talking about where we've been helps other people form a conception of place. It enlists more minds in the meaningfulness of land. It brings the physical world into our shared culture and it makes it more real—in fact, I think stories tied to places may be one of the best ways to foster this type of consciousness. That's what Keith Basso means by "wisdom sits in places," the title of his famously influential study of the Western Apache. Place is a cultural construct, a way to establish common values, and corroborating individual experiences is how we get there.

I come back to a preceding sentence in Falke's piece, one that conflicts, in my mind, with his conclusion: "For the ancient Greeks a place was sacred because people came to it with shared memories and stories." Yes. There are regional-type non-fiction books on my shelf, soon to get kicked off, that I bought in hopes of filling out the world (not stealing hunting spots), only to discover the author refused or disguised the locations. To me, this is like putting a bag over the head of the leading actress. I would never deny the value in evoking mytho-poeic landscapes—those defined only by unknowns, immeasurable depths, and virgin frontiers. But rarely do I find names to stand in the way—and the best names go a long way toward restoring, as Falke says, the sacredness to place. *Lady of the Lake*, for example. *Wolf Voice Lake. Big River Trail.* These are good names. It'd be even better if, at the same time, we set about restoring Native American names to the greatest extent possible. Everyone would benefit from fewer Rock Creeks and Cottonwood Creeks (completely generic titles in places where every creek has rocks and cottonwoods), fewer places named for politicians and bureaucrats that never even saw them, and much more—to use an example from the Washakie Wilderness—in the vein of Ishawooa Creek. It means "danger wood"—a reference to great logjams that form along its narrow bottom and fail under the occasional cloudburst. In addition to being a distinct and excellent word, it'll add to your way of looking at things. So what's the story behind Montana's Bad Marriage Mountain? Choked-to-Death Butte? Bloody Dick Peak? I digress.

Caring about the land means steering the conversation, not keeping it like a secret. While there's a fine line between undiscovered and underappreciated—and no shortage of examples where that line is unwittingly crossed—when the threat of development comes around, obscurity can be every bit as fatal as "loved to death." What if Eliot Porter's *The Place No One Knew* came out seven years before construction started on the Glen Canyon Dam, rather than seven years after? Too often, the popular tide awakens only to a long-mobilized threat. That's what Joni Mitchell was talking about: times when "you don't know what you got 'til it's gone."

◊◊◊

The Absaroka Range, which largely enjoys the protective status of wilderness designation, is not, short of a public lands transfer, facing a rhetorical Glen Canyon Dam. But I do know that it is less loved than it should be; that it deserves more friends than it has; that things could be better. People get away with goofy stuff in there. I most fully appreciated this fact when I patrolled the Absarokas during hunting season. That's the brief window of time when those mountains are crawling with people. While I became skilled, unflappable even, at letting diatribes about Obama and wolves roll off of me, what got me into trouble was that part of my funding as a wilderness ranger came from the wildlife office. Their educational outreach emphasizes grizzly bear safety—for good reason—and I was therefore expected to broach the subject of bear spray.

Many of the horsemen I encountered held a particular vehemence toward the subject. They regarded bear spray like some conspiratorial racket from Washington D.C., designed to rip off rural-conservative voters, get them eaten, and really both at the same time. This, despite the lessons of real-life encounters, which demonstrate that a gun in an actual mauling[*] is as good as nothing, and a can of pressurized capsaicins

---

[*] Most of the time people kill bears in "self-defense" it is because they misread bear behavior and shoot preemptively.

the closest thing to a life preserver.* Eventually I came to suspect that the reason to kill a grizzly went beyond safety for some of these men. Like America's pioneer sadists, who slaughtered for the sake of slaughter, violent conflict seemed essential to their sense of purposefulness. A human-bear encounter, in which only one player survives, may even be one subset of the American Dream. A brutal bit of self-mythologizing with heavily stacked odds; a regressive enactment of the law of the land. "Meet violence with violence" is the cry, and look who all shows up to join the melee. A horseman out of Cody, who had recently killed his second grizzly (both in purported self-defense), was being evoked as a sort of folk hero among the types displaying bumper stickers at trailheads that read "Shoot, Shovel, and Shut Up," and "Wolves: Smoke a Pack a Day."

It's extremely difficult for a court to disprove a shooter's claim of self-defense. The death of one bear in the Teton Wilderness, September 2013, was set into motion when a client and guide from Hidden Creek Outfitters went to reclaim an elk they shot hours earlier.** Despite the fact that as many as five grizzlies had already dragged away and begun to consume the carcass, the men refused to back down. Both of them "forgot" their bearspray back with the horses, but neither of them forgot their handguns, which they fired into the air. The bears drew back—but one of them didn't fully get the message, and when it reapproached the dead elk, the men plugged the seventeen-year-old boar in unison. A grizzly: an endangered species. This, to the court, was self-defense. "While it might not be advisable to attempt to scare off four if not five bears, at least one of which had already dragged the elk carcass 150 yards into a tree line, these individuals nonetheless chose that course

---

* The first round from a panicked shooter is at least as likely to inflict a non-mortal wound (which further inflames an agitated bear), or miss, than it is to kill the bear or scare it away. For this reason, people who don't fire their guns at all in a bear attack have the same rate of injury as those who do. In a study of hundreds of bear attacks in Alaska, people who used bear spray as a deterrent were injured in 4% of attacks, and none were killed. Of those who used guns, 56% were injured, and 6% killed.

** Already, this demonstrates poor form. In order to avoid the obvious, it is imperative that hunters begin processing their kills immediately, and be able to hang what they cannot attend, especially in the dead center of a grizzly bear recovery zone.

of action," the judge explained. Imagine if we did this kind of thing to people. Well, sometimes we do. In 2014, a Milwaukee policeman roused from sleep and frisked a man "clearly" suffering from mental illness. The man assaulted the cop, the cop shot and killed the man, and the cop lost his job—not for defending himself with lethal force, but for instigating a volatile situation that he recognized in advance and could have avoided. You don't have to know much about bear behavior to see that the "course of action" chosen by the Hidden Creek guide condemned a bear to death.

Governmental affiliations aside, it was hard to be taken seriously when I was on foot. My frustrating attempts to converse with horsemen gave insight into the colloquialism, "come down off your high horse." To a fifth-generation Wyoming cattle king, walking in the mountains on your own two feet is a preposterous urban fad. To ride a horse is to live on a ranch, own a truck, have exclusive claim on the word "American." Thomas Turiano introduces Thorofare country by saying, "The Southwest Absaroka have long been the realm of outfitters and horsemen... Parties that explored the Southwest Absaroka as long ago as the 1870s speak in their journals of rogue backwoodsmen employed as guides and hunters." Today, enormous outfitter camps colonize secluded creeks. Forest Service law enforcement chases after camps that disappear in the night, trails with hidden entrances, caches hidden under brush. While neighboring wildernesses limit stock parties to sixteen head in order to curb resource damage, more than one Teton Wilderness outfitter has been granted an exemption to allow *seventy*. The impacts are in the proportions you'd expect: public trails that go through these camps disappear into a maze of trampled high-lines, mud flats, high-stumped trees, and electrified corrals—what feels like a big-ag feedlot. Try to mesh that with Congress' goal for wilderness protection: "Where the earth and its community of life are untrammeled by man, where man himself is a visitor who does not remain..."

Regulating outfitters is complicated by the fact that they necessarily have friends in high places. A guided hunting trip is male bonding in the grandest tradition. Because the cliché of rugged individualism still runs strong in the conservative mainstream, and the Wild West is the ultimate symbol of that (as billionaire and conservative string-puller Bill Koch, who built his own faux-Wild West "town," summarizes: "What I really like about the West is the stand your ground mentality"), a trophy hunt in the Wyoming mountains is, for many of the men who wield the most power in this country, a deeply symbolic ritual. A ritual that can cost well into the six figures. When it does, the rapport between client and guide, businessman and cowboy, is the glue. The rich and powerful use luxury hunts to demonstrate their proximity to tradition, to American sensibility, to "the people"—the people they care to acknowledge, that is. Even if, like Dick Cheney, they're liabilities in the field,[*] a lot of money changes hands, images are conferred, and the modern politician is legitimized by his proximity to a fictional archetype—the personification of American masculinity. Earlier in his book *Hawks Rest*, Gary Ferguson tells how one local Forest Service ranger's attempt to ticket a habitually irresponsible outfitter triggered a damaging rebuke from the Secretary of Defense.

◊◊◊

Among so many other things, the Absarokas are good ol' Boy country. Once, while Jen and I tried to walk around an outfitter camp on nearby Mountain Creek, a camp that swallowed a public trail on public land, we were detained by the hollered greeting, "Whattaya LOST?" A group of jumpy middle-aged men quickly gathered around us. It was a dead end trail and the spokesman demanded to know where we were going. I said we were going to hike over the ridge. He told me it was impassable. I told him we were doing it anyway—and as I experimented with ways to end the debate, the guide repeated three times, with increasing sternness and volume, "Well, we can't have you going in there, fouling up our hunt." Finally I gave up, and Jen and I defiantly headed up trail. As we did, I imagined what a bullet must feel like in the back. It's not comfortable, defying the "shoot-shovel-shut up" contingent where they build forts in the woods and posture with guns.

---

[*] Our then-vice president, who originally hailed from Wyoming, accidentally shot a fellow client on a guided quail hunt in Texas.

Signs of chainsaw use (a violation of wilderness regulation) are almost ubiquitous around Wyoming outfitter camps—as are illegally built trails and garbage. We saw it all as we proceeded to "foul up" Mountain Creek, which is why I suspect the outfitter was so intent on scaring us away. The root of our conflict might best be understood through this quote from Jesse Rodenbough, the then-President of the Wyoming Outfitter and Guide Association: "WYOGA does more than just promote a certain segment of the tourism industry... [It engages in] the unending battle with those extremists who would take away our God given rights granted by the Constitution of the United States." There's no doubt in my mind that I'd object to one or another of the entitlements he's lumped under "God given rights," and skookum outfitters seem to recognize that in me. Outfitting permits, like grazing permits, invite all kinds of creative extrapolations of private property rights into the public domain. That's why, as Jen and I walked, government employees were slaying wolves from helicopters in Idaho Wilderness: somebody's "rights" were being threatened by so much natural order, "jobs were being lost," and, as usual, guns and helicopters were tasked to set things straight again.

Fortunately, these encounters are profoundly far and few between. But they are territorial enough to create the feeling that, during hunting season, you're not completely free to enjoy public land. You're being watched. There was the time that Jen and I were accosted by a group of hunters in the South Fork of the Shoshone. They were the only people we saw in seventy miles. A man started by asking where we'd been—when we told him he said, nodding, "OK. That was you." A day earlier, as we crossed an alpine basin, miles from any trail, we were spotted from a scouting plane.* Since his company had contracts with every person holding a ram tag on the district that year, they worked themselves into a froth trying to figure out who we were and what the hell we were doing

---

* Few hunters would find this compliant with the principles of fair chase, but it's legal—as long as it isn't the *same day* as the hunt—and, more depressingly, it's economically viable. Outfitters have that bottom line to think about, and too often it's made out of percentages of tags filled, not moral precepts.

in their territory. The answer—a skinny guy hiking with his girlfriend—managed to disarm them a little bit.

4

Autumn previewed on September fourth, a day of marbled cloud cover that lightened and darkened and drizzled throughout, but never broke. We followed the Deer Creek trail out of the South Fork of the Shoshone River—a catwalk scratched along the wall of a remarkable gorge. Like the Tsangpo, I said to Jen, though I had no authority to say. But it had such saturated greens and browns, just the right amount of mist, and our two figures seemed tiny enough not to matter. Deer Creek is one of the primary access routes to the Thorofare country: we anxiously anticipated the processions of pack trains that rush dudes in and out of remote tent cities. While we did see plenty of tell-tale impacts—beer cans in the bushes, trail sections pulverized into mud bogs by hurried hooves, and three instances where somebody hooked a discarded horseshoe around a young tree, choking it out as it tried to grow[*]—we saw no people that day. Instead, wolf tracks, the size of my palms and the freshest we'd seen up to that point, plodded steadily up trail for a good six miles before veering off.

Deer Creek Pass delineates a broad topographic shift, from the deep canyons of the Washakie Wilderness to the broad valleys with gently curving walls that characterize the Teton Wilderness. As I compared the two from the top of the pass, I balled my numb fingers into the sleeves of my rain jacket to escape the damp wind buffeting us from the west, and tried to ignore a trail slashed eleven lanes wide in a meadow below us. Our day finished with a rather frantic search for a break off a cliffy ridge, while a storm gathered like a fist above our heads. We arrived in camp bone-chilled and famished. Our rations had shrunk somewhat as our metabolisms apparently doubled.

While Jen set up the tent, I sparked a pile of dead spruce branches and prepared a dinner that would hardly register in my bottomless stomach. Then we hunched before the fire, seeking refuge from the long cold night ahead. Fingers splayed before the flashing light, eyes absorbed by the flames and coals but seeing neither, I realized the self-pity of my situation and decided to pick currants from the wiry thorn bushes around camp instead. After watching too many berries dribble from my wool gloves, I resigned myself to icy bare hands with frequent warmings at the campfire. It took about thirty minutes to pick two cups, which I boiled and mashed for us to eat on the spot. They would've benefited from a lot of sugar.

The next day broke clear but grim with cold. It wasn't that we hadn't known cold since the previous winter: in late July I was hit by almost two inches of hail, and one day high in the northern Winds didn't get out of the thirties. But something in the air said summer was over, and the way I saw things shifted a little. Fall isn't just chilly: it's weakened light, a fleetingness to pleasure. There might be twenty

---

[*] The dark side of the "freedom of the hills" provides cover for a host of senseless and depraved acts.

degrees difference or more between direct sun and the shadow of a tree, so a bare arm sweats on one side while the other goes cold and stiff as a dead man's. The soil doesn't dry one day to the next. Frost hides in the bunchgrass at noon like seed crystals for another night lurking, and these freezing cycles release tangy smells of harvest and rot from the forbs. It's an entirely new perspective on the silliness of summer: grown up and realistic. My sleep was haunted by bizarre dreams that I blamed on a subconscious association between autumn and "back-to-school," even when it couldn't be further from my reality. It never fails to amaze me how thoroughly my unconscious has been commandeered by social anxieties, norms, and taboos—how impossible it is to irradiate those ugly haunts. But when the sun finally rose on another day—we waited for it to hit the tent before moving—I found a temporary solution. I conjured a morning fire from the heap of last night's coals, hunched on my heels warming my hands, and listened to the clear creek run frigid through fresh terraces of ice on the edge of camp. The purity of these elements can make even discomfort savory; cold toes in cold boots the stuff that life is made of. Flames gathered me in and left nothing in return.

I'd lost our trail before reaching camp the night before. Now we wandered through a dream world of meadows and forests, vaguely following the watercourse, sometimes seeing an old cut stump but nothing you'd call a trail. Our steps crunched long curlicues of frost extruded from broken grass stems and the saturated ground. In Swedish they call these formations *piprake*, a term I suggest we all adopt, but people are more likely to know what you're talking about when you call them "needle ice." I stopped caring about the trail and gave up looking for clues. Soon the canyon flared open into a cirque, and that's freedom itself.

Against a rim of breccia above our heads I recognized an outstanding finger of white as a petrified tree. Although we had a long walk and a caloric deficit to think about, we still had to check it out. From below, I guessed it to be six feet tall, but after scrambling up there and framing Jen's picture at its foot, I saw that it was closer to fifteen.

The process begins when wood is quickly buried in sediment,* then suffused with mineral-rich water. As the solution dries, the compounds align with the wood grain, and create a faithfully detailed replica. Magnified cross sections literally show every single cell wall. There are several ways of classifying petrified trees—for my purposes, I simply think of agatized trees as the more colorful ones, created from water with high silica content. Silica is translucent, and showcases the clouding and splashes of other chemical traces—green, red, and ochre are not uncommon. Our tree, however, was calcified. It went through the same process, but with water high in calcium and magnesium. The result was a monument the color of ivory, not unlike freshly split pine, slashed with rusty streaks.

With my hand on its surface I could suspend disbelief and forget it was petrified at all. Had an irregularity on one side appeared anywhere else in the nearby forest, I wouldn't hesitate to attribute it to a woodpecker. Then, for all I knew, maybe it was a woodpecker—a type that doesn't exist anymore—or some reptilian ancestor. After all, scientists have found weirder ephemera preserved in those ash falls and mudflows, tens of millions of years old. For starters, impressions of leaves and patterns in wood grain have revealed great biodiversity in the ancient ecosystem—a forest that was broken into categories of conifers, tropical hardwoods, and ginkgos. The family Sequoia is the best represented—a reduced genus that has one extant and at least five extinct species (just like the genus *Homo*). It is supposed that these Wyoming volcanoes once resembled the kind found in Latin America today, where a broad range of forest types sequence over a great range of altitude. They've also found fossilized nuts and pinecones on the floors of petrified Absaroka forests, and fossilized soils that contain fossilized pollens. The pollens enabled identification of over two hundred total forest species, a list that reads like a veritable cornucopia:

---

* Lahars are the ultimate mechanism. These are debris flows from the flanks of volcanoes, usually associated with an eruption that rapidly melts large amounts of snow or glacial ice. They can carry unimaginably large volumes of sediment—like "rivers of concrete," says the USGS. Much of the Absaroka conglomerate is composed of lahar deposits.

cinnamon, breadfruit, olive, fig. Jim Bridger's cheesy bluff about a land of fossilized birds singing fossilized songs isn't so far off.

A stump visible down slope had three thick roots preserved, and additional stumps and logs protruded from the cliff above. As Williard H. Parsons describes in his geologic field guide, there are places in the Absaroka Volcanic Field where

> Twenty or thirty successive fossil forests are buried one above another. As a forest grew up after a volcanic eruption it came to full size in perhaps a 2,000 year period; then, in a particularly violent eruption, mud flows swept down from the high volcanoes and buried the forest-covered basin, smashing small trees and burying bigger trees as they stood, up to ten or twenty feet above their base.

Jen and I were still many miles from the best known petrified forests (a name that calls to mind something they're not) of the Absaroka Volcanic Province, but chance discoveries are always that much more engrossing.

◊◊◊

From the ancient trees, we gazed straight across the basin to Rampart Pass. Although our map showed a trail ascending it from our side, Jen knew from her time working on both adjoining ranger districts that it hadn't seen a pick or a shovel in generations. We'd listened to a friend of hers, sixty years old, recollect his dad packing stock over the pass, but even to him that was ancient history. As the old Bonney guide to the Absarokas explains: "Beyond [the mouth of Rampart Creek] the Forest Service does not maintain trail or recommend public travel... For an adventurous person, this is one of the outstanding trips in this range, with the trail crossing the Divide on a narrow knife-edged rimrock." In all, at least twelve miles of trail have been abandoned between the head of Open Creek, over the pass, all the way down Rampart, and out to the confluence that forms the Elk Fork.

As we headed up it was easy to understand why. The mountainside consisted of bare bedrock pitching thirty or more degrees. When there was evidence of a trail it was no more than a berm of scraped gravel. Accenting this perilousness were artfully strewn sets of bones, one of which, reduced to a pelvis and femur and ribs, looked big and stocky enough to be a grizzly. When Gary Ferguson crossed this pass on the long hike he wrote up in *Walking Down the Wild,* he was met by the same ominous sight: "In the bottoms of the ravines that lie on either side of the path are the bleached white bones of horses—at least three that we can make out—as well as the remains of one elk, and the skull of a bighorn sheep." When it comes to warning signs in nature, nothing says "danger" like a sheep skull at the bottom of a hill.

Up top, the wind drove us to take refuge on the north side of the pass. Although we found a median between sun and shelter it was awfully cold. A complicated lunch of woody wild onions and powdered hummus on crackers left my fingers as dumb as rubber—still, we couldn't descend before checking up on the Fishhawk Glacier. Compared to the neighboring Beartooths and Wind Rivers, the Absarokas don't have much to show for glaciers, despite sitting right between the two in terms of latitude and elevation. Only three of them have names. But the Dunoir Glacier, for starters, is probably a misnomer to begin with—it's simply too small and too low to move under its own mass and meet the basic criterion. Sunlight Glacier, meanwhile, looks more like what's called a rock glacier, a "periglacial process." Its surface is covered in debris, cutting off whatever ice remains from the replenishing winter snows. That leaves Fishhawk—perhaps the only remaining glacier in this arid range. (Another unnamed candidate lays one drainage to the south.) It hides in the shelter of 11,869' Overlook Mountain, which doesn't even count among the twenty highest named peaks in the range, but rises fast out of wetter country near Yellowstone Lake and sports sheer north walls. Fishhawk has the old ice, the deep fissures, and the dimensions that you want to see in a glacier. We scanned its embattled perimeter with sympathy: hopefully there's something left to see whenever we manage to get back there.

◊◊◊

Rampart Creek is an arrow-straight defile that lacks significant tributaries. In most places, a trail abandoned for as long as that one would be thoroughly erased. But the Rampart trail has been spared excessive downfall by some of the healthier patches of forest in the area (not all the whitebarks are dead, yet) and is refreshed regularly by the passage of elk. As we worked our way down, and our stomachs gnawed, we kept on the lookout for anything edible. Noticing a pattern of bark stripped from the boles of subalpine fir, I realized I just might have tried for a porcupine if I saw one—the only time I've felt hungry enough to say that.[*] We did find chanterelles. These bright orange mushrooms with flaring tops and a gourmet palate were far past their prime, though, and didn't look like much after I trimmed off all the white ground mold. Not the kind of thing you want to pile into an empty stomach, anyway. They still managed to add a peculiar savor to our spicy rice and beans that night.

In total, about four days passed during which I was hungry before I ate and I was hungry after I ate. In the mornings before breakfast, and for the two hours before lunch, I was especially hungry, and entertained elaborate food fantasies. The contributing factors to American health epidemics were the bases for these daydreams: rich food and inactivity struck me as the preconditions for a strong body and mind.

It would be stupid to make it sound like Jen and I were actually starving. As a descriptor, that one's gotten pretty cheap—I'm generally "starving" if I wait until one o'clock to have lunch, for example. The truth is that Jen and I were usually only a little hungry, but it was strange not being able to escape it. Like most people I know—privileged enough to afford plenty of food[**]—I'm not accustomed to being hungry for long, so the secondary side effects I felt, like irritability and weakness, seemed profound. Yes, it was unwelcome. It was something to complain about. It felt a little intense at times. But it was good, too; we knew that. It seemed like something we should be more familiar with: how wilderness looks on an empty belly. It's an equally important

---

[*] Some states prohibited the indiscriminate killing of porcupines, at a time when they were widely despised for the damage they did to timber, just to preserve an emergency food source for the lost and starving.

[**] The average American only spends six percent of their budget on food, far less than on non-essentials.

reality. We weren't motivated to cram in extra little summits and exertions like we had been in the Winds—we focused on following the trail that we had to follow until we reached its end, and that's about it. It felt like we were engaged in something much more serious. As C.L. Rawlins wrote, "It's a mistake to think of the world in terms of a few fair-weather rambles. What's missing is hunger… I lack hunger's art. And it is an art." The art, in this case, imparted a severe disinterestedness to the trackless timber that surrounded us. It was almost scary to consider those canyon walls for too long.

◊◊◊

Jen and I were about five miles out from the Elk Fork trailhead when we finished the last bites of food we had with us: a 1.2 ounce granola bar to split, and scraps of dried apples. Because the sun was warm on the banks of the creek, we also took a minute to jump in a pool of deep blue water. We were confident no one was coming because we hadn't encountered another person—aside from our crossing of the South Fork road—in over six long days of walking. Downstream, the river valley quickly broadened into a great sagebrush flat, squat hoodoos hunkered along the ridges, and already our view extended to the opposite side of the North Fork of the Shoshone, where a formation called The Wall draws a line of charcoal black against the sky. Some of the sagebrush topped my six feet three inches, and one limber pine looked taller than any I'd seen, its canopy flaring upward like an elm.

That's Old West country, if there is any such thing. The Wapiti Ranger Station, which sits just downriver from the mouth of the Elk Fork, is the oldest Forest Service ranger station in the country; the Shoshone, meanwhile, is the oldest national forest. In the last couple miles we finally saw some people, too: characters that disgorged from the scenery like it was a movie set. First, a solo ranger going up in his cowboy hat and khakis, later, an older couple just starting to turn around—plaid and denim, everyone riding horses. Jen and I had been wondering how we'd get to Cody, forty-five minutes east on the highway, to get food. After the couple passed, both of us had the same idea. We nearly paced them out to the trailhead, conveniently arriving as they finished loading the horse trailer. Jen gets elected to talk in situations like that—we hedge our bets on the old-fashioned (sexist) assumption that the girl is less likely to get turned down than the guy. (We've proven this theory in follow-up questions.) It worked. They were nice. On the drive down we all talked for a few minutes, and then stopped. I felt like I'd lost all ability to tell if something was socially awkward or not-really, so I didn't try. As much as anything, there was just surprisingly little to say.

The two dropped us off at Walmart. While Jen went in to buy groceries (ensuring we'd have more to eat than my go-tos: fried chicken and donuts), I sat on a concrete bench facing the parking lot, "watching our packs," and felt very strange indeed. Somehow I forgot my hunger—the beast had turned a corner. But I think the hollowness was still there, and I projected it on everything around me. Coming out of the woods. It's a classic mind-fuck. "You recognize all things as real—paved streets as well as leafy paths, concrete dams as well as canyons—but your allegiance shifts." Another Rawlins.

For a while it was all I could do just to read the words that were shouting at me in bold colors. In my journal, I jotted them down dutifully, like these concepts were as important as they made themselves out to be; as if, taking them together, I could triangulate my position in relation to things exactly. *Cash Advance. Elite Nails and Spa. O'Reilly Auto Parts. Arbys...* Cody, Wyoming, it turns out, is one big collection of chain stores and strip malls, a bastion of retail-therapy power-ups for people about to venture into landscapes that have not yet been completely restructured for the sake of convenience.

Unlike everyone else around (or so I felt), I had reprogrammed my eyes, and this constructed landscape didn't look normal or insignificant to me. It looked like an enormous mistake, a mistake that no one else recognized as such, as they frantically worked toward its maintenance and propagation. It seemed obvious to me that the order of straight lines, strung wires, poles and fences and concrete pads, is not actually what we want—rather, that its deceptive simplicity has made us forget what we want. Our collective ability to conceive beauty, to believe in beauty and sacrifice our lives to its creation and preservation, has been hijacked by an ugly and parasitic pattern that chunks down cinder blocks and plugs in traffic lights.

I've done it, I thought—I've achieved that distance from our culture that allows me to see the bad for the bad and the strange for the insidious. It's made this place into a nightmare.

I'm happy to say I did remain calm. I just kept sitting there, looking around. I watched an employee retrieve shopping carts from the Shopping Cart Corral, with the help of a CartManager XD—a robot, of sorts. Two other workers stood together on break, both smoking cigarettes and facing opposite directions, both tapping on iPhones. There have been other times I've sat in front of grocery stores, grubby from the journey, my turtle-back home resting beside me, and shot the shit with employees on cigarette breaks—sometimes the only words I'd speak all day. That was before the smartphone, and those quiet despondent smokers and I got a chance to look at the sky for a while, to sit with the hills. People are so much less likely to make small talk since they've been able to keep computers running, non-stop, in their pockets—the last, rarest moments of absence have been co-opted by more of the frantic symbol trade.

Powerless to such anxious feelings, I found myself following suit. Jen had left her phone with me and I decided to see how that would sit. I opened only one email before turning it back off: a generic rejection letter for an essay I'd submitted to a website over four months earlier; the last in a long, solid string of rejections to cap a streak of productivity I had the previous winter. This drove me back to my journal. "Whatever it is people want to hear these days," I wrote, "it makes perfect sense I'm not the one saying it."

Before Jen went inside we discovered that a friend of hers from Wapiti, who we'd be staying with that night, was working from home that day, and not in Cody as we thought. She'd have to drive down and pick us up. It embarrassed us to create this extra trip for her—we'd already congratulated ourselves on not having to burn gas for a couple months, and if we'd known we would've walked (hungrily) to her place from the trailhead. But when a woman approached me with a huge smile on her face and said, "You must be Todd," and that I could put my things in the pickup with the friendly dog in back, I knew I'd been rescued from a thought process that had no end in sight. Soon the highway wind was blowing through my funny-looking beard, and I felt amazingly forgiving.

Part Three. **THE COMPROMISED WILD**

It is not nature-as-chaos which threatens us,
but the state's presumption that it has created order.

—Gary Snyder

1

That night in Wapiti, we discovered our stomachs had not shrunk. Jen and I ate berry muffins and whitetail steak, seconds of everything, snacks before and after. We talked with our hosts about unnamed mountains, about the strange and unexpected things one finds in the woods, and, polar bear to least weasel, we studied their startling collection of animal skulls, accumulated over many years trapping and working for different wildlife agencies. There were moments when it felt to me like we'd made it to where we were going—like this could be the conclusion. But at ten o'clock the next morning, packs on our backs, the two of us walked out to the highway to hitch another ride.

In less than an hour from where we stood, traveling west, traffic on US Highway 20 climbs out of the canyon of the Shoshone River's North Fork, crosses Sylvan Pass, and drops into an incomparable scene. The

Yellowstone Caldera spans a horizon almost as broad and flat as the sea. Skeleton forest slashes the view, but doesn't obstruct it. Vanishing-point arms of Yellowstone Lake, and distant blue topography, offer only the least reference points for scale. Somewhere in there sits Lake Village, a developed area near the namesake landform's outlet, where Jen's brother Sam lived and worked—since his vacation in the Winds, he'd already been back on the job for several weeks. This thought almost startled me: the world—a world—rushed on without us. Now we aimed to go visit him there. Jen and I found a nice shoulder to occupy across the street from the Red Barn, a gas station and store and one of the only businesses in Wapiti, and we set down our backpacks. When we saw a car coming, we stuck out our thumbs. And... repeat.

The Smith Mansion, if you're familiar with that road, stood almost directly over us. If you aren't, the Smith isn't like most mansions, which tend to have plumbing, for example. In Annie Proulx's second book of Wyoming stories, *Bad Dirt*, she describes a regional archetype: an "old house that had been gradually enlarged with telescoped additions until the structure resembled a giant spyglass built of logs." Unlike almost any other, this particular log spyglass, the Smith Mansion, points up. It's an outsized piece of vernacular art, visionary like Slab City or the Watts Towers, except that its working frame of reference is rural Wyoming: log cabin. A generator powering a single light bulb enabled the creator, who sometimes labored late into the night as he distanced himself from a traumatic divorce, to build the seventy-five-foot-tall structure alone over twenty-one years. He reportedly slept on a giant swing in an earthen cave; an oversized "doghouse" on the porch boarded his two kids when they visited. But in 1992, when a gust of wind blew Mr. Francis Smith off an eave in a fatal fall, his vision froze to the moment of tragedy—and Smith's arrested creation remains the closest one man can get to a Tower of Babylon.

Despite this rather portent symbol on the skyline, the sun shone warm and friendly on Jen and me. And because we had a lot of great food after days of lack—a couple-pound ham from Walmart, indulgences mailed by my mom—I felt completely carefree. Either a car picked us up or it didn't, as far as I was concerned. I hadn't hitchhiked in over a year and I was feeling the romance. I made a lanyard for my sunglasses from a piece of cordage, nibbled milky fruits from grass growing at my feet, and watched the cars breeze by. It seemed unimaginable that I'd ever tire of standing there, feeling the sun on my face. My only apprehension was that the attendant at the gas station would hustle us along: there aren't many business owners who want anything to do with hitchhikers. It was to my delight, then, that when the clerk did come out, she waved to us: "Come on in, you guys, I'll buy you a cup of coffee!"

I tried to pay for the coffee but she didn't let me. And when I said no to her offer of biscuits, because we had a lot of eating to do already, it was the only time I've ever turned down free food. I did buy two fudgsicles instead, as a gesture of patronage, and when we went back out, emboldened, I told Jen I'd try sitting on the bench in front of the gas station for a while and ask people straight up if they'd give us a ride. Soon two cars pulled in for fuel: a woman and her husband in an empty car, and their two sons in a car full of baggage. It struck me as the best possible situation. In the time it took me to walk over, everyone went inside the gas station except the mom.

"Excuse me, ma'am," I said, as she was unscrewing her gas cap. Her shoulders tightened. "My girlfriend and I are looking for a ride into Yellowstone."

"We're not going to Yellowstone. We're going to Grand Teton," she said.

Obviously, that was her way of saying no, and it was pointless to continue. But I did anyway. "Well," I said cheerily, "Yellowstone is right on the way!" It's true—she had to drive through one to get to the other.

"We're full," she said, and hurried inside.

Unfortunately, that was all it took to sour my position on hitchhiking. I walked back over to Jen. We'd been there over two hours now, and watched hundreds of cars go by. Demonstrating a level of investment that's death to hitchhiking's pleasures, for every subsequent vehicle that passed, I threw a little eye dagger.

It was my own fateful choice, then, to begin framing our impasse in a socio-political way—as a window into the forces guiding human interactions. My first inference was that the vast majority of Americans would rather risk not helping someone with a genuine need than encourage someone who thinks they can get a free ride. Never mind it's in everyone's interest to have fewer cars on the road, to burn less gasoline... forget that today's commute might actually be worth remembering if you share it with a stranger. As a people, we choose not to. Of course, some drivers pass by out of the fear they'll be robbed or murdered, but I'd like to add that the last time Jen and I hitchhiked, our driver remarked with a laugh, completely unprompted, "Who would ever be afraid of you two?" The most likely explanation, I realize, is perfectly banal: we are creatures of habit. We pursue efficiency with mechanical impartiality. (Even I, who make something of a point of picking up hitchhikers, only stop about half the time.) But whatever the reason, the outcome we accept is everyone in their own car.

More to the point, this inefficiency is completely in line with the prevailing ethics. Such waste, as the reasoning goes, is the price of social order—whereas sharing sends a distinctly un-American message. In this country, money represents work. You can only pay for what you can earn, therefore you only deserve what you buy. This is framed as the only reason that anything gets done. By holding a hard line against freeloaders, Americans discourage those who'd cheat the system, those who'd have everyone else pick up their slack. Stuck out there with no car? You deserve to be. Maybe it'll inspire you to work harder in the future.

"The free rider problem" is a broad economic phenomenon that concerns those who benefit from services they do not pay for. Though the very name seems to indict hitchhikers and stowaways as epitomes of social parasitism, actually applying the term here is not so simple. Free riders become problems when they cause the production of a good to become less profitable or dependable. If Jen and I found ourselves joining a crowd of hitchhikers along Highway 20 that outnumbered drivers on the road, and each driver was obligated to stop and load up on us hitchhikers, that could theoretically discourage car ownership to the point that cars became more expensive, until demand eventually outstripped supply. But hitchhikers are *excludable*—that is, you don't have to pick them up, and indeed, almost nobody does.*

Free riding applies to the hitchhiker-driver relationship in another sense. "Free-riding is experienced when the production of goods does not consider the external costs, particularly the use of ecosystem services. One aspect of the problem can be explained by the concept of the 'tragedy of the commons.'" In other words, heedless drivers take advantage of services that they're not paying for: the finite purity of the atmosphere to dispel their gaseous wastes, the ultimate price of subsidized oil. The tragedy of the commons regards the overtaxation of environmental services by unaccountable private usage—the pollution of our atmosphere being a textbook example. Ideally, higher costs and adapting social norms would be used to discourage frivolous drivers from consuming excessive resources, and hitchhikers would help pick up part of the remaining tab by shouldering so much uncertainty and inconvenience. More tangibly, hitchhikers could also be expected to chip in toward the gas fund.

Despite this intelligence, our culture is the expression of popular perceptions, and these operate on unexamined assumptions. In our collective eagerness to prove individual worth, we work—we work fanatically—and we work to create things that are worse than nothing. We encourage terrifically wasteful and selfish tastes. We cheat other people even though it doesn't make us happy. It's good to be able and willing to work, to have that in you, but the only work that's worthwhile creates something better. Instead, we have business after business fostering and mining the substanceless consumerism of stressed-out, materially addicted individualists. Collectively, it only makes us needier and more wasteful. Gold miners create big messes and job security for people who clean up big messes. Cody's "Cash Advance" grafts money from the out-of-luck and keeps them there. If only we figured out what

---

* Part of my desire to examine hitchhiking through this lens came from the realization that, despite living in a region with extremely low ethnic diversity, three of the last four drivers to stop for Jen and me belonged to ethnic minorities. Because it typically requires over an hour of waiting for such a driver to come along, it can sometimes feel as though the status quo—the white middle class to which we belong—*never* picks up hitchhikers, while a large percentage of members of other, less affluent cultures do.

the problem was and what was worth working for—*before* we started working—there'd be a hell of a lot less work to do. But before that can happen, the basic search for control over one's own life implicates us in this great competition for personal freedom, popularly understood as financial independence. It is a truism that the very desperation of this competition exempts us from greater responsibilities. *Hey, I'm just trying to feed my family...* Much is made of the efficiency of competition. Never have I seen these examples weighed against the inefficiencies.

It seems possible that the surpluses of today, which offer advanced education and leisure time for the fortunate few, will also allow the most important work of all to get done—intellectual work that requires great removes of perspective to begin to comprehend, like how to get ourselves out of the mess we're creating, and what the work of the future will be. I know a lot of people are doing such work and I think this country is a relatively good place to be doing it. But there were equally insightful thinkers in humbler times, and the extreme disparity between opulence and poverty in America is not excused by anything.

Begging for a ride didn't bother me. I could only feel so guilty about making practical use of the grotesque surplus of resources coursing in front of me. I knew that some people are going to keep working eighty hours a week because they don't know what else to do; meanwhile, other people will keep working to see how much they can possibly consume, because they don't know what else to do.[*] My projected thumb was a secret message to that rare driver who needed us as much as we needed her or him. But eventually I had to face the possibility that this supposed driver—because there might've only been one in Park County—took a different road that day.

In the end, it didn't matter what I thought about as I stood there. It couldn't make the cars pull over. Our escape—our *deus ex machina*, after four hours of waiting—was Sam, who answered our phone call after getting off work. Then he drove fifty minutes each way to pick us up,

---

[*] That other people are still lacking basic necessities is clear: the fever to secure mass quantities of things doesn't help us understand what to do with them. That's why half the food purchased in America is thrown away, while twenty percent of children face hunger, and there are many times more empty houses than homeless people.

expending his own time and gas, and for that we remain indebted. It meant that Jen and I would be able to volunteer and visit with him as planned. All of which is to say that capitalism, I guess, is working. To all the cars that passed us by—let it be known: we did have someone invested in the system that could vouch for our interests. But by the same token, if we didn't, nobody would've seen us out there in the first place. Jen and I would've happily kept on walking, we would've stuck to the trees. Because at some point, I am convinced, for the innately disorganized and baffled of mind like myself, walking away counts as a contribution to society.

Whoever believes that the marketplace provides sufficient guidance for human responsibility fails to describe my world.

◊◊◊

Jen and I woke beneath the awning of Sam's fifth-wheel trailer at 4:30 am, cold beads of dew covering our sleeping bag. A half hour later, at the fisheries office, the smeared running lights of idling pick-ups and the smell of diesel exhaust floating on a humid chill hit me like a memory from a different lifetime. From there it was out to the pier, where we climbed through a window-sized hatch onto an aluminum boat that swayed on black water reeking of fish. It was named *Freedom*.

By the red and orange lights of the dashboard we stepped into giant rubberized bibs and crumpled foam earplugs into our ears. Our captain-in-training, John, was several years younger than me. He was strong and fast and the way he hunched over the aluminum control panel—with clunky levers and dials like a made-for-TV time machine—reminded me of the punk starcraft of Douglas Adams. We had a noisy forty-five minute chug south to the Flat Mountain Arm (harsh treble from the stereo competing with roaring engines), where three long nets lay anchored. I leaned against the rear port and watched dawn's glow touch down, first on the summit caps of the Absaroka front, then on Frank Island. I'd always wanted to venture out on the waters of America's largest mountain lake—originally given the mystical-sounding name "Lake Eustis," after the then-Secretary of War. But then, I'd always pictured myself in a canoe.

Historically, Yellowstone Lake represented the stronghold of the largest population of genetically pure cutthroat trout in the world. (The state fish of nine western states, cutthroats are further divided into fourteen sub-species, several of them now threatened or extinct. Here, I use the word as shorthand for only one of those sub-species: the *Yellowstone* Cutthroat.) Then, in 1994, "the first verified lake trout" was caught in Yellowstone Lake. Lake trout proceeded to vacuum up the natives: some specimens reveal piles of cutthroats, up to a third of their body lengths, stacked in their guts like sardines. Soon it was hard to catch anything else. By 2011, cutthroat were down over ninety-five percent, while lake trout numbered around a million. Four years after that, and a decade into a Park Service eradication program that ran about $2 million a year, the trend was only worsening. The length of our boat ride helped me understand the advanced scale and complexity of this hidden invasion. Yellowstone Lake covers 136 square miles, and reaches 436 feet in depth.

When the *Freedom* reached its set, Jen and I took positions at an aluminum counter across from the crew of three. As a diversion from our hike, a day volunteering would be both welcome and compromising. It required a different headspace—I was capable of following directions, but it would take some effort. John moved to a standing position where the counter met a window, and as the net mechanically lifted into the opening, he, Sam, and a third crewmember worked rapidly to untangle it, extract fish, and keep the boat on course with an auxiliary set of controls. Watching their hands spring to action prompted a simple thought: I'm too old to work that fast. Not true, exactly, but true to what I was feeling. Jen and I intercepted the fish as they came out of the net. Dead or alive, we drove knives into their sides near the spine, popping the swim bladder. Those that were still flapping would die as a matter of course, but for many, it took far longer than one would expect. Then the mangled fish went into plastic bins for data collection. At the end of the day, we dumped the catch so that the biomass remained in the ecosystem. Unlike most fishing boats, this one didn't harvest—just slaughter, document, discard.

The gruesomeness of our task was not a subject of discussion. The unspoken consensus was "we have a job to do, and we don't allow the suffering of fish to affect it." For me, this was a challenge. Emotional parts of me recoiled from the suffering. But I also wasn't about to object or take a stand—I'd agreed to volunteer because I was interested. I wanted to form a first-hand understanding of a management decision I agreed with in theory, and I also knew that my reaction to the slimy and violent reality was something entirely different to explore, something for later. Elbow-deep in the dirty work, I began to see what this challenge really consisted of: overriding the reactionary area of my brain rather than convince others of its validity. As one may expect, it proved both demanding and unsettling; what's more, it left me feeling isolated in my thoughts. (Take Jen's mom's reaction, who volunteered in the same capacity a couple weeks later. Eyes wide, grinning from ear to ear: "I LOVED IT!")

One important consequence of being out there is that it invested me—it obligated me—to learn more about the issue, something I might not have done otherwise. Before lake trout, Yellowstone Lake had a food chain with three tiers. Cutthroat fed on little crustaceans called scuds, the scuds fed on tiny phytoplankton and algae that make energy from the sun, and that was it—the whole cycle marvelously isolated from other fish species by the great waterfalls of the Yellowstone River.* Adding another trout was not as simple as diversifying this top tier: it added a fourth tier. Lake trout are piscivorous and Yellowstone cutthroats, unaccustomed to swimming predators, comprise eighty percent of the lake trout population's diet.

The most important take-away here is that, despite the apparent simplicity of Yellowstone Lake's aquatic ecosystem, cutthroat trout weren't the only ones affected. Yellowstone cutthroats epitomize a keystone species—directly embroiled in the life cycles of several dozen predators and scavengers, their many influences hold the local food chain together. In this case, the chain is structured around uniquely

---

* How did cutthroat get there? Probably by crossing Two Ocean Pass in the Teton Wilderness, where Two Ocean Creek inexplicably flows directly *along* the Continental Divide before splitting into Pacific and Atlantic Creeks. There is also evidence to suggest that Yellowstone Lake had an outlet to the Snake River, which includes headwater streams within two miles of the shoreline, during the last major glacial advance—a possibility supported by Shoshone oral tradition.

cutthroat habits, for which lake trout are no replacement. While lake trout generally stay deep in the lake and keep to themselves ("freshwater sharks," they've been called), "cutts" spend much of their time near the surface or in shallow water, available to birds of prey. And when cutthroat spawn, they run up adjacent creeks and rivers—regularly placing themselves within reach of terrestrial mammals. Forty-two native vertebrates have been shown to prey on cutthroat directly, employing specially tailored hunting strategies and migrations, while many more enjoy indirect benefits from this infusion to the food chain.

By connecting grizzly bears to phytoplankton, Yellowstone cutthroat trout form a bridge between the two great and vastly different ecosystems that characterize the southeast (and utterly singular) quadrant of the park. That bridge has completely burned through in places. The new predatory cycle struck in tandem with an accidental introduction of *Myxobolus cerebralis*, the exotic parasite that causes whirling disease. Of the tens of thousands of spawning cutts once counted in a given year swarming Pelican Creek, one of the lake's largest tributaries, not one could be found in 2009.

The current scarcity of Yellowstone cutthroat has sent shockwaves through the food web in what biologists call a trophic cascade. The long list of victims falls into categories: former cutthroat eaters, forced to find something else to eat (osprey numbers fell ninety percent), and the "something else to eat" upon which former cutthroat-eaters settled. Trumpeter swans are struggling again as bald eagles target their cygnets; elk calves are more aggressively sought by grizzly bears. Other consequences are harder to quantify. River otters fertilize less riparian flora with their trout-rich scat. Out-of-work pelicans take their operations out of the Yellowstone drainage altogether, creating unknown pressures in unknown places. While opponents of the Yellowstone Lake fishing program posit that lake trout offer a welcome increase of biodiversity (+1 species), such optimism requires a gross oversimplification of how ecosystems actually work.

The contrast between lake and cutthroat trout habitats also enables the fishing operation. Gill nets don't discriminate which fish they kill, so lake trout are sought where cutthroat usually aren't—that's been determined by radio tracking. Yet the efficacy of netting is subject to the law of diminishing returns. After the most predictable lake trout haunts have been fished hard, pure pockets become smaller and scattered, and the proportion of targeted predators goes down as the incidental take of prey goes up. After all, one fish is trying to eat the other, causing great numbers of both to swirl in constant motion through three dimensions inaccessible to the naked human eye.

If the entire population really did explode from some homespun operation (the figure of speech "bucket biology"—which implies a million fish may propagate from a single bucket of minnows—is not an exaggeration), a miniscule number of lake trout could easily repopulate the entire lake again. That's where things get really tricky. Even though I was only on for a day, I acutely felt my position as a hired gun, working under a specialist I'd never met. I "did my job"—and it was a high-impact one, profoundly callous to one particular life form. So much gore and writhing, so many strange gulping mouths and unblinking eyes. How our actions could solve the problem, and when the war would ever stop—these were questions that loomed large in my mind.

Whenever I find myself in such a position—conflicted, and unable to explain the big picture of what I am doing—it helps me demystify the atrocities of history, from environmental to civil rights. Though the line between natural and unnatural has been blurred from a thousand angles, one duality I can stand behind says, "Nature is not cruel—that implies intent"—whereas humans are different. We are creatures of vast, ambitious intent. We do what we need to do to achieve the ends we think we want, and this blinds us to side effects that we cannot defend. The Buddhist's first mandate, "Do the least harm," is the simplest possible reminder that we should take the time to understand our options before we act on them, so that we don't become enlisted by the very causes we fear and hate.* But few of us feel like we have the time.

Then, as Jan Dizard points out, the minimization of suffering is not a moral we learn from the world around us. "Is there not ample evidence of nature producing, on its own, a surplus of pain?" Lake trout

---

* Or, as this quote, often attributed to Albert Camus, puts it: "In such a world of conflict, a world of victims and executioners, it is the job of the thinking people not to be on the side of the executioners."

preying on cutthroat trout; cutthroat trout swallowing scuds and drowning them in stomach acid; bears that feed carelessly on salmonids in bounty, eating only the heads or biting out the eggs. Every step down the food chain is another exponent of suffering.

While it seems unlikely that lake trout can ever be completely eliminated from Yellowstone Lake, there is hope that the current gillnetting program can reduce their numbers enough to restore the cutthroat fishery to its age-old functionality. The downside to this path is that it guarantees ongoing management of the ecosystem ("job security," as a fisheries employee might say)—the slaughterhouses of Yellowstone Lake will float on. It's not a comfortable thought, but look at the choices. What do we want our first national park to be? A replication of "natural" conditions, supported by industrial-strength management—or the playing out of a unilateral and shortsighted stocking decision, made a generation ago, at the risk of a shattered ecological tapestry? If nothing else, this lose-lose makes a case for minimal tampering in the future. Yet to this day, state fish and wildlife departments continue to introduce exotic species (and even novelty hybrids) to a large percentage of fish-supporting lakes on public lands, wilderness areas being no exception.

◊◊◊

What, exactly, Yellowstone is supposed to offer has always been a matter of broad interpretation. From a giant civic center of tennis courts, swimming pools, and social galas, to a showcase for ambitious and novel feats of architecture and engineering, to a living classroom of nature lessons, to pure wilderness, "red in tooth and nail"—Americans have had a difficult time agreeing upon what they mean by "Wonderland." 2015 escalated a debate over implementing blanket cellphone and wireless service across the natural area. Do people go to Yellowstone to get away, or to share it live on social media? As the debates rage on, Jen and I prefer to extricate ourselves. We know only to seek an understanding of the land directly—which is not to say I'm altogether comfortable with what I concede by doing so.

That afternoon after work, Sam took us up one of his favorite mountains above Sylvan Pass. Landlubber I am, it was a relief to step back from the water, and up against sky. The air was surprisingly clear over the Washakie Wilderness and I was almost pleased to find that, despite all the time we'd spent stitching it up with our footprints, the horizon looked as perplexing as ever. In the opposite direction, I studied neighboring Avalanche Peak, forested in what looked like steel wool. Former USFS entomologist and writer Jesse Logan called Avalanche "the epicenter of whitebark tragedy," and perhaps there really isn't a more succinct illustration of the changes characterizing Yellowstone today: a mountain where nearly every tree is dead, the squirrels, bears, martens, and nutcrackers seemingly departed, and an empty wind now reigns. A home for the Once-ler. Then, a white plume caught my eye on the Central Plateau. Due west of Lake Village, the plateau is one of the rising magmatic domes of the park, a reminder that Yellowstone's supervolcano is forty thousand years past due for the sort of explosion that could darken the sun for years. At first the plume resembled a colossal geyser, but in a matter of minutes it bloomed into an unmistakable forest fire. Sam said he hoped it would go big. I took that to mean all those days killing fish were weighing on him.

2

Jen and I weren't motivated for another shot at hitchhiking the next day. We puttered the morning away and fell back on Sam for another ride after he finished work. It was alarming to realize that, as we drove out the East Entrance, we still weren't settled on where we wanted to be let out. All along, we'd kept our plans loose so we could follow our inclinations as we went—that was for fun as much as anything. This time was a little different: it was the weight of the decision that kept us putting it off. From the very beginning, we understood that escaping from the North Fork of the Shoshone would be our route-finding crux.

Our map didn't help. Even though the USGS has mapped the Absarokas into 7.5 minute quadrangles just like everywhere else, the data hasn't been polished into sleek plastic recreation maps like all the neighboring ranges.* Absaroka travelers who can't pay $8 for every 55 square miles or so are stuck with the map put out by the Forest Service, which features low-resolution, 200 foot contour lines, and inaccurate—I would go as far as to say *egregiously* inaccurate—depictions of trails, some of them in places that trails could not exist.

If Jen and I sought only the safest choice, it would have been the first trailhead we passed, just outside the Yellowstone boundary, where the river leaves the highway in a sharp turn north, and a major pack trail connects out the headwaters. But this North Fork Trail is also the most familiar to us, and the furthest from where our last leg had let off. Continuing downstream, back toward the Elk Fork, we passed many other canyons to choose from. Unlike the North Fork, however, none hosted trails that crossed over to Sunlight Creek—the next major drainage to the north—and many didn't claim trails at all. As the spine of the divide rose in elevation and the road continued to drop, our options entailed longer bushwhacks up a still-rising mountain crest, increasing the danger we'd be cliffed out of entire watersheds.** Like

---

* On the locator map for local Beartooth Publishing, which has mapped the ecosystem from the Winds to the Tobacco Roots, Crazies to the Big Holes, the Absarokas are a more than conspicuous omission. Similar holes have surfaced in other data sets. Says geologist Margaret M. Hiza, "As my thesis work continued, I became increasingly aware of how little was known about the (Absaroka Volcanic Province) as a whole, even though it is located in an area famous for its geologic features... Even more astounding is the fact that the AVP has never been completely mapped in detail. Only general maps based primarily on aerial photographs exist for much of the province today."

** It bears repeating that, more than any other mountain range I know, the layered breccia cliffs of the Absarokas have the power to seriously shut down impulsive wandering. A lot can hide within a 200-foot contour. The North Fork scenery (boosters of what's also known as the Buffalo Bill Cody Memorial Highway all quote Teddy Roosevelt, who apparently called the North Fork of the Shoshone "the 50 most beautiful miles in America") excels in ruggedness and verticality. Starting from the door of Jen's old bunkhouse in Wapiti, we've gone on day hikes that gain 6,000' of elevation—Teton-caliber relief. And while other mountain ranges have rock formations with names like "Haystack" or "Elephant's Back," only the North Fork has "Bart Simpson on a Skateboard" ("An unfamiliar intersection between geology and acrobatics," as Tim Cahill remarked about Absaroka formations elsewhere); that's just one of a number of outlandish hoodoos that are part of the Wapiti Formation, a volcanic deposit that weathers erratically and reaches depths of five thousand feet. Another clue to its formidability: in spite of all the

Francs Peak in the Washakie, the highest North Absaroka peaks are nearly the furthest east.

On the other end of the spectrum, Sweetwater Creek was the most aesthetic choice for our route north, and many times I'd dared myself to commit to its fateful challenge. It meets the North Fork directly across the highway from where we emerged on the Elk Fork. Near its upper end, about twelve miles up from the river—most of that bushwhacking—the creek goes over what is called Sweetwater Creek Falls: a cascade guessed to be the biggest waterfall in Wyoming. The amazing thing about this grandiose title is that nobody seems to have settled it. While the Falls can't compare to Yellowstone's Lower Falls in terms of volume or sheerness, suffice it to say the creek drops about 1,600' in half a mile—over five times the drop of Wyoming's most famous waterfall.

There was definitely something appealing about Sweetwater's challenge. And there was definitely something unappealing. I know that moving over fourth class breccia with a heavy pack can take hours to the half mile, and the implications of getting turned around after so much thrashing—in terms of both logistics and morale—were heartbreaking. My deciding factor ended up being a completely irrelevant one. The map showed a ranch filling the bottom of Sweetwater, and I loathe negotiating private land on foot: following arbitrary fence lines alongside hills, getting chased by barking dogs, that sort of thing. (I later discovered from Jen it had been abandoned after a fire many years earlier.) At an obscure canyon three miles upstream of Sweetwater called Clearwater Creek, I suggested we pull over. It looked so wonderfully overlooked.

◊◊◊

---

specialized training and applied technology at the disposal of modern rock climbers, nobody touches those soaring, vertical walls. Featurelessness is one thing—people find a way—but loose and crumbly is another. I'd even hazard that an infamously short-sighted line from a 1918 issue of *Scientific American*, which declared of one of the Tetons, "The summit has never been attained and probably never will be," might yet be sincerely reapplied to some of the gothic masterpieces of Absaroka backcountry.

Back on the trail, I didn't feel as fresh as I thought I should. Our hope, when we set out from Lander, was to draw a line across the ecosystem with our footsteps; this had a decided purity to it. In the last few days we'd found ourselves buzzing back and forth across our walking route in car seats. Each drive added something to the trip—meeting people, new sights and flavors—but they also wore away at the headspace we'd been creating. Here was the worldview of "nodes and connectors," encouraged by so much transportation and information technology, in which we are taught that the end (be it airport, webpage, income bracket, or scenic viewpoint) is all that matters, and we mustn't distract ourselves en route. Each drive jogged me back to the privileged and very modern circumstances that enabled our style of trip, and now I had to get over it again. Luckily, I had good help.

Clearwater was a hot and dusty place that day. The trees were all burnt dead, while a belt of brushy cottonwood regeneration stuck close to the creek. The wild rose bushes were notable, though, bristled into a knee-high weave with crimson fruit hanging thick as Christmas ornaments. We didn't walk far before we saw an unusual pile of fresh bear scat. Roughly the size and consistency of a bison patty, it was composed of a pink paste flecked with thousands of white seeds. The bear had been gorging on rosehips. As we continued on these piles began to appear regularly on the trail. Then, in a large thicket of cottonwood saplings, a sudden commotion broke out—canopy thrashing, branches snapping. We never saw the animal, but *bear* was an awfully logical guess.

Unfortunately, with our late start, we already needed to think about finding a camp. The canyon was narrow with very steep sides. Downfall choked the bottom. If we had a decent trail we would've punched further out of the rosehips and bear sign, but the map only showed two miles' worth, and we lost it long before we got that far. Then the canyon forked and our branch became narrower yet. I suggested we make camp before running out of options. We walked around the bottom until we found a space in the jackstraw large enough for our tent, then another for our kitchen a little ways away. It would work just fine. Soon I had water heating over a crackling fire; Jen reclined with a book.

When a twig snapped both of our heads shot up. A grizzly was nosing around the foot of a Doug fir near our tent, hardly fifty feet from where we were sitting. I was gripped by an immediate physical response: my heart, my breath, my mind, everything sped up. I grabbed for the bear spray, fortunately within arm's reach, and stood. "Hey bear," I said. The animal lifted its eyes to us, froze, then turned on its heels and took off, leaping over logs as it went. Soon it was out of sight.

"My heart is pounding," I said, turning to Jen.

"Mine's not," she said, and she really did look perfectly calm. "I don't know what's wrong with me."

I've seen bears differently ever since I was bluff charged by a sow grizzly with cubs when I wasn't carrying bear spray. I still love to see them—but I can also imagine them doing something besides running away. It's like the time I went cliff jumping when I was seventeen. We floated down to a sandstone bluff on Montana's Jefferson River. The popular consensus is that it's fifty-five feet tall. It wasn't especially hard for me to jump off. But the feeling of freefall disturbed me—it felt like death itself—and the next time I went rock climbing, I had a visceral imagination for what it would feel like if something went wrong. It didn't feel like an innocent game anymore.

We slept with the rain fly off that night. Watching the stars wasn't half my reasoning: I had bears on my mind, and didn't want to feel too closed in. Sometime before five in the morning I heard a branch crack. My eyes sprung open; I held my breath. Leaves rustled. The bearspray was in my hand without thinking: I paranoiacally brought it into the tent for once. Then I turned on my headlamp and stepped outside.

"What are you doing?" asked Jen.

"There's something out there."

"Well I have to pee," she said, and scampered past my legs. I slowly scanned my little LED around the perimeter of camp and stopped when I saw the reflection of eyes. Tapetum lucidum, "the bright carpet." That's the membrane at the back of the pupil that gives most animals much better night vision than people. A pair in your headlamp's glow is an effect well suited to horror movies. These were spaced wide, not high enough to be a moose, the color of pie tins. I held my light to them tensely, like it had the power to immobilize, until the animal had

THE COMPROMISED WILD 141

enough. One light eclipsed, then the other bobbed forward until it too blinked out, and I was left with the heavy sounds of something big creeping away. I went back in the tent, laid down, and stared walleyed at the stars until they dissolved in pale.

◊◊◊

I felt rather stupid for putting us in such an obvious position to encounter bears. Every campground in the North Fork—all eight of them—prohibited tent campers that summer. As I've mentioned, a rash of bear conflicts gripped the ecosystem.* So many things were working against the animals.

Terrible whitebark nut production, drought and record heat that stunted the productivity of forbs and berries, low elk numbers, the above-mentioned cutthroat dilemma, record tourism numbers, an exurban development boom in every county surrounding the park. Grizzly counts for the ecosystem were strong going into the season—over seven hundred—but that meant they had their own kind to compete with on top of everything else. Jen and I could indulge the feeling of boundless wilderness all we wanted, but when it comes to population dynamics of a large omnivore like the grizzly, the entire Greater Yellowstone is best described as a claustrophobic island; the sea level rising. In a hundred years or so, absolutely zero genetic exchange has taken place between those bears and the closest neighboring population in northern Montana.**

---

* In the most recent incident, on August 7th of that year, a nurse at the clinic in Lake Village was killed by a grizzly on the Elephant Back Trail, a trail that Jen and I walked in a couple idle hours starting from the employee trailer park where Sam lived. And perhaps the most chilling of the recent bear-related human fatalities took place off the opposite end of the North Absaroka Wilderness. In 2011, a sow grizzly walked around the Soda Butte Campground, pawing and biting people through their tent walls, before dragging one camper out and partially consuming him. As far as "why": she was starving from an invasion of tapeworms, had cubs to feed, and weighed her fear of humans against these uncompromising demands of survival. Nothing says it can't happen again.

** It just so happens that summer marked the first grizzly sighting in Montana's Big Hole Valley that anybody could remember. A perfect middle ground between the Crown of the Continent and Greater Yellowstone ecosystems, two grizzly habitats so close yet so far apart, the

It's worth repeating that the Greater Yellowstone Ecosystem, both as a concept and unit of management, was first popularized in the context of grizzly bear studies. When brothers Frank and John Craighead recorded their subjects hanging out, for example, at Yellowstone dumps, checking out the elk situation on a private ranch, coming back for the trout spawn, then wandering onto the Shoshone National Forest to eat pine nuts, they realized that there was no point in talking about a park wildlife population. There were only populations that used the park at times, and otherwise negotiated paradigms of management more complex than Yellowstone's specific mixture of recreation and preservation.

In 2015, thirty-five grizzly mortalities in the GYE were proven to be human-caused (1 out of every 20 bears), and many others were the subjects of inconclusive investigations. At least ten percent of the entire population died. Over all these struggles loomed the prospect of delisting—a grizzly hunting season for the first time since 1974.

I was happy to see bears in the Clearwater. But to see them was to disrupt them, and the last thing I wanted to do was cause them more trouble. September is a pivotal month in terms of surviving winter: if possible, a single grizzly will put on one hundred pounds. That's no small task, when all you have to work with are rosehips.

◊◊◊

It took us the entire next day to fight our way out of the burn and into the subalpine of upper Clearwater Creek. In my attempt to lead us I faced one unhappy decision after another—which downfall-choked canyon wall to traverse, whether to drop low or stay high. Among other things, we found ourselves wishing the Clearwater climbed faster than it did. Steep canyons mean changing conditions—as long as one biotic community keeps segueing into another, the worst can only last so long. While Clearwater Creek wound imperceptibly upwards, its steep walls—

Big Hole could facilitate just the sort of genetic crossover that Montana grizzlies need—if only they were tolerated by the rural ranching culture. Researchers don't know which ecosystem the bear started from.

trenched in bedrock, incised with steeper side canyons, and crosshatched with burnt logs—had us grossing great quantities of arduous elevation while netting next to nothing.

Somewhere in the thick of that endless gut, as we pushed through a grove of alder on a short game trail, we met three wolves head-on. Unlike most wolves I've seen, those three didn't seem alarmed so much as genuinely confused by us. They quickly fell back into cover but, forgetting their typical caution, they remained curious—staring agog like they couldn't believe their eyes.

By afternoon the creek had gotten small enough we could hop across it in most places. We gave up on the steeps and began working the gravel banks, scrambling the palisade of an occasional log jam, splashing through narrow slots of dark rock sculpted with mossy grottoes. It might not have been any faster, but it offered a welcome change from all the dusty side-hilling, the stobs attacking my shins. We broke into alpine early the next morning. The remainder of that day reduces in my mind to a series of spectacular scenes. The top of Nipple Mesa, one of the broadest plateaus in the Northern Absaroka, is a Martian environment. It is inhabited by microscopic vegetation, inexplicably round boulders, and expanses of colorful mineral soil. Needly, ice-white crystals in conical shapes lay scattered on coarse, dark sand. From one side to the other we couldn't see a tree in the world, just the bulk of nearby mountains, each profile unique. The nipple itself—and no, there is no other word for it—sits on the southern end of the mesa and sports a jaunty crook. Against a horizon of haze, it looked like a teetering shanty tower at the edge of the earth, a madman's observatory. We kept to all fours on top, to resist the wind.

After retrieving our packs just south of Sunlight Peak, we stopped to gaze into the fabulously secluded headwaters of the Sweetwater. A group of twenty-four mountain goats lounged on a hidden bench like luxuriant white tigers in their new coats of luscious fur. A tarn below Sunlight gleamed turquoise from deep behind a great moraine. Its outlet was a series of springs, founting from the side of the mountain, feeding great fertile blooms on the raw tundra. As the water braided across the basin it streaked saturated pigments of jade and mustard beneath walls of volcanic debris.

And that afternoon, as we dropped into the North Fork, I remember shuffling along in rapture, camera-hand compulsively clicking, before a graveyard of great white spruce. It would be difficult to find a living forest that offered a more intricately conceived autumn palate. Fallen trunks tangled through with bright red huckleberry, whortleberry in lemon (leaves) and lime (stems), white and yellow sprays of pearly everlasting, and the feathered textures of swaying grasses. Whorls of fireweed flashed every hue, pink to plum to persimmon, simultaneously. Lastly, a symbol of hope: whitebark pine, though hardly represented among the burned snags, was making a good run at colonizing the ruins.

◊◊◊

The Absarokas were built in three major episodes—formally referred to as groups—that roughly proceeded from northwest to southeast. Grouped are relatively distinct geologic formations that "interfinger" one another, overlap and blend—and those consist of contemporaneous ash-falls and lava flows and pyroclastic flows and lahars, expelled from a constellation of scattered volcanoes and vents. It looks as messy as it sounds. But the general idea is that the Washburn Group occurred first, then the Sunlight Group, and then the Thorofare Group, with a few overlaps in both time and space. On the North Fork we were firmly in the middle of the Sunlight Group, and our route up Clearwater led us into its heart.

I see parallels between these mountains above Cody and the career of the most famous artist ever born there. James Johnson Sweeney described the first exhibition of Jackson Pollock, one of America's greatest abstract-expressionist painters, in 1943: "Volcanic. It has fire. It is unpredictable. It is undisciplined. It spills out of itself in a mineral prodigality, not yet crystallized." Jackson Pollock reached international renown for the "drip-paintings" he created between 1947 and 1950. The way he painted was as famous as the images themselves. Some called it action-painting, and compared his process to a shamanistic dance: Pollock paced the perimeter of a canvas lain flat on the ground, slashing the air with a stick dipped directly into the paint can, seemingly oblivious to those around him. While critics praised Pollock for giving form and beauty to "chance," few artists from Dadaism to Postmodernism, Pollock included, were comfortable claiming this influence. Instead, he maintained that his work tapped greater, subliminal forces. "When I am in my painting, I'm not aware of what I'm doing," he wrote. "I have no fear of making changes, destroying the image, etc., because the painting has a life of its own. I try to let it come through." Elsewhere, he simplified this explanation: "I am Nature."

Two monster volcanoes dominate the creation story of the Northern Absaroka Wilderness. Neither of them look like volcanoes today. They have been so extensively dismantled by tens of millions of years of glaciation and water erosion that they are identifiable only to the learned and attentive. Time has beaten their telltale cones, once 15,000' high, flush with the seas of rock they emitted; glaciers have scooped and wormed their other dimensions. The named summits in the area today have been distinguished more by erosional patterns than the piling of ejecta.

From early on, great geologists were attracted to the unusually crisp cross-sectional diagrams of volcanism of the North Absaroka. Margaret Hiza explains:

> These ancient volcanoes are similar in form to Mt. Rainier, Mt. Fuji, Mt. Kilimanjaro, and other modern stratovolcanoes, but because they are old and inactive, yet well-preserved with canyons cut through them by glacial activity, they afford geologists a unique opportunity to study the inner plumbing system of volcanoes.

Joseph P. Iddings was the forerunner, and most accomplished, of these geologists. When he named a new family of volcanic rocks, distinct for their high potassium content, the "absarokite-shoshonite-banakite series," he brought these words, endemic to native peoples of the GYE, into technical discussions around the world. It was Iddings who sleuthed out the Sunlight Volcano, king of the Sunlight Group, along with other volcanoes to the northwest. His time in the area must have been what adventurous geologists' dreams are made of—it's difficult to imagine such exciting exploration and rewarding discoveries could ever befall a more receptive mind. His discovery of Monument Peak, near the northern edge of the province, prompted this ecstatic poem:

> I have found where ye dikelets converge
> Where ye breccias chaotic'ly lie
> Where ye low-dipping lava-flows gradually rose
> To a cone that once reached to the sky.
> But all vestage [sp] of cone disappeared
> Like an ant-hill before ye bear's paws
> When ye snow and ye ice in a glacier combined
> To scratch it away with its claws.
> In its place a flat basin remains
> Within a rocky, precipitous wall
> Where ye gabbro and diorite reach a coarser grain
> By ye side of which all else looks small
> Then, Hurrah! For ye gullet of fire
> That belched forth ye hot lava streams
> That threw up ye breccias, and spit out ye tuffs,
> But was choked up at last, so it seems.

And a pity it is the poetic form fell from favor among research scientists. Today, the summit of Sunlight Peak stands three miles southwest of the core of the late, great, Sunlight Volcano. The third highest peak in the Northern Absaroka Wilderness, it is the only of these three within ten miles of the defining Yellowstone-Bighorn hydrological divide. So, Hurrah! As far as reference points go, it is a useful surrogate.

What later became the Sunlight Mining District—a major cherry stem that pinches the wilderness's outline into a lumpy "L"—Iddings fittingly named the "Great Dike Region." Jen and I approached the hub of these dikes from the south, before turning west. For nearly two days we watched this incredible starburst of dark walls gathering, slicing indiscriminately through ridge and canyon alike, toward their nexus at Copper Lakes. The *Bonney Guide* explains this "dazzling center" to readers by referring to a USGS geological map, where "tiny red lines… radiate outward in a glorious sunburst about four inches in diameter."

A dike is a plane of rock, more vertical than horizontal (if not, it is a "sill"), that cuts through the surrounding rock. Dikes are often created when magma wells up at extremely high pressure below a clogged volcano but fails to blow the cap—so the hot liquid pushes outward, fracturing the earth, injecting into cracks and hardening there. When dikes are harder than the surrounding rock they can erode into long, straight, and sometimes uncanny walls. A concentration of dikes is known as a swarm, and on our closest pass to Sunlight Peak, I gained some insight into that term. Dikes crossed and collided in a way that brought to mind crazy flight patterns, contrails in the sky.

◊◊◊

As an academic subject, geology has a reputation for being dry and uncompelling. Assigning an age to a rock requires numbers; it requires math and chemistry. And these symbolic languages, corresponding variously to subatomic particles and epochs of time, lend themselves to casual manipulation. Yet giving rocks *meaning* never ceases to be an extreme exercise in perspective, for which there is no shorthand. It requires an original act of imagination. Problematically, the tedious and rule-intensive parameters of scientific discipline don't always encourage the imagination, while the disinterestedness actually discourages one from "feeling" it. When this is the case, the terminology symbolizes nothing of this world, and the subject becomes dead to us. (I speak for my own experiences in chemistry class.)

Geologic time contests the significance that we give to our lives, our culture, and our species. It is a form of storytelling that casts our entire planet as the protagonist. Earth, we learn, is an unpredictable dispenser of disasters and harmonies that convulse to the surface before being redigested, deconstructed, metamorphosed, and leached. The circulatory system of this planet is whimsical, not as vigorous as it used to be, and thoroughly mortal.

I find it disturbing to regard a piece of Archaen rock with the knowledge that, in three billion more years, the world may well be annihilated by a red giant sun two hundred times its current size—meaning this planet is already past its half-life. No rock born today can reach such a pedigree. Even worse: a pebble of Devonian limestone. Made from the cemented shells of thousands of generations of arthropods, limestone production could end in the next 500 million years, as the earth may have already become barren of life from a runaway greenhouse effect—and that's if humans don't bring it on a lot sooner.

These bigger pictures of life and metaphysics challenge the naturalist mindset. They illuminate the need for philosophy as a counterpart to science. My tendency is to revere nature as I see it; I am not especially receptive to, say, the debate over an open and closed universe. I am more than a little intimidated by the night sky. I am attached to this world, and life as it exists here, and I want some version of it to go on forever. I am much less disturbed by the thought of my own death than the thought of the world gone cold, green buds unfurling for the last time, one galaxy bashing into another. It doesn't matter if I'm long gone and forgotten.

Life wants life. I think of all those animal sparks, that have died without expectation of an afterlife, as part of the same truth—a common striving—that is fundamentally right. And in this sense humankind may truly represent something transcendent: we refuse death, this is our curse. Our fervency may generate the power to sow life on other planets. In this sense we may represent the future of life, the new nature, after all. It's a high-stakes bet, incredibly unlikely, and we'll have to risk everything just to find out. Still we live as though a miraculous escape is inevitable, and infinite is ours—in so doing, we hasten the day of reckoning.

◊◊◊

It was slow progress along the divide of the Shoshone North Fork and Sunlight Creek. Our travel was restricted to an unconsolidated spine of deranged geology. We crept painfully over the distinctly silhouetted knob of Land Mountain, and after that, its arduous satellites. At an unnamed point a short but effortful distance to the west—a triple divide of the Lamar River, Sunlight Creek, and Torrent Creek—we reached the Yellowstone boundary for the first time (on foot, that is). From there, the ridge mellowed and the few remaining dikes were less bothersome than fun. As we gained the last rise before our destination for the day we passed three backpackers going the other direction. We were surprised to see people, no doubt about it, but more surprising was how, less than a hundred feet from one another, we all elected to share quick waves but not a single spoken word. I got a kick out of what I interpreted as a seasoned understanding, a mutual respect for the spirit of the place. Our voluntary silence said more than words could have.

Jen and I ran out of water long before we reached the rim of One Hunt Creek. Her stance seemed enlightened: "If you're doing everything right, sometimes you have too much and sometimes you don't have enough." It's true. Some days we find a spring or a snowfield halfway through and carry too much weight for nothing. When we don't find one—and we've had some real surprises—we get thirsty. So we shoot for the middle to understand both extremes, accepting the famine because we accept the feast. It's a strategy that serves in other fields, too, because it isn't necessarily to your benefit to have everything you want, all of the time.

We dropped about five hundred feet back into the North Absaroka before finding a good flat spot in One Hunt Creek. Surprise, it was an old horse camp. There were abandoned food cans (Vienna Sausage?), gallon jugs, cut rounds, a nasty fire pit, and a stump initialed by chainsaw. Common crimes against wilderness. When you see this kind of impact, it is tempting to condemn horse parties wholesale. Of course, it's not that horse use is categorically irresponsible; it's that slobs on horses can carry more disposables and bigger power tools than slobs on foot can. It's one thing to be ignorant and careless, it's another thing to be ignorant, careless, and powerful. So when pack animals are employed as agents of bad habits, I fault the very availability of cheap power, though it appeals to the irresponsible and responsible alike. Here, our sweat can keep us honest.

By 8 o'clock we were in the tent for good. Rain slapped nylon. The wind, which trashed us all day, gusted angrily between abrupt windows of calm. During those reprieves we could track the noise of the gust as it tore away through distant trees. I tried to visualize its design: it never occurred to me that wind, more than the whole sky moving, might paint isolated strokes or flow in streams.

We were entering the longest stretch of country unknown to us on the entire trip. Neither of us had been from mile 67 to 88[*] along the Lamar-Clarks Fork divide. There were many noble mountains to be checked out, wonderfully remote alpine basins to drop a tent. Yet here was the bad weather. A forecast we saw in Lake suggested that an increased chance of rain might last for three days. Nevertheless, Jen and I wanted to climb Black Mountain, and we woke the next morning undeterred: sometimes one must envision success as a simple matter of resolve. In cold, unceasing rain, we left camp, crossed the basin, and ascended a steep ridge. By the time we topped a summit along the Sunlight divide there was no visibility to speak of, the sleet was horizontal, and it was difficult to stand. We lurched up to the plateau edge that would've led us closer to Black—a steep breccia ridge, peopled with hoodoos, hammered in sleet. Suicide. When I managed to get turned around I couldn't immediately say which direction we'd come from.

So we tried—and established, to our satisfaction, that the situation was out of our control. We got back to the tent numb, wet, nearly shivering. After changing clothes we burrowed into the sleeping bag to let the rest of the day pass us by—wrote letters, talked about most anything. I got completely wrapped up reading *In the Spirit of Crazy Horse* by Peter Matthiessen, a belabored but engrossing chronicle of the prosecution of traditional Oglala Sioux in the 1970s:

> The old Lakota was wise. He knew that man's heart, away from nature, becomes hard; he knew that lack of respect for growing, living things soon led to lack of respect for humans, too.
>
> —Luther Standing Bear

So easily did time pass with rain tapping on the tent, so grateful was I for our minimal refuge, dinnertime took me by surprise. Before we fell asleep, I told Jen it wasn't such a bad day and meant it: I was never

---

[*] The Park Service guards its border with National Forest closely, and once sent rangers to walk its forlorn lines every year. That's why, uncharacteristically, these mileages are marked on some maps.

checking my watch or wishing the time away. I told her we weather a storm well together.

But then the next day was the same. It wasn't worse, but it begged the question: how much longer can we keep this up? When an eye of the storm passed over at 1:30 pm, we decided to make a break for it. We packed everything wet, then hurriedly scampered out the steep, slick headwall of One Hunt Creek toward the divide. The rain resumed before we got there. But at least we had a trail for the time being, and the low clouds made the route ahead look hauntingly beautiful.

We had a trail, but it wasn't like most national park trails. Long sections lacked any vestige of tread. Instead, orange markers flagged the route, and most of them were knocked over under a heavy blanket of fresh snow. Even though we'd been there before, the fog kept throwing us. Approaching Hoodoo Mountain, an ordinarily open and cheery spot, I hounded after trail clues like it was a lifeline, only to lose it again and again. Near the eponymous rock features, which looked especially ghostly through slashing streaks of horizontal snow, we at last picked up a consistent tread. We weren't about to give that up. So we abandoned our ambition of sticking to the rugged divide, and dropped further into the park.

◊◊◊

In the earliest chapter of park tourism, when many Yellowstone visitors were self-sufficient on horseback, Hoodoo Basin was one of the park's most touted attractions.[*] In audience to the excitement was the incising wit of Rudyard Kipling. One chapter of his *American Notes*, which is based on his 1889 visit to Yellowstone ("Today I'm in the Yellowstone National Park, and I wish I were dead," reads the famous first line), has proven to be a timeless commentary on the touristy hype of national parks. Kipling recalls,

---

[*] It is named for an outcrop of spindly, wax-dripping figures that are typical of the flanks of many nearby peaks, and was touted by superintendent P. W. Norris as the "Goblin Labyrinth." The more time one spends in the Absarokas, the less remarkable the spot is.

all that I had not seen—the forest of petrified trees with amethyst crystals in their black hearts; the great Yellowstone Lake where you catch your trout alive in one spring and drop him into another to boil him; and most of all of that mysterious Hoodoo region where all the devils not employed in the geysers live and kill the wandering bear and elk, so that the scared hunter finds in Death Gulch piled carcasses of the dead whom no man has smitten. Hoodoo-land with the overhead noises, the bird and beast and devil rocks, the mazes and the bottomless pits—all these things I missed.

Kipling's sarcasm isn't entirely fair. At least, these sites all have *some* basis in reality: even Death Gulch is real, more or less. Thomas Jagger took a picture of a pile of eight dead bears there in 1897, but it takes some subterranean voodoo, plus a rare inversion, to trap the gas in such lethal concentrations.* "Hoodoo-land," meanwhile, mazes and pits aside, has largely been forgotten. Modern reliance on the road network makes it one of the more remote areas of the park, and the backcountry permit system severely limits how many people can ever go there, even if they want to.

So it's funny to think that Hoodoo Basin reached its height of popularity before the era of park tourism. Hoodoo Peak is a four-way divide between two branches of the Lamar River (Yellowstone's greatest backcountry river valley) and two branches of Crandall Creek (a great fan of a watershed, composed of five major tributaries, that drains into Clarks Fork of the Yellowstone). To the south of Hoodoo Peak, as we had just experienced, are miles of gently rumpled alpine tundra; exceptional traveling and hunting ground. When Jack Haynes visited the area in 1924, he recorded a testament to that fact: "I saw a large, ancient Indian camp ground northeast of Parker Peak [Parker Peak defines the west edge of Hoodoo Basin]… The area consisting of three or four acres was covered with tepee poles—hundreds of them." This site, corroborated in the notes of other visitors, was the largest recorded Native American habitation site in the park; fancy it was located at about 9,500'. It is supposed these wickiups belonged to Mountain Shoshone—Sheepeaters—whose traditional habitations took economical, pole-based

---

* Now Wahb Springs, after Seton's fictional grizzly, who in the final pages of *The Biography of a Grizzly* is called to that place because he is ready to die. It's not fifteen miles away from where we were, down in Cache Creek.

forms. But as a topographical link, the locale was utilized by many other tribes, and over many centuries.

In historic times, Hoodoo Basin played its most pivotal role during the Nez Perce War of 1877.* That year, over 2,500 members of the tribe traveled 1,170 miles from their homeland in eastern Oregon toward the hope of sanctuary in Canada. (They were apprehended just forty miles short of their goal.) It was late August when General O. O. Howard pursued the Nez Perce into nascent Yellowstone Park. He lost them after they turned off the Bannock Trail at today's Nez Perce Creek. By the time they reached the upper Lamar River, the Nez Perce enjoyed enough of a lead to risk a couple days' rest. But as Howard persisted in tracking them from the rear, two additional divisions of the US Army blockaded Paradise Valley and the lower Clarks Fork—the safest escape routes from that rugged region of the park. So the Nez Perce feinted a move into the unguarded North Fork of the Shoshone, and when Colonel Sturgis abandoned the Clarks Fork to cut them off, the exiles hurried down Sunlight Creek and out the Clarks Fork to the Bighorn. The coordination achieved between Nez Perce scouts could, one thinks, hardly have been improved with cell phones. Almost two more weeks would pass before another, fresh army division briefly intercepted the Nez Perce at the Battle of Canyon Creek east of Billings. The tribe's strategies during this war are still taught as part of a basic military education.

---

* "War." Today, we'd probably choose a different word to describe the armed pursuit of an entire community of men, women, and children, themselves fleeing an illegal internment effort.

3

"America's Best Idea," in reference to the creation of national parks, was a commonly heard refrain in the year leading up to the 2016 centennial of the National Park Service (NPS). Needless to say, it is a bold claim, and sure to bewilder those more directly benefited by the Civil Rights Act, for example. Calling the parks the best idea we ever had does, however, accurately describe the NPS in the eyes of many, who have traditionally demonstrated a level of allegiance, even zealousness, toward the NPS that is basically unimaginable in any other government bureau. (In one illustrative incident, Secretary of the Interior John A. Carver complained of an agency manual as having "the mystic, quasi-religious sound of a manual for the Hitler Youth

THE COMPROMISED WILD   155

Movement." He then felt it necessary to elucidate: the NPS "isn't a religion, and it shouldn't be thought of as such.") This sterling reputation deserves more than mockery. Geographically, national parks are places of superlative natural splendor, which is a lot in itself. But on top of that, they have also been tasked with a ridiculously serious job: getting modern people to revalue the welfare of this planet before it's too late.

Climate change, wasted resources, polluted resources, extinction—and uniting them all, overpopulation. So many of the greatest crises facing life on this planet stem from human denial of natural consequences—a deluded exceptionality. While this theme fits into a multi-millennial trajectory of self-reflexivity in human culture, many of us still retain innate affinities for the wild and primitive. We *want* to be outside—and this basic fact creates hope that, by simply reintroducing individuals to nature, a more responsible consciousness can be sown. For designating nature's most spectacular places, making them accessible, accommodating crowds, and offering interpretations that engage the mind, national parks are suited to the task. So we arrive at the concept of parks as salvation—panacea for a self-destructing race. Only here have we "clearly proved that our rapacious society [can] hold its hand," as Wallace Stegner wrote in his namesake essay from 1983, "The Best Idea We Ever Had."

Demonstrating self-restraint wasn't exactly the reason for creating national parks,* but it's in there somewhere, and historians trace its thread throughout. As John Muir summarized on a Sierra Club outing in 1895: "If people could be got into the woods, even for once, to hear the trees speak for themselves, all difficulties in the way of forest preservation would vanish." A 2016 *National Geographic* article proved the endurance of his theory by documenting NPS efforts to draw in certain demographics at nearly any cost. "Does it matter how the parks fit into [young people's] lives?" the author Timothy Egan asks, before

---

* At least, a not-insignificant portion of the momentum behind the designation came from well-connected financiers like Jay Cooke. In national parks, Cooke saw a broad-reaching promotional device for the Northern Pacific Railway.

answering: "Not really." If he's right, the NPS mission boils down to this: bring in more people. Period.

A subsequent quote in Egan's article, from Superintendent Jon Jarvis, compares operating the national parks to running a business—a matter of tapping markets. The summer that Jen and I walked through Yellowstone on our way home, the NPS was repackaging itself and launching its largest-ever publicity campaign.* Among other Internet-age offerings, they deliberately projected some images of national parks as crowded places, to appeal to people who are drawn to crowds. Their efforts paid off. In 2015, Yellowstone visitors broke four million for the first time—up 16.6% from 2014, which had been the second busiest year. 2016 broke the record again, and the national park system as a whole set comparable records. While the advertising campaign blazed forth, it was fair to wonder if the other, more fundamental part of their mission—that is, increasing American awareness of the environment—was making similar strides.

I first encountered the above quote by John Muir, *all difficulties in the way of forest preservation would vanish*, while reading Wyoming author Jack Turner. He offers it as the most concise formulation of what he calls "Muir's Mistake." Mistaken is the assumption that, when a materialist sensibility encounters non-materialist values, the latter will override the former. Let us now entertain the possibility that it will not. Says Turner, "[Muir] could not have known that even the wild would eventually succumb to consumer culture," an unfortunate tendency that I find consistent to my experiences, here, there, and everywhere else. Materialism is not threatened by intangibles so much as ingenious at reinterpreting and appropriating them, perverting and subverting them.

I don't feel critical of national parks so much as critical of our expectations for them. That is, the landscapes infatuate me; I have no special allegiance to the agency that claims and publicizes them. It seems

---

* Ironies of Wyoming's accompanying campaign—the slogan "Roam Free," coupled with images of the same wild bison that are rounded up and shot each winter when they wander outside the park boundaries, according to the demands of state Departments of Livestock—will not be explored here. But let it suffice to say: nearly one thousand Greater Yellowstone bison were being destroyed on a yearly basis at the time of Wyoming's ad run, as much as a quarter of the population.

obvious to me that the power of these isolated places will not save the planet from the short-term interests of all the people who depend on it. Timothy Egan's professed ambivalence as to what teenagers actually do in national parks has been playing out in a larger sense, and much the way you'd expect. "Rangers are often overwhelmed as they deal with the growing catalog of tourist misdeeds," reports Todd Wilkinson. "In 2015, Yellowstone staff issued a record 52,036 resource warnings to visitors." Once park infrastructure reaches capacity, any additional increase in visitation is reflected in disproportionately large spikes in car accidents, life flights, road rage, illegal camping. And, one may suppose, visitor dissatisfaction.

More insidiously, in national parks-cum-tourist traps, unintentional and outmoded attitudes toward nature are disseminated through a circus-like pop culture,* science in the parks faces an embattled history of politicization and gag-orders, and, worst of all, the dire implications of runaway human appetites run unchecked, despite valiant agency messaging efforts, and a certain smugness among their outdoorsy clientele.

Outdoorsiness, it turns out, can be as hollow of an image as any other.

◇◇◇

> *When the symbols provided by the social group no longer work… the individual cracks away, becomes dissociated and disoriented, and we are confronted by what can only be named a pathology of the symbol.* —Joseph Campbell

We can ask a lot from these places, yes, because they have a lot to give. But if we do, we must back our demands with proportional commitments to their stewardship. Even the economic justification, superficial as that measurement is, is there: every dollar currently invested in park management stimulates a nearly ten-dollar return to the economy. As we've redoubled our efforts to popularize Yellowstone,

---

* Two emerging sub-genres of tourist infractions: social media-derived publicity pranks, and all things drones.

however, we haven't made good on sustaining what's there. More people pour in, crime goes up, ranger numbers go down (in 2015, the lowest in 54 years), and the $600 million, fifty-year maintenance backlog, in this park alone, continues to grow. It's a fact we're wringing the golden goose dry. One ranger described the 2016 NPS visitation spike "as if it had been under siege." Arches National Park closed after a line of idling vehicles backed up for more than a mile along a busy highway outside the park, and similar jams are common not just in Yellowstone gateway communities such as West Yellowstone, but throughout the park interior, as well.

Agency-wide, total visitor numbers spiked by tens of millions the year that Jen and I walked through; my own informal surveys of Yellowstone visitors suggested that nobody could refrain from lamenting the crowds within their first sentence or two. Parks are great insofar as they represent a national dedication to environmental health, but popularity is not the same thing. Our commitment to them must be systematic to be more than symbolic; it must be accountable to something more than consumer appetite. "Yellowstone won't be saved if we stay on the same course," superintendent Dan Wenk warned one reporter.

◊◊◊

A common criticism of wilderness designation is that, rather than promoting a relationship between people and nature, it imposes a mandatory distance. (Opponents call the designation a "lock out.") As one who hunts in the wilderness—be it mushrooms, big game, photographs, or self-knowledge—and otherwise sets out for weeks on end there, year-round, answering to no one, I consider this platform disingenuous. Nowhere else am I so free to engage nature, and free to learn from it.

But in national parks, the complaint gains footing. National parks are expensive. If one college student wanted to spend one night in the backcountry of Grand Teton National Park, it would cost her fifty-five dollars.* And national parks are restrictive. In Yellowstone, Bear Management Areas exclude human use for much or all of the hiking season, across hundreds of thousands of acres.**

Of course, there are reasons behind it. The NPS is mandated to provide "for the enjoyment of the people," and at the same time, keep the landscape "unimpaired for future generations." Since most people enjoy nature in a way that impairs it, the push-pull of these dueling mandates has been given a name of its own: the Park Paradox. No matter what the NPS does, you could make the argument that it is either accomplishing both of these objectives, one at the expense of the other, or neither.† In the present example, all arguments find traction, and endless debatability. Yellowstone has as many smart and talented people invested in its future as could possibly be hoped for: you can't just write off the sophistication of the present balancing act. Yet I am convinced that, when it comes to unimpairment and enjoyment, one issue informs the other. Therefore, I will make the case that Yellowstone is not accomplishing either of its mandates very efficiently—and it all comes down to our culture-wide fixation on popularity.

In order to connect with nature—to care about it—you need to have a relationship with it. If this relationship only goes one-way (nature through the window of a van, or nature explained by a man in uniform), it's something less.‡ To speak for myself, the paved and processed face

---

* $30 entrance fee (good for a week) + $25 backcountry fee. The park argues that the backcountry office is expensive and the people that use it should incur those costs. What they are really saying is that tourism is cheapest when you deal in volumes, and that volumes are their business. For better or worse, they're right.

** The Gallatin BMA is closed May 1 through November 10, in my closest-to-home example. The Clear Creek BMA, meanwhile, is an example of a relatively small unit that, by blocking the mouths of several major canyons, effectively closes a much larger area.

† To take these arguments to their logical extremes: if the park did nothing to manage human use, it would at least leave the people's freedom unimpaired—just not the resource. If it shut people out entirely, it would still arguably provide for their enjoyment, by preserving a resource of the mind (wildness).

‡ The natural world can, of course, be wonderfully engaging even after it is translated into a non-physical subject. The popularity of nature shows on television, or the sorts of "weird insects" books I loved as a kid, are proof. But as a form of human engagement, physical nature is a distinct and uniquely powerful form of experiential learning, one that has no replacement, and

of Yellowstone has never spoken to me. The license and responsibility to explore the backcountry, meanwhile, has invested me irrevocably in the wellbeing of the place.

This necessity of interaction is problematic, as I've mentioned, because when a human interacts with nature, they influence it. When four million people visit Yellowstone each year, the average visitor can't be trusted with the fragile living assets of the park—she represents a culture that is divorced from nature, and lacks a respectful, non-acquisitive way of interacting with what it sees. Therefore, the average visitor gets shuttled around "the Grand Loop Road" instead, herded in and out of parking lots, onto boardwalks, and in circles around visitor centers. Along the way, she is bombarded with messaging. Nature is a public service announcement, it's a drive-thru, it's a spectacle, it's a museum—and it's always, barely, out of reach.

◊◊◊

Maybe Jack Turner's indictment, "Muir's Folly," isn't quite fair. Maybe the folly is that one condition of Muir's prescription ("If people could be got into the woods") is assumed to necessarily give rise to the second ("to hear the trees speak for themselves")—when in reality, it is possible to provide for one while effectively preventing the other. Maybe, in cacophonous Yellowstone, people can't hear anything for themselves.

The modern American is incomparably more sensitive to the context of their own culture than they are to the natural world. As national parks become increasingly complex cultural constructs, millions of annual visits have little or nothing to do with first-hand experiences of nature. It's no exaggeration to say that, as Jen and I brainstormed our ultimate hike across the GYE, we both worked from an unspoken agreement that we'd avoid the park boundaries as much as practicable.

The official line is that there are even off-trail camping permits available for Yellowstone—but I've never succeeded in getting a

---

that is what is lost when Yellowstone becomes synonymous with mass tourism. People can watch movies about Yellowstone at home: they don't need to drive three days to do it.

backcountry ranger to so much as admit to me that these permits exist, and several have explicitly denied it. Overworked national park gatekeepers find themselves, consciously or no, fogging the line between "not recommended" and "not allowed." Elsewhere, cultural norms do the trick. Most visitors are reconciled to enjoying the landscape from crowded roadside areas. If you come strolling out of their picture frame, and cause an elk to withdraw beyond a photographer's telescopic vision, you may be publicly chastised.

◊◊◊

Drawing a hard line between humans and nature is an admission of defeat. The presumptions underlying this segregation are dispelled by the many cultures that have coexisted with wildness for thousands of years: cultures that engage the natural world on a regular basis, see themselves as part of it, foster humility and restraint, and pass down traditions that replenish what they take away. (It should go without saying that our culture is not one of them.) These are the best examples we have for what long-term human survival can look like. From them, we may conclude that love and respect results from understanding, not boundaries or distance.

Less than 1.1% of Yellowstone's 2015 visitors spent a night in the 91.5% of the park that is recommended wilderness. Not only is the average tourist losing his initiative, the park does not facilitate adventure. Vanishing down a rocky trail, to sleep in your own tent and bury your own poop, costs more than visiting multi-million dollar visitor centers, playing with multimedia exhibits, flushing toilets, watching movies, and talking to living history actors.

Even after hundreds of nights in the backcountry together, Jen and I are constantly learning. We are constantly being humbled. We try to understand what it means for us to be out there, sharing in it. We know and understand incredibly little—and yet, this process continues to be the most valuable and engaging of our lives. With every day we spend out, we improve our ways of approaching the landscape: how to pass the night; how to recognize a plant from its leaves; how to proceed.

It seems very reasonable to ask national park backpackers to visit a ranger station and apply for a permit before they head out. It wasn't possible on our trip. And it seems little to ask that they stick to an itinerary. Yet throwing such a constraint on top of the September storm cycle that Jen and I were dealing with would've been dangerous.

Extenuating circumstances aside, the pleasure of backpacking is simply too tied up with the capricious demands of your exercising body, its sudden aches and importunate drives, to survive regimentation—everything returns to the unencumberedness, the tests of volition, the pursuit of feeling. Setting off with a pack on my back, not knowing where I'll end up, matching the tune of my muscles to the length of my gaze: this is my most visceral definition of freedom. That is, it's how I know *belonging*—the unspeaking conversation between physical self and worldly presence. Spontaneity is so fundamental to the experience that I almost want a different word for how they make you do it. I am of Jack Turner's school on the subject: "In every manner conceivable, national parks separate us from the freedom that is the promise of the wild." And if you can't already tell—yes, this is the preamble to the part of the story in which Jen and I break a rule, and then get caught.

In the process of trying to spend my life outside, I realize now, I have become an almost habitual breaker of certain park regulations. I've taken the time to form an understanding of the ecological and cultural intent of the rules, therefore I retain my greater conscience. I feel responsibility toward my understanding of the world, not to the letter of the law.

This doesn't put me above the other rule-breakers: for seeing myself as an exception, I'm like every other asshole. In saying as much, I simply hope to explain what brought us down into Miller Creek, that wet and nasty mid-September day, as objectively as I can.

◊◊◊

That was the second time Jen and I walked together down those switchbacks into Miller Creek late in the afternoon, thereby committing ourselves to spending the night in the park, and the second time we had no backcountry permit in our possession.* The first time, three years earlier, we were improvising a seventy-mile loop out of the North Fork of the Shoshone. While we knew that any ranger would be likely to ticket us, the route made sense in every other way, and it also seemed likely we wouldn't see anyone. Then, all too predictably, our first glimpse of the Miller Creek Guard Station revealed horses in the pasture. Rather than suck it up and continue through on the trail, I suggested we slip around the cabin by the creek. It turned into a prolonged and awkward thrash through log jams and brush, a lot of frantic whispering. The sneak "worked," but was probably unnecessary, and frankly, I get embarrassed just thinking about it. Years later, as Jen and I walked down the switchbacks for the second time, we had a good laugh remembering the time before. Those laughs ended as soon as we saw a turnaround of fresh horse tracks coming up from the cabin.

I was resolved, this time, to face the music. Putting safety and common sense above the shame of a violation notice, we begrudgingly followed the horse tracks down. On the trail, slick with mud, I watched how the horses had skated from side-to-side, punching holes in the loam. When we encountered this group, I reminded myself, I'd need to be able to accept either outcome: the ticket or the warning. But it galled me to imagine a ranger throwing the book when we couldn't match the damage they'd created if we tried. I was resolved, but not at peace.

Then, to our astonishment, we found the cabin empty. The horse tracks continued down trail. Dusk was falling early beneath sodden-wool cloud cover, so we appropriated the dry, covered porch. After hanging up our dripping wet tent, and setting our dinner at a simmer, I was shaking out the sleeping bag when, from the other side of the porch, I

---

* Our hiking days in Yellowstone tend to fall into two categories: days we don't see any other hikers (the majority), and days we see dozens. All my days in the upper Lamar have fallen into the first category: on five different multi-day trips I've taken in the area, I've seen a total of three other parties. All three of those parties consisted entirely of NPS employees. For this reason, the upper Lamar serves as one illustration of the extreme inconsistency in Yellowstone visitorship: human density in the roaded frontcountry is essentially urban, and over 1000 times greater than the backcountry. The categorical nature of NPS regulations, applied uniformly across both areas, creates some constraints that are absurd.

heard Jen's voice. A wavery "Hi?" that died in the dark woods. It made my heart sink. Someone was out there. I walked over to see headlights bobbing toward our sanctuary. Three guys in Park Service slickers. What was this: a stake out?

In a true wilderness setting, rangers are a welcome sight: an opportunity to swap stories, discuss the terrain or the weather. In an over-worked, under-paid, losing-battle tourist setting, as often as not, you prepare yourself for "forest cop."* I wasn't sure what exactly you'd call this—we were way out there, yet we were exactly where we weren't supposed to be. This wasn't the Alaskan bush, where cabins don't have locks, and strangers combine forces against the elements—this was an intensively managed recreation area. This was trespassing on federal property, and it suddenly seemed quite serious. The weather fed my pessimism, and the three men didn't seem any happier to see us.

"Is it just the two of you?" the first one asked, as he reached the steps of the porch.

"Yes."

"Thank God," another exhaled.

This was my first clue that things might turn out all right; a realization we might not be who they thought we were. Still feeling a cocktail of shame and having-known-better, I hurriedly cleared our things out of the way and muttered a confessional of sorts. "We're just passing through… didn't intend to come into the park at all… we don't have a permit or anything… let me get this out of your way." Backpedaling is apologizing only because you got caught.

Picking up on these signals, the three were anxious, actually, to comfort me. "Oh, don't worry about it, you're not in the way." They welcomed us to use the porch and headed inside. "Come on in and we'll give you a cup of coffee." Despite their accommodating words, we moved our tent to the mouth of the horse corral (it turns out these three were traveling on foot), and gobbled our dinner before heading back to the cabin, eager to bury the awkwardness of the first encounter. We quickly learned that these were "just radio guys," the same three we saw days earlier, and the only people we would see in eight days. We laughed

---

* I, too, have been called "forest cop." It's not like it's an easy job.

about the brevity of our initial encounter while walking along the ridge: "I just thought, they probably don't feel like talking right now," one said. A savvy inference if I've ever heard one.

It was a profound pleasure to sit and make an hour of conversation while rain hit the windows. We established a few mutual acquaintances, and all three were excited to hear what we were doing. Before we went to bed, one of the men, the one that I initially mistook for the "bad cop," gave us the biggest compliment of the summer. "If everyone did what you two are doing," he said, looking us in the eyes, "the world would be a different place." His words stuck with me, a vital reminder: if you start getting paranoid and judgmental, desperate to avoid people, they're probably what you need the most.

◇◇◇

The next day we joined the cabin crew for coffee, then cleaned up their Mountain House hash browns and eggs, before getting a late start. We wore rain pants for the soaking wet brush, and within minutes put on rain jackets against a steady drizzle. My boots started and ended the day squishing wet.

A short distance down the Miller Creek Trail we took a barely recognizable junction toward Canoe Lake. After expecting to spend the day in old burn I was delighted to reenter virgin forest after a mile or so. Tree identification is almost stupidly easy in the Greater Yellowstone. Compared to Florida, where hundreds of native trees intermix, knowing the differences between four pines (four at the very most, and never all at the same time), two firs[*], a couple broad leaves, a juniper or two, and a spruce, will serve you almost anywhere. This, despite the great diversity of habitat: the ecosystem's recent, catastrophic history of ice and fire is largely to blame. Where we were now, the forest was almost completely lodgepole pine.

If charisma didn't count for anything, a lodgepole pine—not the bison or the grizzly or the wolf—would be the icon by which the world

---

[*] One—Douglas fir—is "false" and shares its genus with just one Asian relative. Subalpine fir is our only true fir.

knew Yellowstone National Park. Lodgepole comprises about eighty percent of the forest canopy within the park's boundaries, often in extensive and nearly homogenous tracts, and this habitat type floods outward into all the bordering national forests. Scenery aficionados that have road-tripped Glacier National Park's Going-to-the-Sun Highway, or Utah's canyon country, will have their enthusiasms severely tested by the generically forested green tunnels of Yellowstone; environmental sympathies aside, at one point or another, every lodgepole walker finds their thoughts paraphrasing Ronald Reagan's unsentimental declaration that "when you've seen one tree you've seen them all." The lodgepole is, fittingly, more pole than anything else.* What more can you really say beyond its bole is straight and narrow, the bark is flaky and grey, the cones are small and hard, and the plume of living branches is high and out of reach?

There is a reason lodgepole pines do so well in these places. They are experts at living with wildfire. Most organisms cope, at best, with wildfires; Yellowstone lodgepoles love them. Literally, they are "pyrophiles." Compared to lodgepoles elsewhere, these ones carry a markedly high percentage of serotinous cones, cones that open only to an environmental trigger. In this case, the trigger is fire (meaning they are, more specifically, *pyriscent* cones, but this word is seldom used), and the scales are sealed with pitch that softens at about 140 degrees. A wildfire of the right intensity will wipe out a mature stand, but also provoke a green groundstorm of lodgepole saplings after a couple of years. These upstarts can reach hundreds of thousands to the acre. To travelers, the phenomenon is known as "dog hair," and moving through it is the only time you'll wish you had a machete in the northern GYE. By resetting itself in this way, lodgepole forest curbs outbreaks of parasites and pathogens like dwarf mistletoe, bark beetles, and blister rust, while putting the specie's competitors (aspen being an exception) back several decades.

---

* Interestingly, though, the common and Latin names of the species are at odds. *Pinus contortus*—"the contorted pine"—suggests something entirely different. It references stunted specimens found along the Pacific coastline.

A couple sharp elk bugles issued through the mist-wrapped forest. Moments later we walked up on a big bull. He took off running—by holding his nose high in the air he kept his eyes on us, the tines of his enormous antlers almost wrapping his haunches. Because this good, old forest hadn't burned in a while, it's what foresters disparagingly call "decadent." As in, it's just asking to be cut or burned. But there's a notable level of understory development that can only be found in such places, and I often remember them best. Mosses and lichens take to the cool, moist environment created by a dense canopy, and in turn help insulate the soil, retain moisture, and encourage larger trees. The product of these slowly formed relationships is an intricate fantasy world you won't often notice; when you do, you're liable to get lost in there.* I took a picture of a prime Chocolate Chip Lichen, which looks exactly like the kind of chocolate-chip cookie an evil witch would give you. Then I gushingly declared a blue sponge lichen, Easter Foam, to be my favorite. It looks like a prop from a 1950s fish tank, an accessory of Ray Bradbury. Meanwhile, Fairy Clubs and Powderhorns surged throughout the whortleberry—minarets of Lilliputian mosques—others, blister-lipped elephant trunks... the similes go on and on. Lichens are all and none of these things.

By the time we arrived at Canoe Lake (a tiny tarn shaped like a canoe—in no way is it canoe-worthy), the rain had congealed into blots of snow. We approached the pass to Timber Creek forlornly, our hopes for a tree with a dry, sheltering skirt steadily winking out. There wasn't one. Instead, the wind froze our soaking raingear into crinkly space suits. Snow lay deep on the route to come—up and along the divide—and it seemed like, if I stopped long enough to eat lunch, my body temperature would never recover. We started down again, needing, now, to find this sheltering tree, when find it we did. A trio of them: their combined canopy exceeded my highest hopes. There was no longer any question we'd be pitching camp early.

And that's what a four-mile day of hiking looks like.

---

* "These comparatively invisible things, although everywhere present, are nature's delicate underclothing, which she is in no haste to exhibit except to her intimates and admirers," as Alfred Barron so memorably put it in 1885.

The next day was not the recovery day we were hoping for. Heavy cloudbanks barring the horizon rolled slowly over our heads. Even though our week-old weather report was right (if grossly understated), insofar as the three-day storm stopped spewing, it no longer mattered. The wind was the enemy, and falling snowflakes or whirling spindrift was all the same to us. We'd spend the entire day exposed on a high and difficult ridge, breaking trail through deep and drifted snow, slipping on loose rocks, while our gaiters waited in our resupply box for Cooke City.

I won't forget the frustrations of that day, how I prayed under my breath for an escape off the ridge, trudging on with no resolve. But I'm no more likely to forget moments such as this one: two ravens soared around an unnamed summit like Halloween kites on strings. Wind whipped a taut flag of snow dust from the top, and when the sun hit a stretched spot in the clouds, the peak gleamed against a north sky churning mottled charcoal-grays. Or when we spotted, through a window of stunted trees, a lone bighorn sheep gazing over the edge of a cornice. Then we passed behind a screen of trees, and the view from the other side revealed only the ewe's disappearance. An empty ridgeline left swinging before the trackless terrain of Closed Creek; the speechless sky.

Such moments flooded me with certainty. Here I was finding what I was looking for. To be subjected to the strength of unadulterated elements; to taste the intermixture of misery, beauty, and surprise; to sense the reinforcement of wordless beliefs. As the tracker Paul Rezendes writes, "When we live our lives pursuing pleasure and avoiding pain, we only live half our lives." Now, nobody wishes for shit weather. But at the same time, we need to see it all, if we're going to live. And sometimes we want the earth to rise and smite us, even if we hate it when it does. When Jen and I reached the spur to Closed Mountain, the one mountain on that leg that we went in certain that we would stand on top of, I didn't regret passing it by. Wreathed in weather, stately and inhuman—the timing was so wrong. To frame that deity as a "climb" at all seemed inappropriate. I gazed with a reverence reserved for the unattainable. Slashed heavily across its south face was a pitch-black dike pointing toward Hurricane Mesa, the other great volcanic center of the Northern Absaroka. Praise onto the places we cannot go.

THE COMPROMISED WILD 169

◊◊◊

Waldo Tobler's first law in geography states: "Everything is related to everything else, but near things are more related than distant things." Perhaps the exception that proves his rule is the relationship between Heart Mountain and Hunter Mountain.

Hunter Mountain is an unremarkable spot on a ridge, a ridge that was just coming into our view to the northeast. Dozens of miles away in the other direction, isolated Heart Mountain stands like an enigma, 3,000' above Cody, Wyoming. Heart is crowned in Paleozoic sedimentary rocks, while the bottom is Tertiary—hundreds of millions of years younger. It's like the mountain flipped upside down. Still a matter of high speculation, some believe that the upper mountain is the remnant of a one thousand square mile block of earth that was once connected to Hunter Mountain. An incredible emission of volcanic gas buoyed, lubricated, and then slid it into place. As geologist Robert J. Carson writes:

> From the breakaway at the northeast corner of Yellowstone National Park to the farthest remnant of the mass, the distance is more than 60 miles… Along the failure surface is as much as 6 feet of carbonate breccia—limestone and dolostone that got pulverized during the sliding.

This "carbonate fault breccia" is a described geologic layer, metamorphosed by friction, then "injected" into the Bighorn Dolomite above.

> Based on thermodynamic and mechanical calculations, Craddock and others proposed that the velocity was 280 to 760 miles per hour and that the whole event took place in less than four minutes!

As Chief Plenty Coups once observed, so eloquently, there are "things that are beyond us." No shame in admitting it. The thought of mountains, moving across the Greater Yellowstone at the speed of jets, is one example.

4

When we finally got a chance to drop off the divide we took it, and down we went, into the lingering aftermath of the Clover-Mist fire. Has an inferno ever been given a more innocuous name? For burning over 140,000 acres in and out of the park, the Clover-Mist was the second largest player in Yellowstone's historic "summer of fire," 1988.

As of July 14 of that year, there were a total of six Yellowstone wildfires burning, but they were hardly a matter of national attention. Then the Clover and Mist fires blew up to a combined 7,000 acres. Images of apocalyptic smoke columns, towering against otherwise empty skies, made for irresistible media coverage. For three months after that, Yellowstone fires never ceased to be news, and frequently made international headlines. Eventually, the Clover-Mist complex alone would comprise an amalgamation of at least seven different fires, all of them started from lightning strikes.

On the day of the first blowup, it just so happened that Vice President George H. W. Bush, the newly nominated Republican candidate for president, had a dude ride scheduled into the Lamar—the river that collects the waters of both Clover and Mist creeks. The ride had to be cancelled. It might not be a total coincidence, then, that the very same evening, the park tweaked its official policy toward wildfire. At that point, Yellowstone had been experimenting with a policy of "let burn." This ever-controversial strategy treats wildfires as the natural phenomena that they are: normal and conducive—if not critical—to land health. But after fifteen years of relatively cool and wet summers, the policy hadn't fully been put to the test. Now, with Yellowstone cast in the brightest spotlight since its designation, the park declared it would fight fire unless a determination was made otherwise. And when the Clover-Mist made another run on July 21, garnering more critical attention and again carrying political implications, another change was made: Yellowstone's default would be to fight *all* fires. It might be said that these policy revisions didn't change much (except in tax dollars spent: more)—yet the two-step between media and management still serves as an uncomfortable reminder of the vulnerability of science-based policy to popular perception.

◊◊◊

By 1972, various agencies had been experimenting with various philosophies of land management in Yellowstone for exactly one hundred years. And after this century of confounding, expensive, and often unhappy surprises, almost everyone involved could appreciate the idea of restoring Mother Nature to the director's chair. It sounds like an easy way out—a way to save face, while remitting oneself from harder decisions. But as Aldo Leopold inconveniently pointed out, all the way back in 1927, "The balance of nature in any strict sense has been upset long ago, and there is no such thing to maintain." His observation has become more pointed with every passing year: environmental processes we take for granted increasingly rely on human intervention. That leaves us first with the question of what a natural balance would even look like today, and, complicating that, how much "nature" public opinion can stomach. In the case of Yellowstone fire policy, the NPS didn't just have natural wildfires to fear—fires of the sort that made the park what it was when they found it—but human-exacerbated "super fires." Then, as now, any way forward had to start by seeing mother nature for what we have reduced her to: a patient in detox.

The modern firefighter's predicament is informed by its many parallels to another legacy of over-reaching land management: predator control. Both policies arise from a tendency to overlay natural processes with human values. When specific aspects of a wild equilibrium are declared "good," and framed in opposition to others, which become "bad," the logical next step is declaring war on the bad parts in hopes of maximizing the good. Such myopic scale-tipping is also a tried and true method to make the entire equilibrium tank.

In the case of predator control, park rangers subjected the fates of entire wildlife species to the standards of human civility. Herbivores were good: peaceful, picturesque, endearing to polite society. Wolves, coyotes, and mountain lions, on the other hand, were bad—destructive killers, distrustful of human presence, less likely to pose for the camera. Once that was determined, they set about killing as many predators as they could. (Yellowstone bears escaped the purge because of a propensity to ham it up.) The well-documented outcome of such policies was an as-hoped for explosion in elk numbers, which closely coincided with an equally dramatic deterioration of the greater biotic community. Suddenly, malnourishment was the limiting factor of ungulates rather than predation, and that meant incapacitated animals prone to disease and parasites. Even worse, edible flora was decimated, especially on winter range. Invasive plant species moved in, some of which altered the chemistry of the soil. Beaver, whose preferred food sources were annihilated in this landscape of starvation, almost disappeared, along with the healthy riparian areas and augmented water tables that their dams promoted. Erosion skyrocketed. Similar, contemporaneous scenarios played out elsewhere, including on land managed for wildlife habitat on Arizona's Kaibab Plateau. A benchmark study there found that, because of the destruction of range quality by overgrazing, "carrying capacity was reduced on a large area to an estimated 5 to 10 percent of original conditions." In an unmanipulated paradigm, the "good" that we humans sought, in coexistence with the "bad," exceeded that in our own lopsided arrangement by at least a factor of ten. Slowly, land managers in Yellowstone realized the poverty of their product. But rather then stepping back, the knee-jerk reaction was to interfere more, and since they were already killing predators, they would have to start killing prey, too. So that's what they did. Things didn't start making sense again until 1994 when wolves, the most precise form of long-term game management possible, were reintroduced in three places throughout the Northern Rockies. (Almost a quarter of a century later, the galvanizing force of western land management politics could still be summarized thusly: indignation that natural order is not as predictable as we think it should be.)

To bring it back to fire control, decades of successful firefighting meant none of the benefits of fire. Firefighters found that their meddling on one side of the fire regime committed them to meddling on the other. In areas outside the park, prescribed fires offered an important tool to dial back the destructive effects of fire prevention. But inside the park, prescribed fire never got through all the tape, and conditions steadily worsened. Dead wood piled on the forest floor, disease and aging tree populations limited regrowth—the threat of larger, more destructive fires on federal lands increased with every passing year, and expensive new developments, housing a powerful political constituency, crowded the perimeters.

◊◊◊

In controlled scenarios, managers and scientists can make highly informed decisions based on empirical data. But when political interests become invested in specific outcomes, the difference between right and wrong has nothing to do with conditions on the ground. Wildfires, unfortunately, fit into broader, patriotic narratives. As Stephen Pyne writes, "Fire control by the federal government began when the U.S. Cavalry rode into Yellowstone National Park in 1886. They were greeted with fires, which they fought; their example inspired eager successors."

Thereafter, "the firefight-as-battlefield motif persisted, rekindled dramatically during… the Yellowstone conflagrations of 1988, when the military again mobilized for fireline duty, bringing the saga full circle." Fighting fire became a matter of national identity and prowess—and "letting burn?" Cowardice bordering on treason.

The day after the park re-declared itself the sworn enemy of all wildfire, July 22, 1988, the leading front of the Clover-Mist bumped up against the treeless divide of the Absaroka crest, where Jen and I walked over a quarter-century later. An absence of woody fuels there stalled eastward progress for nearly a month—but the possibility of fire crossing from national park to national forest land was additionally contentious. The Forest Service, which manages its reserves for a calculus of interests including timber production, had an even harder time justifying a fire than the park did. And local politicians, representing the people who hunted and owned homes in the area, had the least appreciation for a natural regime of all. They blustered and fumed and leaned on the NPS with all the weight they could muster. In the end, though, it didn't matter how "approving" anybody was—here was a pretty clear message that Rocky Mountain forests are going to burn, whether we like it or not. On August 20, the 78th anniversary of the most cataclysmic fire blow-up in western history,[*] strong winds and hot temperatures licked up 160,000 new acres of flame across Yellowstone, and sent the Clover-Mist hurtling east over the alpine buffer into at least three different drainages on the Shoshone National Forest. That day entered the annals of park history as "Black Saturday"—but it wouldn't be Yellowstone's biggest-burning day that summer, not by 70,000 acres.

The decision to go to war with the '88 fires cost our country hundreds of millions of dollars. Many experts conjecture that, aside from a small subset of the effort tasked with protecting structures, all

---

[*] The Big Burn ripped about 3,000,000 acres in three days across northern Idaho and Montana, beginning on August 20, 1910. Despite the fact that humans have exacerbated the conditions for such catastrophes, catastrophic changes are also thoroughly natural.

that money and sweat failed to improve the outcome*—so it's tempting to moralize the episode as a very expensive lesson. However, that would imply a lesson has been learned. Today, a frequently heard firefighting joke is that the plan is to "throw money at the fire until the snow puts it out." A critical summary of 1988, this scenario continues to play out on an annual basis. We simply can't help ourselves.

◇◇◇

You might say that the slowest thing to adapt to the 1988 fires is popular knowledge and understanding. Even though no people died, and losses of wildlife and private property were astonishingly small, you would never know it from the political wake. In the immediate aftermath, regional politicians described a park "destroyed by the very people assigned to protect it." By over-representing areas of high intensity burn, the media fostered the impression that the entire park scorched sterile. Caustic public criticism found vindication in the unrelated: the winter of 1988-89 proved colder and snowier than normal, and in the spring, hundreds of elk carcasses melted out of meadows. Bitterness lingers to this day.

It's hard to rationalize through the emotional response to fire. Fire turns places that look green and alive into the exact opposite. All demographics hold sentimental views of how nature should be; environmentalists aren't the only ones. That's why the benefits of wildfires, though proven by science on any number of levels, remain poorly accommodated for in twenty-first century policy.** The Forest

---

* In some instances, it made things worse. When the town of Cooke City was threatened by total destruction, it wasn't by a wildfire, exactly, but an escaped back burn. In other words, firefighters lit the fire in hopes of creating a buffer that would protect the town. But then their fire jumped their fire line, and manifested the very threat they hoped to prevent, burning down some of the town's outlying buildings. The debacle cemented a verdict in the minds of many locals: as voiced by Cooke City resident Lee Holt, "It just looked like another government scam."

** In 2015, a state representative from Bozeman, with a name uncomfortably similar to my own, proposed suing the federal government up to $10,000 a day when wildfire smoke appeared in Montana communities. The pretense was public health; the implication was that all fires can

Service, for example, re-instigated some version of "let burn" in 2012. Two years later it was explained to me in a briefing that, immediately preceding the policy shift, the agency fought 99% wildfires on national forest across the United States—whereas the next year, after the policy shift, crews fought "only" 98%. One additional fire in a hundred was allowed to exercise its admittedly important function... and all I could think is that one fire in a hundred would've burned out before they got to it.

Only part of this endless war is a refusal of science. Across America, more than a quarter of homes built since 2000 sit in what is called the wildland-urban interface. The fates of these buildings are intermingled with the forests: if one burns, the other likely will, too. The pressure to protect homes has made firefighting more deadly, and the prospect of "let burn" politically loaded. The health of forests must be weighed against the sanctity of private property. The number of places where any fire can be let go is shrinking: a disproportionate amount of exurban development occurs in the increasingly arid west.

Stakeholders of the drying forests are in a double bind. We're damned if they burn and damned if they don't, and we have to fight them either way. We should all feel lucky our kind held no omniscient final say in land management 2.1 million years ago, or there's little doubt we would've forbade the volcanism that created Yellowstone—in spite of the knowledge such explosions are necessary to set into motion the dynamic legacies that sustain our present and future.*

◊◊◊

As Jen and I descended further into Cache Creek, we could see no mature trees. From the ground beneath our feet to the opposite mountain ridge where the canyon turned out of view, there was only a chicken scratch of gray snags and downfall; one isolated fuzz of

---

be prevented by replacing forests with intensively managed tree plantations—therefore that's what we should do.

* I wrote this sentence rhetorically. Shortly thereafter, I learned that NASA is researching ways to "defuse" the Yellowstone Hotspot.

regeneration lent a smear of green. In the twenty-seven years since Yellowstone Park's biggest fire season, a diversity of growing conditions created no "typical" '88 regeneration. From suffocating dog hair, to cemeteries of snags standing ankle-deep in sagebrush, or even reverting to meadow, the variability depends not just on the intensity of the fire but on the very localized climatic conditions of the intervening years. That is the beauty of wildfire. It isn't neat or clean. It is wild and disruptive. And an erratic "routine" of disruption—be it a supervolcano blowing every 600,000 years or so, a wildfire every few decades, or the seasonal fluctuations that can feel like a diurnal occurrence in the high country—maximizes biodiversity. It makes the GYE the exciting, surprising, instructive place that it is.

Robin Wall Kimmerer is a talented biologist and author whose studies of mosses along a river in Wisconsin contributed to the creation of what's called the Intermediate Disturbance Hypothesis. As she summarizes, biodiversity is highest when "disturbance is just frequent enough to prevent competitive dominance and yet stable periods are long enough for successional species to become established." The implications of her discoveries have wide-reaching applications. She goes on to explain how the hypothesis applies to fire regimes: "Creation of a mosaic of patches by mid-frequency burning creates wildlife habitat and maintains forest health, while fire suppression does not."

As for Yellowstone, two-thirds of the park did not burn in 1988. Of the third that did, only about half of that was "subjected to crown fires that give the impression of devastation." As Jeff Henry recalled from a reconnaissance flight that summer, "The thing that struck me the most from the air was how the Clover-Mist was not a single block of fire amounting to 36,000 acres, but instead was an aggregation of an almost uncountable number of separate fires burning within an overall perimeter." Just as regular, medium-sized fires benefit the whole, so does a mixture of various intensities within that fire, including some proportion of heavy scorching. Even though Jen and I were seeing an area that hadn't returned to its pre-fire condition, there was a lot of life there. Several harems of elk were thriving on extensive forage; the first long-tailed weasel of our trip went dodging through a pile of stream-transported branches. The boon has been going for decades now: in the spring of 1989, elk populations began a climb toward eventually-historical heights. The park set record visitation numbers, gateway communities reported increasing revenues, and rangers had a fresh narrative to share.

In the cobbled bottom of Cache Creek, I found two old ram horns, the keratin scaly like dry-rotted wood. My first conjecture was that the ram might've died in the fire. But why should it have? Life goes on here, thriving and dying. No fire can change that.

◊◊◊

Yellowstone Interpretation 101 tells us exactly what should happen in the wake of a forest fire. Lodgepole pines and aspen, which largely depend on fires to reproduce, take off in a sprint toward the sunlight. In forty or a hundred years, they create a canopy that accommodates shade-tolerant trees like subalpine fir and Engelmann spruce, and the scene knits back to climax. The concept of ecological succession is a beloved one because it is simple and logical. It goes long way. It is also too simple and logical to tell the whole story.

One of the most basic assumptions of the successional model is that, despite yearly variances, droughty decades, and wet spells, somewhere there is a state of normalcy—as though all the myriad faces of destruction, recovery, and climax that an ecosystem displays express different aspects to the same, foundational average; the way it's been, the way it'll always be. Well, today that average is shifting. September 2015, when we walked through the headwaters of Cache Creek, was the hottest September on record, and it initiated a streak in which every month except one set such records for a year. 2016 would be the hottest year on global record, right after 2015, right after 2014. The same heat and dryness that preceded our winter storm on the Absaroka Crest resumed for the two weeks that followed, and while it made for happy walking, it did not foster the resurrection of forests that generations of Yellowstone visitors understand as right and good.

A recent addition to the concept of ecological succession—a rather critical asterisk—is that of tipping points, "points of no return, beyond which landscapes will not revert to historically documented conditions."

That is, the idea isn't new—evidence of climatic shifts have been widely accepted for hundreds of years—but it's only recently been used to describe the compounding changes we are seeing year to year, right now. We often can't recognize when tipping points have been crossed, just by looking at a growing forest, because climax communities create their own microclimates. Mature forests enjoy higher retention of water, more shade, and lower temperatures. This enables them to persist as artifacts of the conditions when the forest last reestablished—sometimes to an extreme degree.* The suitability of a biological paradigm to a specific site is most crucially determined following a disruption, when the microclimate is lost, and biota need to reestablish those conditions. Tipping points also apply to fauna, and they definitely affect the practicality of restoring endangered species. In some cases, it's not just that an animal was killed off—it's that the land stopped suiting its needs.

Even on the smallest scales, imperceptible variations in aspect or soil type foster strikingly different communities of life. In Paul Schullery's required Yellowstone reading from 1984, *Mountain Time,* he recounts how, on the scoured west face of Yellowstone's Mount Everts, "about three times as many plant species [grow] on the north side [of a minor ridge] as on the south side, and there is only one species common to both." Here we may begin to imagine the degree to which the ecosystem that emerges from today's fires may not resemble that which preceded it. As "the fire regime on the Yellowstone Plateau [switches] from being climate-limited to fuel-limited," expect grasses to take the place of trees. 2016, the year after we returned from our walk, would not only be earth's third record-breaking hottest in a row, but Yellowstone Park's biggest fire season since 1988. Most surprising to observers was the degree to which 1988 regeneration, usually seen as a fire buffer, torched readily in the Boundary and Maple Fires, and constituted a large proportion of those burns—possibly derailing the lodgepole

---

* The Tree of Ténéré, an acacia in the Sahara Desert, was legendary for its isolation: over 250 miles from any other tree. Its presence recorded the wetter climate that fostered its germination. As conditions dried out and the water table lowered, and all of its neighbors died, that tree's roots followed the water over a hundred feet deep into the sand. It was destroyed by a drunk driver in 1973.

regeneration process. For me, such occurrences lend urgency to a growing imperative to get out and see a place from as many angles as I can; an impending sense of loss powers my compulsive picture taking. When biomes I know and love may burn next year, never to be the same, each picture with a tree, a plant, or an erosional surface in it, no matter how incidental, becomes a historic document; a memento of a vanishing time.

◊◊◊

On the slopes that surrounded Jen and me, most of the dead snags were lodgepole pine. Engelmann spruce skeletons—with barrel trunks, rifled grain, and stubby, jointed branches, like the arms of T. Rex—dominated the bottoms. But many of the green saplings I saw were whitebark pine, and it was easy to forget that vast tracts of the Absarokas have lost well over ninety percent of their mature whitebarks since 2000. This high-altitude species is especially susceptible to warming temperatures and the many consequences thereof; a fungus introduced from Europe around 1900, white pine blister rust, cripples or dispatches many of the survivors. Consequently, the whitebark pine nut, a staple of Douglas squirrels, grizzly bears, and many creatures in between, is in awfully short supply.

Whitebarks thrive in burns because their saplings require an open canopy to get started. Which poses the question: how do their smooth, egg-shaped nuts find these burns? This tree simply cannot be discussed independently of a bird called the Clark's nutcracker. These members of the Corvid family harvest whitebark seeds (technically, they're not nuts) from a radius as large as twenty miles. Back near their nesting sites, usually found on steep hillsides, the birds cache their favorite food in the ground the same way a farmer would plant a kernel of corn. Swipe a trench with the beak, put a few seeds in the hole, and flick some soil on top. One nutcracker may deposit thousands of tree nuts in a season and is bound to lose plenty of them—octopus-trunked trees memorialize especially fertile caches. It's been suggested that the propagation of this species, and entire forest type, depends entirely on its flighty little gardeners; it's just one more example of how the big picture hinges on the most incidental-seeming players.

Despite all the saplings, the basin in Cache Creek is too low in elevation to be prime whitebark habitat. But more than most trees, I've noticed isolated whitebark populations growing off the extreme edges of their expected range, both high and low, with nearly a 5,000' range in total. Even though the wildest outliers aren't likely to produce cones, it gives me hope for a mutated specimen here or there that might, allowing this expressive and revered tree—which is already described as functionally extinct in most of its twentieth-century range—to persist.

If nothing else, our age of ghastly hubris will offer an interesting opportunity to watch for some real miracles to play out. But that doesn't mean we can count on it—that's the nature of miracles. Even if the whitebarks do eke by, it doesn't let us off the hook for risking it all in order to see.

The segue from pristine alpine to downtown Cooke City occurred in fast-forward. One minute we were breaking through dry, knee-deep snowdrifts on Republic Pass, the next thing we knew the snow had thickened to slush and the trail channeled a gushing rivulet. In the last big meadow on the Republic Creek trail we plopped down in dry yellow grass, our toes in the sun, and realized town wasn't more than an hour away. An older couple walked over to talk to us. I recognized the woman—she'd worked with me as a volunteer on the East Fork of Hyalite Creek the previous fall, and, uncharacteristically, I even remembered her name. It was good to talk, and to learn a little about their lives together. Gail met her husband while working in Yellowstone in 1978. In the decades since, they'd written their story all over this many-faceted ecosystem: Jen and I related to their special fondness for Sunlight Basin. It only made sense for the four of us to introduce ourselves in this way, by touchstones of the landscape. That day, the husband carried an overnight pack, hoping to hike over Republic and into Cache Creek the next day, but the low snow line worried him. We consoled him there'd be two fresh sets of boot tracks to follow, and after saying farewell, I felt prepared to enter town again. As antisocial as I can be, here were these connections, this camaraderie, with the only two parties we saw in nine days.

Wilderness is often accused of being elitist. The charge is that not everyone is equally capable of wilderness travel, be they short on time, money, or physical health. I ask—what would it mean for wilderness to *not* be elitist? Admission may be impractical, but it's free. Outfitters provide for the disabled. The North Absaroka Wilderness cannot be relocated closer to a population center. Meanwhile, private owners claim at least 36% of Greater Yellowstone counties. That's far less than most counties, but it still amounts to millions of acres that exclude the unpropertied and unconnected altogether—and there are individual men in this country who personally claim estates significantly larger than Yellowstone Park. In the interest of reducing everything to the dollar, we blind ourselves to the most blatant forms of elitism.

At its most convoluted, the elitism charge presumes that wildernesses are protected for the recreational opportunities of the wealthy, while the rest of society pays the costs. It completely ignores the foundational justifications for wilderness, those that benefit society as a whole. These are also known as "natural services." You don't hear about them very much because everyone completely takes them for granted. Michael McCarthy summarizes these services as "climate regulation, composition of the atmosphere, provision of fresh water, flood defense, control of erosion, maintenance of soil fertility, detoxification of pollutants, pest control, provision of fisheries, waste disposal, nutrient recycling, and more subtly, provision of a vast genetic library offering potentially life-saving new drugs and other products." A different type of service is Wallace Stegner's theory of wilderness as a psychological resource—the peace of mind, enjoyed by all, that try as we might we will never quite pave over everything. Earlier that summer a group called Great Old Broads for Wilderness volunteered to work with me in the Lee Metcalf Wilderness. (I was employed as the wilderness ranger.) These were a dozen or so "women of a certain age" (like Gail, but Gail actually belonged to a different volunteer group) who enthusiastically scoffed at the notion one must be young, fit, and independently wealthy to partake in wilderness. We cleared trees off the trail, cleaned up campsites, pruned back the dogwood and ninebark, closed user trails, picked up trash. Some of the members hardly ventured beyond the trailhead, but everyone received equal measures of mountain air—plus, the huckleberries were thicker down low.

The creation of wilderness in Wyoming is full of such stereotype-busting individuals. Local conservation pioneers include racial minorities such as Robert Harris and Nell Scott, members of the Shoshone and Arapaho tribes respectively, who helped designate the Wind River Roadless Area in 1937;[*] the blue-collar working class such as Mike Petrovich, a hard-rock miner who in 1958 drove an old pickup at his own expense from the rough-scrabble town of Rock Springs, Wyoming, to Salt Lake City to speak on behalf of three hundred of his fellow miners in support of the Wilderness Act;[**] and the elderly—in 1978, Dubois hero Mary Back offered this testimony for a Dunoir Wilderness area (adjacent to the Washakie): "Wilderness is said to discriminate against the old, the infirm and the poor. I am all three. Wilderness for me is a challenge, not a denial."

Jen and I switched wet boots for sandals and made short work of the rest of the trail. In Cooke City we met Jen's mom and brother, out to visit for the weekend. They treated us to dinner at the Miner's Saloon. I was in another strange frame of mind: in the wilderness, it's easy to focus. But in the Miner's Saloon, the diversity of human experience, the number of perspectives, complicates everything. When Tammy asked the waiter what vegan French fries were, he gave a skating explanation that hybridized the concepts of not eating meat and not eating gluten— "…We can also talk to the cook, about the strength of your allergy." For minutes afterward, I replayed this surreal interaction. Meanwhile, I drank two PBRs, ate a blue cheese bacon burger, and heard all about the happenings back in Bozeman. The "Paleo diet" had erupted on the scene. It all became a little noxious in my ears. Not the specifics—it

---

[*] This designation being a visionary, locally tailored predecessor to the Wilderness Act.

[**] Imagine: conservation was not always so politicized. Voters had not yet been hoodwinked into seeing healthy landscapes as threats to their quality of living. Most of them, therefore, intuitively understood them to be the opposite. I said it once but it's worth repeating: only one member of the House, out of 435, voted against the Wilderness Act in 1964. Today, it would split along party lines, and not pass at all.

wasn't personal—just the big old crazy world. Of course I always say that, and to put it in perspective, this time wasn't so bad. This was Cooke City, after all. Violent Femmes and Little Feat on the stereo mesmerized me, and eventually all I had left to do was space out and watch people float through the noise and buzz of cheap beer, like puppets in a shadow play.

Part Four. NEW WORLD, OLD WEST

Nobody ever headed in that direction
with any idea of heading toward the future.

—William Kittredge

1

At a picnic table in front of the Cooke City Chamber of Commerce, it took Jen and me over an hour to repackage food for the next leg of our trip. We poured cheese crackers from cherry-red boxes into reusable bags, sought crumble-proof storage for piles of grocery store cookies, and shuffled dozens of little Ziplocs from rows into columns and back again. To vacationers stopping to use the free wireless or bathrooms (all out of toilet paper, to my dismay) it was a foregone assumption that Jen and I chose that spot to draw attention to ourselves: throwing a bake sale, perhaps? When Jen left to do laundry at a hotel I stayed back, "watching our packs" as I do so well, and gabbed with the few individuals that stopped long enough to sit down.

In hindsight, the theme was obvious. One road-tripper wanted to talk about the Pacific Crest Trail (PCT), an opener to asking what we were about. Another told me the story of Grandma Gatewood, the first woman to hike the Appalachian Trail (AT), and subject of a recent magazine story. A third proudly claimed a cousin who completed the Colorado Trail. How unexpected this was—in such a short time, three parties, unprompted, wanted me to know that walking a long way made sense to them.

When we got home, I was able to more fully appreciate that 2015 was something of a breakthrough year for "long trails"—less fringe, more mainstream—and that our trip belonged to this greater cultural climate, whether we related to it or not. Incredibly, hiking was even making it in Hollywood—the oldest and perhaps least likely sport to do so. Cheryl Strayed's book *Wild*, a 2012 #1 best-seller about the PCT that was released as a movie in 2014, prompted twice as many hikers to line up at the southern starting line in 2015 than in any year prior. Another movie, based on Bill Bryson's book about the AT called *A Walk in the Woods*, apparently entered theaters around the time we reached Dubois.

I also learned that long trails were being adopted into the world of athletics as a category of endurance sports. In August, a New York Times article declared F.K.T.s "the hottest acronym in the outdoor-adventure world." (Maybe that's not saying much). F.K.T. stands for "fastest known time," and refers to unofficial speed records for backcountry routes. While the pursuit of speed records is far from new, the popular standing of it is, and, as I sensed during our time in the Winds, a great and diffuse race was on. A man set the overall speed record on the AT that summer, and a woman set the self-supported record shortly thereafter,[*] both to great publicity. A website hosting dozens of discussion boards dedicated to the subject popularized the treatment of other scenic trails as racetracks, while smartphone apps like Strava offered digital arbitration of times. That summer the Colorado journalist Jonathan Thompson would write about hiking in the company of mountain bikers who, locked into competition on a crowded public

---

[*] F.K.T.s are separated into three categories. If a competitor did *not* cut switchbacks to shorten their time on a peak, that, too, is specifically noted.

trail, bellowed *"STRAVA!"* to clear everyone else out of their way. All things I would thankfully remain ignorant of for the rest of our walk.

But it leads one to wonder, sometimes: *is it all really just one big race? If so, our "performance" that summer should shame me into silence. If not, why are so many people treating it as one?*

◊◊◊

Scott Jurek's celebration party after setting the new speed record for the AT, for which he received three citations from Baxter State Park, helps illustrate the conflict of motives. Promotional photographs show Jurek on the top of Mount Katahdin—the official end of the trail—surrounded by a crowd of admirers, who hold smartphones in front of their faces in what I call "the cyborg salute." Jurek is covered in sponsor logos, from his head to his feet, and he sprays champagne from a shaken bottle over the top of the mountain. For those critical of Jurek in the ensuing debate, the specific appropriation of Mount Katahdin was part of the problem: not only is it the highest point in Maine, but the focal point of that state's largest wilderness area. Juxtapose Jurek's party with the words of conservation godfather Sigurd Olson, who helped draft the Wilderness Act:

> How often we speak of the great silences of the wilderness and the importance of preserving them and the wonder and peace to be found there… They will always be there and their beauty may not change, but should their silences be broken they will never be the same.

And so unspools that timeless debate about the uses appropriate to such places. Henry David Thoreau climbed Katahdin on an expedition in 1846 and his experience lives on in the chapter "Ktaadn" from his book *The Maine Woods*. Setting out, Thoreau sought an encounter with "grim, untrodden wilderness," as so many Katahdin visitors do today. In his time, the summit was known as the home of an Abenaki mountain god named Pomola. Pomola commanded weather cycles from this elemental perch and forbade human trespass. Though conscious of the prohibition, Thoreau remained intent on climbing the mountain. "It is a slight insult to the gods to climb and pry into their secrets, and try their effect on our humanity," he admitted. "Only daring and insolent men, perchance, go here." (He seems to have missed the actual summit in fog.)

Throughout his venture, Thoreau remarks on a surprising number of human impacts: white pines culled from the remotest lakes, a ring bolt in a boulder, a random brick in the forest: even in the mid-nineteenth century he's worrying about the resilience of wildness. And, as usual, his prose is packed with enough prescient one-liners so as to seem forever relevant. On the way home, after his party smoothly navigates the fierce-looking Aboljacarmegus Falls, Thoreau discovers with disappointment that "savage and awful" nature, which he so admires, had lost something of its aura. "There was really a danger of [the rapids] losing their sublimity in losing their power to harm us. Familiarity breeds contempt." And by familiarity, he simply meant completing a journey without injury or disaster—not throwing media events on a sacred and traditionally forbidden summit.

If Jurek's motivations were really as simple as he says they were—that is, drawing attention to the vegan diet, and inspiring "one more person to get outside, enjoy and protect the wilderness"—then he should be concerned about the way he came across. Because the image he projected was something different: the recreationist as rock star, exploitational conqueror, and self-interested representative of the "me" generation, hell-bent on drawing attention to themselves. The language used elsewhere by F.K.T.ers reinforces this theme of conquest. Megan Michelson, on extreme-hiker Heather Anderson: "This was a slugfest now, and she moved with brute-like intensity." In a *New York Times* article, Jennifer Pharr Davis (the holder of several F.K.T.s) describes a record-holder as a "titan in the field," one who "endures excruciating pain" to "dethrone" a competitor, before complaining, "There seem to be just as many people who will belittle and berate an F.K.T. for being too fast as who will be in awe of such a raw display of endurance."

To me, belittling is a somewhat natural response, because tunnel-visioned displays of human ambition are exactly what I hope to escape in wilderness. So, I say, let's not turn this into Monday Night Football. In the light of Pharr Davis's macho tone, her admonishment of the public for withholding praise is that much more revealing—she gives herself away. Her overriding value is not natural integrity but social relevance, and for many of us, it is wrong to twist the meaning of this continent's least social places toward that end.

I belabor the point because the competitive approach is an addictive one. It requires only the narrowest perspective and the most self-serving behavior. Branding rugged vistas as billboards for your personal trademark is draining the vitality out of the wild faster than ATVs in Recapture Canyon. The more we reinforce this value system in one another, the more we are distanced from what we need, and the more frantic the competition becomes. In wilderness-cum-athletic clubs, the curse unsettling us is foisted as the cure. One reporter quoted a hiker named Paul Nuckols, of Springfield, Massachusetts, who made the point better than I can: "Doing [the A.T.] in 46 days is like going through the Metropolitan Museum of Art in one minute and 17 seconds."

◊◊◊

During one quiet moment, a woman wearing makeup handed me a pamphlet before hurrying away. It was titled, "If at first you don't succeed, don't try skydiving. 101 of the World's Funniest One-Liners." Jokes that I recognized as such intermixed with a different type of one-liner—such as, "God made mankind. Sin made him evil," and "Evolution: true science fiction." Just like that, my idleness recast as delinquency, a chilly breeze started up canyon and the sun went behind the mountain. I couldn't wait to draw back in the timber, pitch camp.

One block south from the liveliest part of Cooke City[*] the ground falls down a steep embankment into Soda Butte Creek. Our tent felt right at home among the historic refuse and large spruce trees that line its banks. Soon the ring of stones I kicked free of forest litter hosted a popping cooking fire. While the water heated I went to check out a decrepit cabin, tree fallen across its ridgepole, less than a hundred feet away.

---

[*] Which sounds meaningless in a town of 140, but it's a hot stop for Harleys patrolling the scenic byways.

In the buttered light of sundown, a haphazard time capsule of cans and bottles scattered across the cabin's floor made for a captivating discovery. This collection, gleaned (I imagined) from dozens of intimate soirées, chronicled a good half-century of product design—so many intersections between an idle soul, the scroll of time, and one disposable of beer. Among the even older newspapers employed as insulation on the cabin walls, I noted one Firestone advertisement: "Budget your car needs." Sale prices indicated over 1000% inflation through the intervening years. When I emerged blinking from the cabin, I saw that eight horses had escaped their corral to browse the edge of our camp, and a thought occurred to me: we'd stepped into a Rocky Mountain vagabond's dream. Here we were, a couple hours' walking time from two different wilderness boundaries, the smoke from our private campfire drifting unmolested across Main Street, tall straight trees and the clear waters of Soda Butte Creek to sustain us.[*] The only thing missing was a cheap grocery store—one that tosses food the day it expires into an unlocked dumpster.

And it was tempting to conclude that Cooke City is as thoroughly forgotten by American culture, as legitimate of an artifact, as it looks. But, like all the other mountain towns in western Montana that would have you think you discovered them, Cooke City has inflated real estate and its own sorts of infamy. "Cycles of prosperity and recession have long characterized the American economy, and in that long-running game of crack-the-whip, the West has been at the far end of the whip," writes Patricia Limerick. Some people call this the Old West, some people call this the New West, but what's amazing is how much stays the same.

◊◊◊

Geographically, Cooke City is more or less interchangeable with Colter Pass. Because the Absarokas and the Beartooths form parallel fronts lining its sides, it doesn't feel like a pass so much as a domed

---

[*] I missed the memo saying the creek had been poisoned with Rotenone just a few weeks earlier.

valley floor.* The name is a tribute to John Colter, one of western history's greatest known walkers. As Lewis and Clark and the Corps of Discovery headed home from their two-year exploration of today's northwestern states, the first trickles of the coming flood of civilization were already flowing, and in the Mandan villages of North Dakota, the expedition encountered two frontrunners. Among the returning corps members, only John Colter—a low-profile man noted for a court-marshal right out of the starting gates, as well as superior marksmanship—wanted to join them. He took leave and turned right back around.

In a demonstration of just how fast the west was changing, no sooner did Colter fall out with his new partners the next spring than he found work building a fur trading post for a man named Manuel Liza. Fort Raymond, Montana's first, opened for business late in the fall of 1807, which isn't to say they had any customers. Liza put Colter to that task: contact every native band he could find and tell them to start killing beaver and buffalo. Incredibly, Colter was dispatched not only alone and on foot for this mission, but during that transition time of hypothermia weather now known as hunting season. His mysterious odyssey may have lasted six months and made him the first known white person to see what's now Yellowstone Park.** No man of letters, nearly everything about Colter's trip is speculative, based on the second-hand remarks of others—including which direction he circled among Sunlight Basin, the Wind River, the Tetons, and Yellowstone Lake. We know only that Captain William Clark roughed those features into his 1810 map, immediately after talking with Colter.

Colter did not, of course, discover the pass that bears his name. He may have happened onto it by luck, assisted by the preceding footfalls of uncountable generations of Native Americans, but it's even more likely a guide led him there. More than just a pass, the passage through Cooke

---

* While the pass itself is the gentlest to turn the ecosystem's great eastern front, the Clarks Fork Valley on the east side conceals a spectacular inner gorge, and the basin breaks over a barely navigable mountain front. Road traffic must choose between two other passes to the north and south, both of them much higher and steeper, if they wish to continue east.

** Unsurprisingly, this rather meaningless title is contended.

City bridges two geographical hubs serving legendary realms of mountain country: the Lamar Valley to the west, and the Clarks Fork to the east.

Today we call Colter's route the Bannock Trail, as it achieved especial importance over a generation after the explorer's symbolic traverse in 1808. In a cascade of cultural revolutions during the early nineteenth century, several Northwestern tribes—the Flathead, Bannock, Nez Perce, and others—acquired horses, instituted wildly productive bison hunts, and then saw bison populations in their region crash. In regard to Idaho's Snake River Plain, homeland of the Bannock, trapper Osborne Russell noted: "In the year 1835 large bands of buffalo could be seen in almost every little valley on the small branches of this stream; at this time [1841] the only traces which could be seen of them were the scattered bones of those that had been killed."

As the bison hunt became an increasingly committing proposition for the Bannock, Colter Pass—the smoothest connection between the Snake River Plain and the Bighorn Basin, a bison-rich ecological extension of the Great Plains—became crucial. Travel peaked between the years of 1838 and 1862. Its final traverse for this purpose was in 1878 when, famished from starvation rations on the Fort Hall Reservation and cut off from their traditional food sources, the Bannock made a run for Canada in the mode of the Nez Perce just the year before. (In fact, Nez Perce passing through Fort Hall tried to incite that tribe to join them. But the Bannock, beguiled and fragmented by an on-again off-again alliance with the US military, were not yet prepared to accept a common fate: they'd even enlisted in the Battle of the Big Hole to fight *against* the Nez Perce.) In the wake of the Nez Perce's defeat, the Bannock War was a sad and inglorious episode, a bitter slamming-shut to the freedom of the plains that Colter Pass once represented. As one historian summarizes, with some exaggeration, "The main band of marauding Bannock was defeated by a group of [Yellowstone] tourists." The tourists, in this case, were almost a hundred strong, and included a detachment of soldiers.

◇◇◇

In 1851, the Fort Laramie treaty ascribed Colter Pass and eight million acres of its environs to the Crow Nation. In the grand scheme of manipulative Indian War diplomacy, that looked pretty generous. Unfortunately, not only did it force the Crow to forsake the freedom to follow bison herds and live according to their traditions, it was anything but inviolable. Lakota and Cheyenne enemies, who pushed the Crow out of the Powder River Basin not long before, would retain power in the area through 1877 ("Custer's Last Stand" wasn't until 1876). After these powerful adversaries weakened, it created an opening for white settlement, a far more profound threat to Crow autonomy, and the 1851 Treaty would prove to be only the first draft of an agreement that would get stingier and stingier.

A group of prospectors discovered gold in the mountains above Colter Pass in 1870. And just like the Forty-niners before and the Klondikers to come, Cooke City—originally named Shoofly, after a top-producing mine—hosted its own gold rush. The growth was quick and dramatic enough that, by the time Chief Joseph and his band of Nez Perce fled through the area in 1877, they intentionally deviated from the Bannock Trail in order to avoid the burgeoning settlement, which already featured an ore-grinding mill, two smelters, and housing for over a hundred workers.*

Crow title was of little consequence to early miners in Cooke, except when it came to attracting capital. Due to the sketchy legality of the operation, investors were scarcer than gold. Jay Cooke Jr., a Philadelphia banker who largely financed the Northern Pacific Railroad, was the first best hope of the outpost: so desperately was his investment courted, it's his name immortalized on maps today. During his one, ill-timed visit to Shoofly in 1880, for the purpose of appraising claims, all relevant geology was hidden under ten feet of snow.** Frantic to hold his interest, the miners started shoveling. On Cooke's last night in town, in

---

* Some accounts would have you think otherwise. In one imaginative piece of journalism, the Nez Perce run everyone out of town with "battle drums," then loot a smelter for bullion which they fashion into silver bullets to keep up a running battle. We get a sense of how the West was a fiction that wrote itself.

** Details of Cooke's visit are inconsistent: some believe he arrived in July, others speculate that he never came at all.

what would seem an act of true desperation, the townspeople suddenly announced they were renaming Shoofly after him. Cooke's subsequent $5,000 commitment to the operation fell through—but it may have been enough to convince the U.S. government that the writing was on the wall. They officially took the land from the Crow, without pretext, in 1882.

◊◊◊

Since then, the New World Mining District has ridden out additional booms and busts, not all of them related to mineral development, and each wave contributes another high-water mark of flotsam to the surrounding hills. Jen and I got a sampler as we walked out of town the following morning—from bullet-ridden Studebakers folded into ditches, to the Cooke City Store built at the town's population zenith (1,200 people in 1886), to motor sports shops that cater to "extreme" snowmobile tourism of the twenty-first century. The residential street we selected transitioned into a jeep trail that switchbacked up the base of Miller Mountain. After it seemed we'd left town for good, one contour spit us out below a bustling construction site, where flatbeds and beeping skidsteers congregated around the skeleton of a new house. Cube-shaped, two stories high—how do I explain.

The thing just about made my blood boil. Private development is the greatest threat to Yellowstone. Although a majority of the ecosystem is public land, the fraction that isn't occurs in disproportionately important places. River valleys and creek bottoms, for example, are not only the most intensively developed habitat by far, they're far and away the most fragile and biodiverse. No matter what the billboards say, the limiting factor for ungulate numbers is not wolves—it's winter range. Then you must consider the repercussions of low-density, exurban development, the fastest growing category of land use in the country, and an epidemic in the west. Trophy vacation homes like the one we saw, isolated on mountainsides with their full sets of accompanying infrastructure, couldn't create wider or more enduring impacts if they tried.

Some of these flip-flopping investments spend more time on the market than they do under ownership. Of course it looks grandiose to live perched on the side of a Yellowstone mountain—but how many people consider what it feels like, day after day, to live miles up a gravel road with your yard an unfunctionally steep side-hill of fire-killed snags? How much is the view going to matter to you as you deal with all the very real inconveniences of your choice; how long before you're numb to this particular perspective, when you see it every day and never have to work for it? Of course, most people never actually call them home. They're second homes, recreation residences, or investment properties. I turn again to Sigurd Olson, who warned,

> A vista divorced from the open air is only partially enjoyed. If we could see all there was to see from indoors, if we became content to have the beauty around us encompassed by the four walls of the cabin, we would lose what we came to find, and that we must never do.

He doesn't even get into the possibility that, if we succeed in selling this image to people who don't understand the West because we want their money, everyone else will lose what they're trying to find, too. We need people to love this place, yes, to "invest" in it. But when that love takes the form of possessiveness, the injuries exceed that of ignorance alone.

◊◊◊

Our jeep trail eventually devolved into a web of ATV roads, far more than appeared on our map. We were entering the New World Mining District. Old maps of this area show a dense mosaic of mining claims gridding the area, and the names of these claims evince a very human spectrum of outlooks on life: you have *Cold Rain*, *Horrible*, and *Revenge*, and then you have *Sunnyside*, *Peach Tree*, *Silver Wonder*. Situated near the high point of our day's walk, the McLaren Mine was, by many standards, the most successful in the district. That is, it monetarily rewarded the efforts of its investors. But today we can say that, in a broader sense, it was also the greatest failure—for leaving behind a poisonous blight on the ecosystem, and an enormous burden on a legacy of taxpayers.

The New World Mining District owes its fruitfulness to what geologists call a skarn formation. When molten rock rising from deep within the earth invades overlying sedimentary strata, strange syntheses can occur. Skarns. It is a very unfortunate coincidence that the New World skarn happens to crop out at the apex of a major hydrological triple divide. Henderson Mountain hosts the headwaters of Daisy Creek (the furthest reach of the Stillwater River), Fisher Creek (which heads off the Clarks Fork River), and Miller Creek (which joins Soda Butte Creek and then the Lamar River). All three rivers go on to join the Yellowstone—the longest undammed river in the lower 48. In the dead center of this fragile lacework of nascent watershed, spanning two sides of Henderson Mountain, is the McLaren: an industrial worksite poised to create superlative damage.

As Jonathan Thompson explains:

> Acid mine drainage may be the perfect pollutant. ...All you have to do is dig a hole in the ground. ...Oxygen "rusts" the iron in the pyrite, yielding orange iron oxides. And hydrogen, sulfur, and oxygen atoms bond to create sulfuric acid, which dissolves zinc, cadmium, lead, copper, aluminum, arsenic, and other metals. Naturally occurring, acid-loving microbes then feast on the metals, vastly accelerating the whole process. ...Once the process is catalyzed, it's almost impossible to stop.

Three years before our walk began, the McLaren was leaching between 10 and 20 tons of iron a year into Miller Creek, staining the creek bed red for its entire length, and creating a dead zone that plumed into Soda Butte Creek—one of Yellowstone National Park's most scenic watersheds. A twenty-million-dollar remediation project, the most expensive ever tackled by the state of Montana,* finally corked the Miller Creek source. But tailings piles from the McLaren off the west side of Henderson, which stain the entirety of Daisy Creek before leaving loads of aluminum, copper, iron, and zinc in a large and rare high-elevation wetland full of beaver dams and willow swamp, still have not been addressed.

---

* Montana has been the site of far more expensive *federal* mine-remediation projects.

Jen and I reached Bull of the Woods Pass by lunch and ate in the shelter of a hedgerow of fir. To the south, Pilot Peak and its sister Index stood in stark black, back lit against the blue sky.

Pilot Peak is the sentinel of the North Absarokas, hidden from Cooke City by its own foothills, despite a clean, 4,600' rise in barely two miles. From the east and west it demonstrates textbook "horn" (Matterhorn-like) architecture: glaciers whittling from opposing faces gave its top a parabolic taper.* During glacial climaxes, the top of Pilot protruded as an island from rivers of flowing ice—making it what geographers call a nunatak, or "lonely mountain." Which is a perfect description of what it looks like now. The mountain gazes over the bewildering contours of the lake-studded Beartooth Plateau, Montana's most formidable mountain range and close kin to the Winds. All in all, Cooke City's geologic contrast is analogous to the Dubois area, though its higher elevation and precipitation create an entirely different biome.

Our view north from Bull of the Woods was captivating in a different way. Below us, slopes of dark spruce and fir broke off to sharply delineate the boundary of a great meadow. Mount Abundance, a layer-cake of volcanic debris, anchored the scene. Its slopes skirted down to a willow swamp, defoliated by the last week's winter storm into red thatch. It was almost startling to see such a memorable vista, so close to home, for the first time—to realize that, if I'd been shown a picture of this impeccable composition at any other time of my life, I would've failed to recognize it. Why is this important? Perhaps it isn't. It just feels like it should be—and the feeling is strong enough to keep driving me on, to know what these places consist of. We descended through a short talus field—some of the only limestone on our trip—before breaking out onto an open bench. By lurch and stutter-step I tried to avoid stepping on Mormon crickets. These medieval tank-

---

* The mountain isn't as symmetrical as its European counterpart. From the north-northeast and south-southwest this Hershey-kiss effect is lost; Pilot has the profile of a floppy leather boot. Or visualize A. Bart Henderson's original appellation from 1870: "Dog Turd Peak."

looking fatties hatch in swarms, and, I always think, must make for epic coyote all-you-can-eats. (Pre-Columbian human feces have been discovered that consist entirely of hoppers.) They tend to materialize wherever I'm about to put my foot down. So did broken pieces of snowmobiles and bleached beer cans—come winter, snowmobilers throttle their machines toward nearly every summit of that horizon, wilderness or not.

Like so many wild places, the twenty-first century Stillwater River owes its splendor to a fluky restraint of American enterprise as much as natural history—both of which make its current integrity seem equally unlikely. The canyon below was once America's most unlikely mail route (Nye, Montana, to Cooke City, traveled by cross country skis) and a prospective railway. It is also the setting for the greatest mine that Cooke City never built.

◊◊◊

In late 1990, the Montana State Department of Lands received a proposal for an understated operating plan from a company called Crown Butte Mines, Inc. Despite their listed headquarters in nearby Billings, Montana, Crown Butte was actually a newly minted subsidiary of a major extraction corporation from Canada called Noranda Minerals. Noranda already logged, drew oil, and operated mines elsewhere in the state and around the west; for Crown Butte, they amassed leases and rights to 2,600 acres of private and public lands centered no more than three miles from the boundary of Yellowstone National Park. They called their claim the New World Mine.

While the company expected to find appreciable quantities of copper on the land, it was the gold and silver that gave Cooke City a name—paired with modern mining technology—that made the New World such a lucrative prospect. Crown Butte projected a total mineral value of $800 million dollars. And the upper-nine figures are hard for a town, population low three figures, to ignore. But weigh the 114 year-round jobs New World could have created for a ten- or fifteen-year timeline against the inefficiencies of remote one-time-use infrastructure and remediation; factor in how the corporate profits would end up with a foreign company that our country *could not tax* because of antiquated mining laws; then throw on the industrialization of an alpine basin of singular ecological value in one of America's most cherished natural areas—because that's what a surprising number of local townspeople did, before deciding the price of business simply wasn't worth it. Cooke City, 1990, was nothing if not a unique wilderness town—a little gloss and a lot of genuine, moldering history, valuable for being exactly what it was—and a crucial cross-section of its residents were drawn in by that ineffable quality only after they'd succeeded in resisting the mainstream prosperity of Everywhere, USA. Rarest of all, those locals remembered all that, even when they were courted by the potential for enormous wealth.

A homespun group (everything in Cooke City is homespun, except the Exxon) called the Beartooth Alliance laid out the case. In doing so, they divided households, made enemies of neighbors, found some powerful allies, and galvanized nation-wide opposition to the New World Mine. Beartooth Alliance founder Wade King received death threats at his home; anonymous calls to the police framed him as a drug dealer loitering outside bars. The face-off became emblematic of a larger, national conflict between free enterprise and government regulation. Right-wing militias and anti-federal movements protesting the Clinton administration attracted record numbers, while thinly disguised efforts like the group People for the West! propagated a now-familiar rhetoric equating corporate sovereignty and the dissolution of public land with patriotism and righteousness.

In August of 1995, President Bill Clinton placed a moratorium on further mining claims on public land in the New World Mining District. This was mostly a symbolic gesture—even the president couldn't challenge Crown Butte's existing proposal. But it ensured against a larger boom that could've spurred the patenting—or privatization—of more public land in the area for token administrative fees.[*] That December, the World Heritage Committee of the United Nations, which monitors

---

[*] The General Mining Law hasn't been updated since its creation in 1872—coincidentally, the year that Yellowstone became the world's first national park.

and creates awareness of international treasures, placed Yellowstone National Park on its "in-danger" list.

Over five years of mounting public opposition passed before Crown Butte finally pulled out, and left behind a $22.5 million fund for the reclamation of historic mines. That's one way of putting it, anyway. You have to hand it to their public relations, because the Canadian company also netted more than $40 million from the U.S. Treasury, in federal land and other assets, for not doing anything—and achieved some semblance of generosity in the process. But it would be another fourteen years before the chapter finally closed. Mineral rights to the upper Stillwater remained in the hands of a retired schoolteacher from Livingston, Montana, who refused to sell to the government. After she died and her nephews inherited the estate, five years and eight million more dollars finally moved the 1,468 acres of claims back to the Forest Service. (One more reason to get up and see the place: it has a very high pay-per-view.)

Had the New World Mine come to pass, it is likely the entire facility would have already run its course by the time Jen and I walked through; Crown Butte Mines digested back into the Noranda Corporation. But the world would not have been a better place—with wealth further concentrated in the few hands that violated the area, more roads and building platforms on national forest, and millions of tons of tailings dozed into impoundments for toxic water. Reclamation of the site would've only begun—the process of healing that is never completely finished.

◊◊◊

We couldn't walk through the upper Stillwater without noticing the scars of earlier mining activity—from imperfectly restored assays scatter-shot over mountainsides, to the network of motorized trails which, that day, hosted men in camouflage driving UTVs in anticipation of the earliest rifle season in the state. We reached the Absaroka-Beartooth Wilderness by mid-afternoon. Though the boundary line slices randomly across the basin, our crossing corresponded with a geologic shift: swells of Precambrian granite from the Beartooth uplift bubbled up, and within half a mile we reached Lake Abundance, the first real lake we'd encountered since our last night in the Winds nearly four weeks earlier. (The only other named body of water we passed in that time, Canoe Lake in Yellowstone Park, has no visible inlets or outlets.) Camp that night was unusually quiet. When a fish jumped on the still water it almost made me jump. We luxuriated in our full camp routine: after a splash in the lake we rinsed our clothes, set a cooking fire, took a good hour to read, and then, with dusk and the prospect of sleep, the world shrank to a sanctum of glowing orange coals and languorous thought.

From there it was down Lake Abundance Creek into the great Slough Creek drainage. Slough Creek is one of my favorite watercourses of the ecosystem—one that I've backpacked in every season, alone, with friends, and with family. The largest pack of wolves I've ever seen was in there: thirteen members of the Prospect Peak Pack. Aside from that, I'm not sure how to explain what's so extraordinary about its subdued scenery except by saying that it looks like it should have a road. So rarely is such a river valley—long, broad, and blessed with level meadow bottoms—kept in a pristine state, a first visit to Slough Creek is like rediscovering an animal thought to be extinct. My eyes rove its borders with suspicion before accepting what I already know: here is a great, protected place, acre by acre of far greater ecological worth than its equivalent of so much rock-and-ice wilderness. Slough Creek is one of very few places where grizzly bears can still reach spawning cutthroat trout in privacy, where bison winter beyond the telescopic eyes of road-bound Yellowstone safaris.

The route we followed was originally blazed by a Cooke City miner named Joseph "Frenchy" Duret. He built the trail to connect what is still known as Frenchy's Meadow—where he homesteaded a hay field—to Cooke City, where he sold cattle and poached game meat and kept a couple mining claims. As we started up a tributary on the opposite side of Slough Creek, we were only about a mile from Frenchy's grave. Depending on where your sympathies lie—with the ambitions of the pioneers, or the ecosystem they were striving to conquer—Frenchy's grave is either a marker of tragedy or divine justice. Frenchy was torn apart by a grizzly on June 12, 1922: "Pieces of grizzly fur, strands of hair, torn bits of flesh, the blood-soaked ground and chewed rifle stock all bore mute testimony to the struggle that ensued," reads an unexpectedly juicy and lost-in-the-woods historical marker the Forest Service placed above his hand-carved grave marker in 1960. Frenchy was no stranger to the Great Bear. As his widow boasted to *The Park County News* in his obituary, "Mr. Duret has been credited with killing upward of 200 bears during his long residence of 20 years in southern Park County. He had already killed six bears so far this season." In fact, Duret had already trapped and shot that grizzly—but the bullet was poorly placed, and his trap didn't hold.

◊◊◊

Slough Creek forms a low pass with the Boulder River; end-to-end the two watersheds make an incredibly obvious halving point for the 944,000-acre Absaroka-Beartooth Wilderness. You might even say that Slough Creek and the Boulder are the hyphen in "Absaroka-Beartooth," partitioning two great mountain ranges that otherwise form a contiguous block in the largest single wilderness unit in the GYE.* How this ancient travel corridor escaped a modern road is one of those greatly consequential accidents of conservation, almost as miraculous as the Wilderness Act itself. It could've been the dozer's first stop: in a preliminary survey of what would later be the Yellowstone Ranger District, John Leiberg described Upper Slough as "well stocked with forest, carrying the greatest quantity of timber of any of the townships" in the Forest Reserve.**

Moreover, it was already accessible to machines. A scratched-in wagon path served (and continues to serve) the Silvertip Ranch on the

---

* Growing up in Bozeman, we called the western half, simply, the Absarokas. But geologically, that is misleading—the Absaroka Volcanic Province terminates definitively at Silver Pass, less than halfway north. Taking this into consideration, the great GYE mountaineer and scholar Thomas Turiano calls the mountains south of Silver Pass the Northern Absarokas, lumping them in with the kindred North Absaroka Wilderness, and the mountains north of Silver Pass the Western Beartooths. East of the Slough-Boulder, then, would be the Eastern Beartooths.

** Intriguingly, his report also makes explicit reference to stands of Western White Pine in upper Slough Creek, a species unknown in the ecosystem today.

park boundary, thirteen miles out from the closest road, and it once continued to Frenchy's place a couple miles beyond that. To the north, on the Boulder River side, a road ran twenty-some miles from canyon mouth to alpine meadow and the outlandish mining settlement of Independence. Because of this, when the area was scoped for logging and development in the 1970s and conservationists rallied for wilderness designation, they initially considered Slough Creek and its pass a lost cause, and concentrated instead on the rockier and remoter tracts of both ranges separately. But some harebrained ambition eventually persuaded them to go for the entire thing—and my life, at least, and the lives of many animals, to say a lot more, is so much richer for it. Today, Frenchy's fields lie fallow in a conservation easement; willows ecstatically tangle his thresher.

As we ascended the west side of the valley, Jen and I reentered the Absaroka Volcanic Province. These were quick switches we were making between entirely different mountain-building processes, differences that manifested in contrasting soil types and erosional patterns. The Beartooths, like the Winds, are born of the Laramide Orogeny; they heaved from below. The Absarokas, as we've seen, largely bombed down, spilled out, and slid from above. Other differences rippled outward among the flora and fauna, which, though mostly incidental, seemed inevitable at the time. On the granitic east side of Slough Creek, the only bison of our trip stood knee-deep in the grass of a once-burnt glade between polished pewter domes; on the volcanic west side, we left the burn above a steep, "V"-shaped canyon that quickly enveloped us in damp, primeval wood. Where deliquescing mushrooms and paisley lichens patterned the ground, we fell into step behind a waddling porcupine. Never has a member of the wild kingdom come off more nonchalant. Sitting back on chunky haunches in the trail, she looked at us over one shoulder, coy as a stuffed animal, before shuffling on. If I were a bear or a wolf I would've learned the porcupine's defenses the hard way that day—these long-suffering beasts are occasionally photographed with muzzles like pincushions.

2

*The subject of walking is, in some sense, about how we invest
universal acts with particular meanings… from the erotic
to the spiritual, from the revolutionary to the artistic.*

–Rebecca Solnit

On first glance, hiking is a means to an end; it's a form of transportation. But hiking is not just walking. It is walking to walk, and the closest thing to an end-goal is a return to where you started. The purpose that motivates us, then, is a non-physical product: some psychological import that can inform our days. Yet the preconditions for such gains, and even their most basic defining characteristics, remain perfectly abstract. While hiking remains the means, its relation to the end is uncertain. For this reason, the most botched hikes often offer the best stories, and a completely aborted endeavor (like the "snowbridge" group I described in the Winds) can provide the most important lessons of all—the better for being unanticipated, let alone desired. Each excursion initiates a fresh confrontation between one's momentary condition and things as they are: that's the only certainty.

Given what Jen and I go looking for—that is, nothing in general, everything specifically—there's little incentive to end a good trip before the sun goes down. Carrying a camp along serves the overarching goal of spending time outside in quantity. Quantity, in this case, provides openings for serendipity: we can't know what will move us. God forbid we relegate the natural world to a space for our own performance. Inviting dusk, dreams, and dawn into the equation facilitates so much ritual; it fosters participation. There's a headspace that unfolds from backpacker routines, be it rolling out the sleeping pad or waiting for the water to boil, that makes me prefer every little chore to its equivalency under electric light. I also know I'm not unusual in this—the preference seems to rise from some intuitive standard of goodness that science is still working to pin down. Parts of us understand that, as one health reporter writes, "A fundamental mismatch [exists] between the conditions that molded our bodies and those that we inhabit," evidencing "that we are born to be in motion, with health consequences when we are not." Michael McCarthy calls this bone-deep understanding "the bond of fifty-thousand generations." Studies suggest that respecting such a bond promotes happiness by almost every standard—backpacking strikes at an expression so primal that it overflows all but the most general terms. Bringing into conversation the mind, the body, and creation, these contrived little journeys don't just stand in for bigger things: they juxtapose foundational complexities in our lives and synthesize higher expression. For entering the process of becoming-who-we-are, they do much more than we can say.

The beauty of artist Richard Long's walking pieces (such as "Line Made By Walking," discussed in the introduction) is not, to me, the visual composition of the product. It is the sense that his efforts isolate the animal-like physicality of the walker, and hearken to an earlier form of consciousness. At best, his actual creations are eminences from the walker's simplified world-view—incomprehensibly simple to viewers, thus compelling. Importantly, he doesn't mystify the process; if anything, he attempts the opposite, by universalizing it. "My work really is just about being a human being living on this planet and using nature as its source. ...I enjoy the simple pleasures of well being, independence, opportunism, eating, dreaming, happenstance, of passing through the land and sometimes leaving traces along the way, of finding a new campsite each night. And then moving on."

When we imagine the artist's goal to be receptiveness to life, any product beyond living itself can seem superfluous. In my mind, the challenge that remains is appreciating this subject's potential not as an idea but as a practice. Though Richard Long's beliefs are known from gallery showings, not from utterances at crossroads or scrawlings in caves, his pieces only really succeed if they inspire viewers to walk to understand the world—not if they sell for six-figures. How, then, does one lead by example, when the lesson is so quiet as to render invisibility? Hamish Fulton is another British artist lumped into the "land" movement. He prefers an even more specific title, however: a walking artist. His entire career is an overt effort to point the viewer away from his products and back toward the primacy of experience. "THIS IS NOT LAND ART," he broadcasted over one photograph. Elsewhere: "AN OBJECT CANNOT COMPETE WITH AN EXPERIENCE."

In 1969, Fulton spent three weeks wandering the Beartooth Plateau to create "21 Pieces of Wood for a 21 Day Walk in Montana." He didn't use wood gathered along his walk—unlike Richard Long, who scuffed lines, nicked wood, and rearranged stones, Fulton strove to "leave no trace." The wood pieces are actually machined dowels, painted black, and linked in a jerky line that evokes a rugged horizon. To my eye, the result does suggest the Beartooths, specifically. A spiny ridge culminates in a broad-headed summit (of course, the artist may have had something altogether different in mind); Granite Peak, the highest in Montana, is not dissimilar. As for how well the piece stands in for a three-week trip—it's enigmatic, I suppose. It makes you wonder. Its very inadequacy may be its excellence. The artist must have hoped that twenty-one pieces would be just enough—and not too much—to lead people to look elsewhere, and seek direct experiences for themselves.

The power of abstraction depends on the recipient's willingness to empathize with the creator. Perhaps I find no visual appeal in Fulton's products precisely because I already like to backpack in the Beartooths: I have my own referents for its power.

From the campfire that night, I studied Granite Peak's memorable profile through binoculars. In west-facing couloirs, the last colors of the sun caught along bright lines of snow. I watched them until they were gone.

◊◊◊

No speed hikers, Jen and I justified more than a couple items in our packs by comfort and convenience alone. If our awareness of the burden (containing up to ten days of food) overwhelmed our awareness of the setting, we stopped and camped. This did not allow us to travel as quickly as ultraliters, but by my reckoning, it allowed us to do something more important: stop and more fully inhabit the places that struck us. Invent a side trip. Stay an extra day in a place that deserved it. This was a practice well suited to the fact that, in contrast to those who know exactly where they're going, we didn't want to know. "Getting there" wasn't the goal—just an eventuality. We dilly-dallied. In the meantime, we would be *there*, with everything we had in us.

Such aimlessness conceals unexpected challenges. There is no shortcut to remaining open and continually aware. One must practice continual vigilance against goal-orientation: the American Way. To call it a lost art is not far off. In his masterwork *The Practice of the Wild*, Gary Snyder describes the trail-less journey as a metaphor for following a spiritual path. He starts by considering the first line of *The Tao* (The Way), which, in my copy, translates as "The way that can be followed is not the Eternal Way." Snyder elaborates,

> The actuality of things cannot be confined within so linear an image as a road. The intention of training can only be accomplished when the "follower" has been forgotten.
>
> There are paths that can be followed and there is a path that cannot—it is not a path, it is the wilderness. There is a "going" but no goer, no destination, only the whole field.
>
> So what's off the path? In a sense everything is off the path. The relentless complexity of the world is off to the side of the trail.

In the Absaroka-Beartooth, like every leg of our journey that preceded it, Jen and I found ourselves spending consecutive days off trail. As our overall route grew into an increasingly subjective record of decisions made and feelings felt, our freedom was not the freedom to clock out and retreat behind blinds of repetition (though there was some of that), but the freedom to indulge curiosity. In regards to our starting and finishing points, far, far more intuitive lines connect the two. But to base any decision on efficiency alone betrayed our intentions, and distracted from the relationship between fascination, landscape, and movement that we were working to perfect. As we got the hang of it, the weight of decision-making (this way or that?) fell away and our motion clarified into a simple expression of desire: desire for this boundless, endlessly alive, forever surprising and instructive world. A procession among perches for one's attention—insights more evocative and finely spun than we knew how to pray for.

◊◊◊

The wilderness experience has been scrutinized from many angles—perhaps too many. I have read discussions about the noises made by airplanes, the visual impacts of their contrails, the clashing color schemes of tent fabrics, the inevitable yet indeterminable unnaturalness of Anthropocene weather. And I have already spent some time on what I consider to be the greatest obstacle to seeing wilderness: the restless and acquisitive modern mind. But there's one more obstacle that I believe deserves mention, if only because it appears to be so much more overlooked—and that's the trail itself.

Despite (or, perhaps, because of) our attachments to them, there are problems with trails. Determining the extent to which this is true is a good thinking exercise. I'll start with some rather hypothetical examples, relating to the quality of naturalness, that I've wondered about more than once. For one thing, it is no secret that poorly maintained trails are terrific agents of erosion. Absent the plant life and organic litter that absorbs water or slows its flow across undisturbed ground, trail beds pirate the loads of sophisticated webs of hydrology percolating downhill, and usher that water away in barren canals. How does this affect the living layer of earth? Deeply trenched, side-hilling trails that lack adequate drains (which are common enough) could disrupt the allotment of surface water over all the mountainside that lies below them—and in so doing, select for different biotic communities than were there before.

As beaten paths divert the movements of water, so they divert the movements of life forms. In the most extreme settings—benches blasted from bedrock—trails provide ungulates ingress into places that were inaccessible to them before. In more conventional forest settings, the layout of trails, with their promise of reduced energy expenditure, may influence large-scale migrations and grazing habits. Even on terrain relatively lacking in natural obstacles, trails invite usage, plain and simple—they insert a bias, directing passers-by toward certain places, away from others. Predator behavior in the proximity of trails must shift in analogous ways. The goal of a trail-bound wolf, and a wolf in trackless backcountry, may be the same—finding prey. But patrolling a reliable path for a scent signal could enable much different strategies than doing the same through noisy underbrush or dense downfall. The ranges of meat-eaters almost certainly enlarge when they incorporate human trails.

How significant are these influences of trails on flora and fauna? I have never seen them accounted for, or even described—but once I get thinking about them, they're hard to write off altogether. I suspect the side effects of trail systems are so often overlooked by champions of wilderness because trails, in general, seem natural enough. Sections of human and animal trails may be indistinguishable: a strip of dirt, usually about a foot wide. Cumulatively, though, there's a huge difference between your typical game trail and a "system" trail. As a 1915 Forest Service pamphlet explains, "Mere ways through the forest, whether marked or not, are not regarded as trails; they are matters of woodcraft rather than of permanent forest improvement. A trail is a narrow highway over which a pack animal can travel with safety..." Engineered to grade, signed, faithfully maintained and logged out, static in space—for your average hiker, as a psychological and physical comfort, the difference is all.

Forest trails were built to provide access to natural resources. That mission hasn't changed with the designation of wilderness, exactly, but the nature of the resource has. Where the resource is wildness, trails compromise that resource by structuring it into a network of nodes (destinations) and connectors (trails): no matter where the trails lead, wildness will be elsewhere. As "permanent improvements" (and exceptionally pervasive ones, at that), they are discouraged almost by name in the Wilderness Act—likewise, as a "mark of man."

To its credit, the philosophy of wilderness trail work has also shifted. While trails once aspired to provide efficient firefighter access to absolutely everywhere, they are no longer seen as desirable in every reach. Large-scale construction has generally ceased; many pre-existing trails are purposefully neglected. The justification for those trails that remain has also shifted, from the provision of human recreation to resource protection. Resource *protection* (and not development) because people will explore the wilderness backcountry whether there are trails or not. In the places they are most likely to go, trails sacrifice a minimal thread of terrain to concentrated impacts (the destruction of vegetation, the disturbance of wildlife, etc.) in the interest of preserving the larger tableau.

Traveling a trail allows for some degree of personal expression—length of stride, foot placement, speed—but at its heart, the trail is not so much a thing as a mode. A mode that we might call "preprogrammed." Like all constraints, trails offer a measure of one type of freedom (freedom from contingency) in exchange for another type (freedom to go anywhere you want). When you accept its terms, you follow not only with your feet but with your eyes and mind.* As you traverse otherwise rugged country, enjoying the luxury of gazing while your feet are mostly taken care of, and taking additional comfort in the knowledge this trail is leading you where you want to go—you are not in the wilderness. The efficiency and peace of mind that you take for granted is the provision of laborers and engineers; gone is so much uncertainty and challenge. Not all uncertainty and challenge, but a singular variety of each: the varieties that characterize the wilderness experience. Even the view, which is essentially unchanged, will be

---

* To psychologists, the term "path-dependency" describes the human tendency to accept precedents rather than improve on them, even when those precedents are proven to be inefficient or counterproductive.

perceived much differently off the trail: less as a backdrop, more as a medium.

On an even broader note, think back before the trip began, and how trails structured the way you first approached the landscape. So great is their influence, so strong is our preference for walking on rather than off of one, most people automatically reduce the incredibly complicated field of information that their topographic maps provide into a single multiple-choice question: shall we take trail A, B, or C? This proscribed vision is broadly encouraged; one old Park Service sign advised, "Stay on Trail Stay Alive." The message continues to be disseminated today, if in more subliminal ways.

Today, there are a surprising number of people capable of running through fifty or a hundred miles of wilderness in a continuous push. They take for granted the standardized surfaces and homogenous movement enabled by trails. Some of these athletes simultaneously lament the loss of wildness, and publicize their runs under the pretense of drawing attention to the fragility of wilderness—never considering, I assume, that the standardization of the wilderness trail is one of the greatest culprits.* It is an irony that seems somehow appropriate: medium and message combine into a sort of self-fulfilling requiem for the resource.

But it is wrong to suggest that wilderness without trails is a choice that we get to make. Trails are inevitable. The siege-like demolition of new trails through the most rugged places may be a thing of the past, but the maintenance of those already in existence, and the proliferation of user routes, is a habit—a passion—of the masses. Trails are democratic; they are involuntary by-products of popularity.

---

* For an article that does more than lead with statistics about the author's daring-do, follow with rueful observations about the fragmentation of wild lands, and leave readers to reconcile the two subjects, see "Passing Through," by Nicholas Littman. "The Great Burn needs silence to maintain its wholeness, but it needs human voices to maintain its silence," he writes, reflecting on a fifty-three mile run that he organized to bring attention to the area's proposed-wilderness limbo. "It isn't just a pretty place to run through." Littman is aware of the potential contradictions underlying his strategy—"I cannot be sure if I am succeeding"—but it's his rigorous thinking-through that's illuminating.

◊◊◊

I am of two minds on the subject. I take great pleasure in building trails to spec, or bringing them up to standard, or tweaking their designs in the interest of efficiency. As a vocation, it has supported me through most of my adult life; trail work is also the only job that I have consistently summoned real passion for, so closely is it aligned with my native interests. Outside of work, I love, for example, studying old maps and tracking the evolution of trails. I love sleuthing out traces of abandoned trails. I even take joy in identifying the prosaic scars of former switchbacks, or obsolete blazes. For me, lines on the land hold stories, and to walk their faded boundaries is to live history. One time, in Desolation Canyon, I ecstatically traced the twenty-mile pack trail to my great-grandmother's childhood homestead, discovering en route the names of her family carved into a boulder. It was the continuity of the line I that made me feel so connected. I have learned to depend on trails, as well: launching up unfamiliar drainages by headlamp, covering eight miles before sunrise, with blind faith that I was going to end up where I wanted to go.

A corollary to my appreciation of trails is my resentment of poorly made trails. When the trail dips down and I mean to go up; when the trail weaves a slalom course between downed trees; when I can't help but notice a far more intuitive route—then the trail is my adversary. I resent these instances more than most (just as I can be needlessly critical of books I am reading) partly, I believe, because I hold some pride in their institution. I idealize their theoretical potential. Contributing to my frustration is a generalized interest in the art of covering ground—an interest which begins with the conviction that bushwhacking selects for an elevated plane of consciousness (animals being our most exemplary teachers), and culminates in a love for skiing across virgin snow, drawing lines that accentuate rolling topographies like ornamental scrollwork. But in the end, these are merely contributing factors. At the heart of the matter, when I find myself cursing the trail for not going where I think it should go (even if I am eventually proven wrong), I think what I am sensing is my own helplessness as a follower. If a trail is there, I am going to take it, and relinquish a lot of my engagement with the landscape in the process. I will be at its mercy and not create shortcuts: that's the trade-off. Travel will almost certainly be easier and safer in return. But when I'm not so sure it's easier, and my confidence in a specific trail's layout wavers, I will be thinking about how often trails describe accidents of history; how much they are creations of the masses, revised and defiled and lacking consensus, with amendments and rebuttals scratched in the margins, and a mainstream so deeply rutted that it is as unsightly as it is hard to escape. How arbitrary the trail can be, how unexamined its presumptions.

How many wilderness travelers never leave the connectors and nodes of civilization? How many walk only where they are led, camp only in established campsites, and never touch ground that is not conspicuously impacted? All of which is to ask: how many wilderness travelers *never set foot in wilderness?* A lot of them—and how fortunate it is, for the wilderness, that they do not. Because in the end, that is the only argument for wilderness trails: to keep as many people out of it as possible. To contain them on a "durable surface" (as instructed by Principle #2, of Leave No Trace ethics), where the impact is already absolute. In this regard, restricting your wilderness experience to trails is the responsible way; for the sake of both observer and the observed, the two must remain segregated.

Yet this is not an argument for building trails everywhere. They remain justified only where there is sufficient use to *create* a trail, were there not a trail provided. Otherwise, off-trail travel is most appropriate, because it creates less cumulative impact than the very large impact that is a trail. Currently, most Forest Service ranger districts oversee hundreds of miles of trails. They are also under-budgeted, unable to maintain their trails in a sustainable way, and most of these inadequately maintained trails—though rarely used—create impacts as a consequence of their very existence. They sit there, hard-packed, discouraging germination, eroding without encouragement. Their existence—and the obligation to provide them with some modicum of maintenance—can spread thin the resources of management agencies nearly to the point of futility.

Being deliberate about it, and making sure we're managing wilderness for what we say we're managing it for, would mean monitoring the use-levels of individual trails. It would mean determining whether or not there is enough use to justify routine maintenance on a given trail, maintaining them to impeccable standards, and abandoning those that fall short. There's no reason to believe that management agencies will ever do so. But it is beneficial, nonetheless, to understand where our methods sit in relation to our stated principles.

◊◊◊

A subalpine park, churned by pocket gophers, flecked with obsidian chips. A protuberance above tree line, another perspective, another conceivable world. A plunge through timber, decomposing stone, bristling currant bushes. A talus field, flowing in slow motion by seasons of freeze and thaw, plowing a fold in the root-woven soil.

Under the spell of a rarefied, trail-less state of mind, a thought struck me more than once: nothing that humans create compares to that which we haven't. We can't approximate this interplay of living elements, this miracle of self-renewal. I have spoken already on why I believe in including place names in outdoor literature. Now I must explain my decision to omit a map: there's no point in fixing it so. The line we drew recorded the give and take between place and time—*who we were*—a story more intimate and whimsical than the one I'm trying to write. Like-minded sojourners must strive to plat their own wonder.

Through those off-trail days we found more evidence of Native Americans than on the rest of our trip combined. What to make of these lost tokens of artful utility? As usual, the first question is that of authorship. The aforementioned Crow tribe, whose reservation once included these lands, is as good a guess as any. At one time or another, their homeland is said to have encompassed everything from the mouth of the Yellowstone River in North Dakota to its headwaters in Wyoming.

The Crow language is Siouan. It is related to a great spectrum of languages scattered from interior British Columbia to the Gulf Coast in Alabama. Linguistic studies suggest that this family of tongues originated on the East Coast, and when the Italians first reached North America, ancestral Crows probably lived in and around what we call Ohio.* Needless to say, the arrival of Europeans disrupted Indigenous America's balance of power immensely. Many Midwestern peoples experienced this disruption long before they ever saw a white person firsthand, as some tribes, such as the Ojibwe and Cree, obtained exclusive access to game-changing trade goods long before others. Finding themselves literally outgunned, some ancestral Crow moved north to settle near Lake Winnipeg—but as the European influence kept pushing west, they were displaced further, first by the Cheyenne and then by the Lakota. Come mid-sixteenth century they joined the agricultural communities of the Mandan along the Missouri River in present-day North Dakota.

All through this time the Crow were not yet what we call the Crow. They were Missouri Valley Sioux speakers, living with the Mandan, sorted into various units. The Crow-to-be differentiated themselves after a leader known as No Vitals had a premonition to move his people west; those that remained became known as the Hidatsa. When No Vitals** and his followers reached the central Montana-Wyoming border they knew they found what they were looking for: broad river basins between expansive highlands, a land of plenty straddling nearly 10,000' elevation. It gives pause to imagine encountering such a place for the first time—a real-world promised land—and then begin learning it as home. Horses hadn't arrived yet, so the exiles hunted bison using stealth and disguise, and otherwise relied on the diverse hunting and foraging opportunities of the fertile mountain-meets-plains ecotone. A description of the Crow and their selected home is incomplete without emphasizing just how

---

* Tribal prehistory is a contentious subject to which some Native Americans object. Here, I am summarizing a story based on academic scholarship. I offer it as food for thought.

** AKA No Intestines. This moniker seemingly relates to a dispute that offers a more specific explanation for the division of the tribe. During a time of hunger, one group procured a bison, which it was customary to share. But they offered only offal to their companion group, who not only refused it as an insult, but then resolved to pick up and leave. "No Intestines" as in, "No intestines for us, thank you. We're leaving."

smitten they were with the place.* After generations of searching, here arose a culture grounded in an unimpeachable love and gratitude for where they lived, a model for a better world.

These initial residents would later be known as the Mountain Crow, as distinguished from the River Crow, a second group that emigrated later and filled a lower-elevation niche. Less has been written about the Mountain Crow than the Mountain Shoshone—the Sheepeaters—but there is every reason to believe that their relationship with high places was similarly robust. This is notably true in the ceremonial sense. Lawrence Loendorf wrote, "There are few groups that put more emphasis on the vision quest ritual than the Crow Indians of Montana." In another week, Jen and I would round a shoulder of remote Crow Peak and remember together a medicine wheel-like circle of rocks, partially sunken into the tundra on an unnamed neighboring summit, which we found one previous summer. The ethnographer Edward Curtis once referred to the Crow as "a powerful tribe of mountaineers"—a description sure to enchant anyone acquainted with the rugged majesty of those mountains today. In fact, the word Absaroka derives from *Apsaalooké*: the name by which the Crow refer to themselves, and of which "Crow" is an imperfect translation. It means something closer to "Children of the Large Beaked Bird."

◊◊◊

The fluidity of Crow history is not unusual. Maps of Native American history give the impression of borders: demarcations as definitive as our fifty states. In reality, the places that members of a tribe could and couldn't be found were in constant flux, and the best map of pre-reservation tribal territory offers only a ballpark estimate of one snapshot in time: a fiction. Tribes merged, fragmented, migrated, and vanished. While twenty-six tribes from Washington to Oklahoma claim official associations with Yellowstone National Park today, perhaps several times that number remain lost to time.

---

* Chief Arapooish: "The Crow Country is a good country. The Great Spirit has put it in exactly the right place... Everything good is to be found there."

Despite an admitted ocean of unknowns, when we found artifacts in the mountains I thought of the Sheepeaters. That's because, even if Sheepeaters weren't the first to use a given high-elevation site in the GYE, they were often the last. While neighboring cultures in the eighteenth and nineteenth centuries reinvented themselves to the way of the horse, Sheepeaters adhered to their traditional, mountain-based way of being. For non-experts like myself, their culture offers a logical starting point for approaching the subject of mountain-subsistence in general.

◊◊◊

Considering their small, self-sufficient groups and affinity for out-of-the-way places, Sheepeaters earned an outsized reputation among developers of the West. A couple of reputations, actually. Among trappers and early explorers, who were also relegated to foot travel for some decades, consensus said the Sheepeaters were friendly and helpful. One of the standout details we have about Colter's 1807-8 winter adventure is that he apparently visited the North Fork of the Shoshone twice, in the heart of Sheepeater country, though it required going out of his way. (Near this spot, Clark's 1810 map is labeled "Yep-pe Band of Snake Ind. 1000 souls.") Even without this clue, Colter's strategic route finding, not to mention the fact he survived his winter tour at all, strongly suggests he received direct assistance from the locals.

The journals of Daniel Trotter Potts are the earliest written accounts we have of Yellowstone. Things were looking bad for him when, in the winter of 1823-4, he lost his company in the Owl Creeks and received crippling frostbite on his feet. But then Potts fell in with a group of Shoshone—Sheepeaters, according to a biographer—who guided him to their wintering ground near Dubois. Though Potts lost two entire toes, and parts of two others, he felt lucky he didn't lose a lot more. He wrote, "I am obliged to remark on the humanity of the natives towards me." They took him into their lodges and dressed his wounds twice a day until he was capable of continuing.

Osborne Russell, who trapped throughout the Yellowstone region for seven years, beginning a generation after Colter, left the most articulate, perceptive, and generally reliable journals of the trapping era. He remembered the Sheepeaters as "neatly clothed in dressed deer and sheep skins of the best quality and seemed to be perfectly content and happy." And no, he didn't talk that way about just anyone.

It is rather shocking, then, to shift forward fifty, a hundred years, to the words of empire-builders, and Yellowstone-area historians. Burton Harris on Sheepeaters, 1952: "lowly, defenseless ...furtive, wretched, and misshapen." Harris's statements are of the sort that, for failing his subject matter so thoroughly, offer unintentional insight into the culture for which he wrote. For example, he summarizes Shoshone culture as having "ranged from the Lemhi, rich with many horses, to the abject Sheepeater or Digger Indians, whose diet often of necessity included grasshoppers and ants."

To Euro-Americans, a refusal of the horse was laziness and cowardice—a refusal of progress. And they'd rather starve than eat bugs. To Sheepeaters, horses offered nothing that dogs and their own feet couldn't do better. There's no doubt that horses revolutionized the plains by opening up a nearly limitless protein source.* But bighorns also provided, and hunting them is an entirely different prospect than bison: the animals run and play where horses are nothing but a liability. Because Sheepeaters didn't need to follow their quarry on seasonal, cross-country migrations, they also didn't need large pack animals to carry their camps. Dogs pulling travois worked fine. Then there is the horse's demand for extensive forage—incompatible with the tight canyons where Sheepeaters wintered. By necessity, every consideration returned to the carrying capacity of the land, and horsepower didn't make the cut: it would have meant throwing away sophisticated and dependable land-based identities and traditions for bedlam on the plains. Speaking as one who is all too familiar with the additional inconveniences that accompany horse work in the mountains, I suspect

---

* Numbering in the tens of millions, pre-Columbian grasslands supported bison herds that compared admirably to the biomass of domestic cattle currently supported by industrial agriculture.

that after the introduction of the horse, an isolated life in high places might've looked better than ever.*

"Some people think: Why live up there, because it's so costly?" This from archaeologist Richard Adams who, between 2006 and 2009, led a survey of a sixty-lodge Sheepeater site (imagine level earthen pads, encircled by rocks, around nine feet in diameter) at 10,700 feet in the Wind River Range. "I think just the opposite. The living was easy." That site, which Adams named the High Rise Village, is now on the National Register of Historic Places. It also spurred some controversy at the time of discovery, having appeared as a terrific anomaly. But after Adams and his crew had time to connect what all was going on there—productive whitebark pine stands and bighorn habitat all around, plus manos and metates for the processing of additional vegetal foods—they quickly found a dozen or more such "villages" at altitudes traditional archaeology never thought to look.

Based on Adams' findings, Sheepeaters were doing more than making do: they were thriving. "The high elevations of the Winds were more dense archaeologically than their surrounding lowlands," summarizes one researcher. Carbon dating at the High Rise Village suggests more than two-and-a-half millennia of continuous use. To take one example of what this life might've looked like, consider whitebark pine nuts: as oily and indulgent as the pine nuts we buy in the store. In a strategy known as masting, whitebarks produce bumper crops every few years, glutting the market in a way that encourages caching by squirrels and birds. Also, humans. During masting years, reports Lois Wingerson, "If the women worked 20 hours each week gathering and processing nuts to be carried downhill at the end of the summer... they would have supplied up to 2,000 calories each day for about 50 people through the entire winter." With such a luxury of time and sustenance, the

---

* It may seem paradoxical that the Shoshone National Forest, which is almost entirely comprised of Sheepeater country, is now the domain of dude rides and mule packers; its motto, "the Horse Forest." But stock use became much more practical after crews blasted trail benches into the rugged topography. Despite the most obvious differences, the Absarokas have selected for something in common from both today's riders and yester-year's residents. It's an allegiance to an old way because it works, it makes you who you are, and it can be more fulfilling than keeping up with the cutting edge.

Sheepeaters were also able to pursue the finer things in life. The exceptionality of their craftsmanship bears testament.

Perhaps the best example of Sheepeater ingenuity is their archery bow—one of the most advanced technological achievements of any North American Indian tribe.* It creatively exploited two resources uncommonly abundant in Sheepeater homeland: the curls of bighorn rams (up through the 1950s, the largest herd of bighorns in North America wintered on Whiskey Mountain, in the northern Winds), and hot spring water (the GYE encompasses more geothermal sources than the rest of the world combined). By softening the curls in hot water, craftsmen achieved a flexible material that had stronger compression strength than wood. Sinew of wild game, plaited in strips with adhesives made from hooves, further augmented the draw strength. The end product was an approximately three-foot bow that could, given a sufficiently strong archer, shoot a stone-tipped arrow all the way through a bison. This is a level of performance that has not been surpassed by modern technology.

Other examples abound. Less dramatic, perhaps, but nearly as surprising to me, is an incomparable artifact found near the top of Sheep Mountain above the confluence of the north and south forks of the Shoshone River. About 8,000 years ago, prehistoric hunters wove a net from the bark of juniper trees estimated to be 180 feet long. It was strong enough to snag charging bighorns.

The resourcefulness, hardiness, and sense of self we may read into this archaeological and historical record give us much to admire in the Sheepeater way of life. A final attribute, harder to put into numbers, is the universal mystique that makes the notion of a mountain-dwelling population so compelling. As Lawrence Loendorf and Nancy Stone wrote,

> Spirits were not all equal: the strongest—those of the *toyawo*, or mountain medicine—lived 'in the wooded mountain areas of the Yellowstone National Park, the Absarokas, the Wind Rivers, and possibly the Big Horn Mountains.' Shoshone bands living at lower elevations also believed that the strongest *puha* (power) existed in the mountains. Consistent with this spiritual hierarchy,

---

* The Crow employed this technology, as well.

the Sheepeaters were recognized as "living among the powerful spirits" and absorbing some of their power. When, in the 1870s, Sheepeater groups were moved to reservations, they were regarded as particularly powerful medicine people.

So why were some historians telling people that "the Sheepeaters possessed few weapons, and had been cowed so thoroughly by their enemies that their principle method of defending themselves was to cower near geysers"? This particularly inaccurate and libelous slant is usually traced to Hiram Chittenden, the first person to lay down a comprehensive history of Yellowstone Park.* As such, he stands accused of an ulterior motive: pushing Sheepeater history out of Yellowstone simplified the Park Service mission, and preserved its benevolent image. One needn't spend long in Sheepeater country to disprove his hypothesis: whatever the perks, living in the mountains requires "unparalleled levels of physiological strength and behavioral flexibility— and no small amount of ingenuity." In other words, nobody winds up there just for being a slouch.

◊◊◊

Our most memorable archaeological discovery occurred near one night's camp. I found a large, crudely shaped circle of ochre chert. At the time I guessed it was an over-sized hide scraper—now I know it fit the definition of a preform, or quarry blank. These plates were roughed out at their geologic source into a size and shape convenient for travel, then kept on hand for future tool production or trade. When Jen came up behind me she looked at my find, looked at the ground, and picked up the most artfully worked obsidian I've ever seen. Its outline was classic "arrowhead": trapezoidal stem, circular notches, flanks converging at a precise tip. But it was executed with a carefulness and control that was impossible to miss. After reviewing my pictures, I'd

---

* Many of the most hostile and resilient rumors deviate little from those laid out in Chittenden's 1895 history, *The Yellowstone National Park*. "Feeble in mind and diminutive in stature," he wrote, Sheepeaters were "utterly unfit for warlike contention, [and] seem to have sought immunity from their dangerous neighbors by dwelling among the inaccessible fastnesses of the mountains."

explain this by the fact that not a single surface was merely flat or straight. The cutting edges swelled out from corner notches before pinching to point, like a very subtle spade, and the butt end held a barely perceptible swell. The side-view revealed sleek and consistent tapering, from a projecting mid-section to precise blades, which drew the inky smoke color out to transparency. What's more, the arrowhead was still sharp. Freshly knapped obsidian can be several times keener than a scalpel of surgical steel, a property that modern hospitals would be happy to exploit.

Of the dozens of prehistoric artifacts I've found, I've only kept one, and that was the first—an obsidian scraper from the Madison River that I found when I was in grade school. Since then, for whatever reason, my admiration for these objects has largely disassociated from my possessive impulse. Part of what I find inspiring about archaeology is that, after leaving something where I find it, there is a unique pull to revisit that place. These are sites of pilgrimage, be they just a few steps off the trail, and at my own discretion I share them with others. Even if I never come back (or can't find them again), the remembered presence adds a dimension to the place that is more deeply affecting than perhaps any other—an intimation of what it means to belong. Craig Childs explores this position in his book *Finders Keepers*, which examines the wide-ranging consequences of archaeological plundering. At one point, he summaries an argument from an ethics columnist Rangy Cohen, who "argues that there is a kind of continuity that makes the locality where the artifacts are found a stand in for the owner." In other words, "Their meaning is often very much tied to the place."

Meaning, in this sense, applies in a personal sense to the finder, a broader intellectual sense if the site is studied in the future, a social sense for anyone else who may or may not find it, and a cultural sense for any descendents of the people who made the artifact. In the last example, even if the nearest living relatives of the creator are unaware of its presence, it is spiritually significant for the piece *not* to be in a private collection—that the intellectual and spiritual property of one's ancestors are not exploited for profit, just as you wouldn't want strangers trading around your grandpa's bones (or, for that matter, to know that a trade in grandpa bones exists, period). For everyone involved, the artifact must be allowed to inform the landscape and vice versa, because therein the power lies.

That said, I recognize that this argument is either unintuitive or unconvincing to a large percentage of the population. Plenty of people I know and spend time with feel entitled to keep what they find; that is true whether or not they know it's illegal. Fellow Forest Service employees, who are trained to enforce the very laws protecting these artifacts, are scarcely more respectful than average. Whether they've always wanted to find an arrowhead, or are massing inventory for a "personal museum" in their basement (true story), many act under the assumption that if you found it, you'd keep it, too. To share one example: two friends were working as wilderness rangers in Wyoming. One of them, a woman from a small nearby town, found an elegant white projectile point. She showed it to the man—a thoughtful practitioner of Tibetan Buddhism. When she moved to put it back, he objected. He told her that if she wasn't going to keep it, he would—to him, leaving it was the same thing as throwing it away. A standoff ensued. In order to prevent a violation of the federal regulations that they were both there to implement, and, more than that, to protect her own beliefs, the woman had to go out of her way to hide it from him. Years later, when I was in the same meadow, the would-be taker of this artifact (last I heard, he lives in a monastery) candidly related this story to me in a way that took my sympathy for granted. But all I could think was that, if he hadn't made a stand, we would've been admiring it again together. It's like trying to debate income equality or consumer responsibility with a jet-setting billionaire. To them, property rights are inherently fair, guaranteed by the patriotism of American self-interest. The very implication that moral shades of grey exist to "what's yours" elicits feelings of defensiveness, distrust, and accusations of jealousy or greed. Indeed—opening up another person's actions to discussion, no matter how trivial, might be the most inherently perilous terrain of our individualistic era.

As I stood and watched Jen excitedly examine her discovery, I was surprised to notice I felt differently that day. My reasons were personal; not defensible. I knew that not only was it the first complete arrowhead she'd found, but a spectacular one. I knew how many times I'd ranted about the selfishness of taking things, and how she always supported me leaving the things I found. I knew all the places she'd left better than she'd found them, picking up trash and rolling rocks out of the trail. She knew the arguments—therefore the choice needed to be her own. For me to speak up then, and add guilt to the equation, would make her decision meaningless.

In many ways, leaving an arrowhead is a symbolic gesture. Jen's was found in steep, loose dirt, creeping toward a gully bottom, far from a trail. In a place like that it's more likely to be lost to forces of nature than it is to be appreciated again. Later in *Finders Keepers,* Childs recounts his discovery of a rare and immaculate piece of pottery. After admiring it, and making the argument to a friend that it should be left where it is ("It's been here for eight hundred goddamned years! ...At least let it die here"), they walk away, and, "Like those before us, we never returned." Until, he did return. Reporters from the podcast *Radiolab* accompanied him back to the site. They discovered that a cliff collapsed and completely obliterated the pot. It is clear from the audio that the great and moral desert explorer's convictions are shaken; his decision to leave the piece seems to have been partly based on his assumption it was safe there. Though that's the story of a crazy coincidence as much as anything, it's no less true that, every time you walk away from something small and wonderful, you have to make some kind of peace with the fact that it may disappear before you return. That it may be destroyed—or, that the next person who comes along probably will take it—and this is surely the greatest challenge to archaeological ethics, as well as any other defense of the commons. If you don't take/develop/kill it, someone else will—the more careless that person is, the more certain it is they won't pass it up. And surely they don't deserve it more than you do, right?

Leaving arrowheads can start looking like so many of the other self-imposed limitations exerting themselves on our society, like truncating your own bloodline out of consideration of overpopulation while your loutish neighbor has five kids, or buying only sustainable and locally harvested vegetables, even when they cost five times as much. It is my suspicion that the people that are most likely to leave artifacts are the type who'd also be most likely to share and learn from them—figure out the who-what-when-and-why, eventually donate their discovery to a museum. (It's not a completely fair assumption, but I'll let it fly.) Even if the taker does none of these things, the object will almost certainly take on some sort of personal significance, and no one else will be any wiser. So why should anything, with such an abstract potential for consequence, and such a burden on personal lot, be left up to the conscience?

Fortunately, I have plenty of answers to that question, and apparently so does Jen—namely, if you stop acting as though your choices matter, life loses meaning. Leveraging your blessings for personal profit also eviscerates them of their beauty and magic. After Jen and I walked away, the arrowhead and quarry blank remained. We hadn't traveled so far to align ourselves with common denominators. Robin Wall Kimmerer:

> Wildness cannot be collected and still remain wild. Its nature is lost the moment it is separated from its origins. By the very act of owning, the thing becomes the object, no longer itself.
>
> I think you cannot own a thing and love it at the same time. Owning diminishes the sovereignty of a thing, enriching the possessor and reducing the possessed.
>
> Barbara Kingsolver writes, "It's going to take the most selfless kind of love to do right by what we cherish and give it the protection to flourish outside our possessive embrace."

3

The human body is the only one designed to carry things as it walks—an unsteady activity that is both encouraged by trails and encourages more trails. As our genotypes have led us carrying things down trails, our phenotypes have evolved in concert. Now that trails have given us the most illustrative analogies for how the brain works,* the relationship has come full circle—E. O. Wilson calls this dance

---

* *Neural pathways* are worn by the directions taken by thoughts, forming evermore connections, freeways, and shortcuts; *evolutionary pathways* are those trajectories of mutations that record the interplay between life form and environment. Every story recounts motion, every movement implies a path…

"gene-culture coevolution." Our habits are formed to our abilities, and the more our culture selects for those habits, the more able we become.

So what do trails tell us about who we are? Consider a popular memory competition in which participants race to memorize the order of a shuffled deck of cards. Unprepared people like myself would rely on the laborious imprinting of repetition, and require hours, perhaps (I'm not about to try), getting it down. But for those at the top of the game, one run-through is enough, and the record is twenty-one seconds.

The winning strategy traces to ancient Greeks, often tasked with laborious memorization, and they named it the Method of Loci—the Method of *Places*. Competitors prepare by dialing in a mental map. That's the entire secret. Houses are common, but gardens, city streets, and other outdoor environments also work. They organize the map along a linear route, as though they are walking through it, and designate 52 sites along the way. They also assign each card's combination of number and suit to familiar people or animals. With these associations in place, flipping through a shuffled deck generates something more than a random smattering of symbols. It follows a sequence of characters along a path—in other words, it turns into a story.

Spectators are right to be amazed. The Method of Loci taps a latent superpower. It's officially called spatial memory, and it's in all of us. While twenty-one seconds for a deck of cards is awe-inspiring, the power of spatial memory is even more impressive when tasked with things besides trivia. To take one famous example, London cab drivers must memorize the relative positions of about 26,000 unordered street names before they begin work. In the process, the hippocampi of these drivers—the brain lobes containing the centers of spatial memory—measurably enlarge.

The freaky capacity of spatial memory indicates the degree to which survival once hinged on the individual's ability to decipher and interpret landscape. For a long time, spatial memory's only measure was human propagation: hunter gatherers learned where to find food and shelter throughout the seasons, just as generalist eaters like grizzly bears patrol wide-flung networks of hundreds of food types, and nutcrackers mustn't lose track of their dozens of nut caches hidden under pine needles (as we've seen, it's fortunate for both parties they'll always lose track of some). These are the true miracles of memory: how we ever survive in the first place, let alone make this world home.

For better or worse, the availability of human food and shelter is no longer tied to a nuanced understanding of the landscape. Our hardware pines like a muscle craving exercise.* The dominance of spatial memory makes sense to me, not because I know anything about physiology or psychology, but because I feel subject to its dominance. Giving it full expression for a day, be that in the mountains or in town, can feel as liberating as the physical activity that enables it.

Once a bodily potential is grasped, ignoring it can become a burden to bear—I know what C.L. Rawlins means when he says, "My body has ripened to constant movement. ...Most of us get sore from long hikes. I get sore without them." I've taught my spatial memory to "feed" just like I have my quadriceps; to devour space and incorporate components into the most detailed and beautiful cognitive map I am capable of. To keep looking. Unturned corners and neglected heights glimpsed along the way develop into aches and longings, and those feelings mature into a yearning, if not compulsion, to return.

In the Absaroka-Beartooth, Jen and I enacted so many deferred dreams. We put our bodies to horizons we'd glimpsed from afar, many times over many years, horizons that had taken on the aura of forbidden realms. We traversed chains of alpine basins cured into lions' manes, shaded timber copses barnacled in hoar frost, cliff bands vomiting aprons of puce, half-digested cobbles. We learned earth's curves by our own measurements, truthed shades of perception against lines on the map, hungered after the biggest patterns like they'd redeem our trying lives. We had no way of telling whether it was the right thing to do—we knew only that it's what needed to be tried, first.

---

* The number of people who are "terrible with directions" seems to suggest that spatial memory can vanish with disuse. Really, it's been reassigned, from spatial concepts to symbolic values—like card values and suits.

The greatest and earliest works of literature predate the written word—they are inheritances from the oral tradition that survived for hundreds of years in the minds of storytellers. It is not by chance that Homer's *Odyssey*, over 12,000 lines long and one of the oldest extant pieces of Western literature, recounts a journey. Scientifically, it can be viewed as a rather magnificent yet perfectly logical outgrowth of spatial memory, in which linear time and physical motion proceed in tandem.

It makes sense to our brains that time and space should develop in concert: historically, good things have not reliably come to those who wait. It's motion that makes us: I was reminded of this after watching *Mulholland Drive* days after the end of our trip. In his director's notes, David Lynch addresses the prevalence of roads and paths in his filmography: "A road, I've been thinking, is a moving fast forward into the unknown, and that's compelling to me. That's also what films are—the lights go down, the curtain opens, and away we go, but we don't know where we're going." This is the story that never gets old. Lynch elaborates on how this form also pervades his creative process: he doesn't use a storyboard. He creates parts depending on the personalities of actors who draw him in. The results are not always logical (far from it), but they feel right. By communicating not just ideas but the all-important mystery, his work makes a deeper, more enriching sort of sense.

Before we left Dubois, I folded a copy of Robert Service's poem "The Cremation of Sam McGee" into my journal, and began memorizing it over our campfires at night. By the North Absaroka, I could recite it to the end, with mistakes. By the Absaroka-Beartooth I was fluid. When a line seemed remotely applicable to the situation, I belted it out in a highfalutin voice for my audience of one. "The trail was BAD and I felt half MAD, but I swore I would not GIVE IN!" was a popular one, or, in a more somber moment,

> Now a promise made is a debt unpaid, and the trail has its own stern code.
>
> In the days to come, though my lips were dumb, in my heart how I cursed that load…

It didn't take long for me to discover the therapeutic function of memorization. Running through those sixty-eight lines was a form of meditation, most welcome when my thoughts started to snag on bodily aches and pains. As the great Montana author Bill Kittredge wrote, "Without stories, we're not much more than what Spinoza called 'falling stones.' Narrative may well be our fundamental survival strategy."

◊◊◊

From a shallow basin near the divide between Mill and Hellroaring Creeks, two watersheds comprising hundreds of square miles, I watched the sky with a level of vacant absorption rare to me. "There is twice as much UV radiation and twenty-five percent more light here than at sea level," writes Ann Zwinger in her beautiful book *Land Above The Trees*. "Psychologically, the great wash of light illuminating the alpine tundra gives one a sense of encompassing comprehension verging on euphoria." Horizon to horizon, clouds stood in isolated clusters across the smoothly graded wash of sundown-blue.

Each collection posed its own peculiarity—a Dadaist flotilla, a spontaneous *objet d'art*, another version of truth. In one corner of the sky, snatches of pattern unraveled like cloth in an acid bath. Elsewhere—how to explain the distance, the relation—a perky cauliflower in bright pink whisped across a backdrop of hammered meal. And if I turned my head the other way, I saw a tower layered in feathered strokes, the cross-section of a high-rise butter croissant, blooming rose and purple throughout. As I stared, the eastern sky massed heavier, fomenting the darkness that would soon blot everything out.

We'd spent much of that day in suspense. We needed to find a route up and over Peak 10,484', a dark mass of bedrock I nicknamed the Jello Mold. But each study through the binoculars, each contemplation of our options for retreat (a steep, loose downclimb off the ridge into a jackstraw mess of burn), shook my confidence that an unroped traverse was even possible. When we finally got our chance, though, the route unfolded before us. We threaded easily through the hoodoos balanced along the Jello Mold's knife-edge ridge. In so doing, fears lifted, and a proportionate satisfaction took its place. Now, with camp made and dinner eaten, I wasn't reclined so much as melted to the ground, my head on my backpack mindlessly content.

From the summit of Peak 10,484', the end of our trip was practically in sight. I could clearly decipher the skyline of the Madison Range, further west than our walk would take us. The Madisons served as my primary work area for the previous two summers, and I took the time to envision the hydrological context of each major peak. Also visible was the Hyalite cluster at the northern end of the Gallatin Range, the last topography we'd cross before dropping down into the Gallatin Valley. Bozeman. To hold my eyes to that spot—to see it was right there—unsettled me. I imagined a flag sticking up from the hole between the Hyalites and the Bridgers, Bozeman's mountain range to the northeast, and felt the disappointment rush in.

But the disappointment was fleeting. Nothing said the finish line had to be so definitive—our walk had a major advantage over more exotic vacations. It didn't rely on novelty. It wasn't an outlier of experience. It was an expanded definition of home, I was starting to feel that, a fleshing out that was literally grounded in our daily lives. As Bernd Heinrich explains, home is not just a partitioned stake of what you own. It "is also the surrounding territory that supports us. 'Homing' is migrating to and identifying a suitable area for living." Later in his book *The Homing Instinct,* he describes pigeons, "circling near their lofts in apparently aimless flight. …Through time and experience, and longer and longer ranging excursions, pigeons enlarge the area where they are home." Finding home is deepening one's context—understanding where you are in relation to everything else—a process far more enriching than the squabble to extend boundary lines of personal possession.

Studying the map, I realized that our route on that leg alone threaded through the destinations and turn-arounds of seven other multi-day trips Jen and I had taken together over as many years. All told, our summer's route built off of dozens of trips we'd made just for fun; over a decade of combined backcountry work experience; books read and maps pored over with friends. It drew a thread of unity through so much of our lives. As we proceeded north, ideas for future explorations popped up left and right. There were so many more things to learn about, things to live to see—that's how trips go. Go in telling yourself that exploration is a phase to be indulged and then gotten over, and you will be surprised, "Sorcerer's Apprentice" style. Interest expands by exponents.

What I felt at that moment was the very opposite of an escape. It was confrontation: renewed acquaintance with what is most essential. Here, Jen and I re-dedicated ourselves to the place we chose to live, in an investment that would enrich whatever came after.

The Greater Yellowstone is, quite simply, the most beautiful and complicated thing I've endeavored to wrap my head around. My efforts, while of necessity incomplete, cannot go unrewarded. To trust in the dynamic of this system, as it plays pattern off of pattern into an order so sophisticated it is often misidentified as chaos, is to know completeness.

◊◊◊

Three days passed during which we counted over thirty mountain goats a day. Burly, compact things, standing less on foothold than optical illusion, foraging some incipient ground cover—scraping, even, crustose lichens from rock faces with terrible yellow teeth—they looked utterly of-the-place. At one time, the harmonious sight of goats among cliffs would've lent support to the spontaneous generation theory of the origin of life: if rotting meat gives rise to maggots, and toads materialize from the right recipe of muck, then it makes sense that forgotten outposts of the Absaroka Province would conjure these ghostly "beasts the color of winter" (in the words of biologist Douglas Chadwick) to find fuller expression of their contours. Not only do we know better today, but the presence of mountain goats in the Greater Yellowstone is actually the least mysterious of all four-legged residents, recorded in a paper trail. We're the ones that put them there.

In the early twentieth century, when bleating herds of domestic sheep ravaged alpine pastures of the GYE every summer, they exposed bighorns to diseases like pneumonia and pink-eye—diseases for which the natives lacked all immunity. Scourges ensued that were not dissimilar from the unbelievably destructive smallpox epidemics wrought on Native American people. In some GYE ranges, like the Crazies and the Bridgers, bighorns died off completely, and remain absent to this day.

The problem with that, as humans perceived it at the time, was not localized extinctions per se, but the hunting grounds underutilized by quarry that bighorns left behind. According to this way of thinking, replacement species would do just as well, and mountain goats weren't hard to get a hold of: they're native to Montana, mostly west of the Continental Divide, and as close as the Beaverhead Range, about a hundred miles from the GYE.

Goats had no trouble fitting in. Those that Jen and I first saw in Clearwater Creek—less than a dozen miles from the Washakie Wilderness—were many days' travel from any introduction points. It's fair to say that goats would've expanded their range into these mountains eventually. It's puzzling, in fact, why they hadn't yet during this epoch—because in the long view, goats are native to the GYE. Due to range fluctuations corresponding with glacial advances and retreats, mountain goat remains pop up as far south as Mexico.*

Nevertheless, as introduced goats "naturally" continue to expand, and native bighorns "naturally" continue to struggle, it's hard to make total peace with the situation. Bighorn Peak in the Gallatins, Sheep Mountain in the Western Beartooths, Sheep Point in the Lionshead—in all these places I have seen families of mountain goats, but never the eponymous bighorn. And while the one doesn't appear to directly displace the other (the two species exist in harmony in many places, none more photographed than Logan Pass in Glacier National Park), there remains this unanswered question of how goats change the places they occupy. That herd of seventy I saw in the Madisons is seriously altering the diminutive, slow-growing floral community above treeline on which it subsists, and that in turn affects everything else—from butterflies to contour lines.

Many decades after those first, disruptive goat introductions in the GYE, we're still not acting like we know any better. Out of the blue, Utah introduced mountain goats to the La Sals in 2013, and neglected to provide for any sort of native plant survey, first. That invaluable task fell to an impromptu citizen's group scrambling in at the last minute. Only

---

* Winter range on high, wind-scoured ridges, sets the population threshold for goats. They are especially conservative when it comes to expanding their ranges.

after the fact do we understand what the trade-offs were; only then do we realize what we had to lose.

◊◊◊

Our route continued to serve up a curious mix of geology. Jen and I walked past walls of ash, silt, and volcanic clasts lain in crisp, horizontal layers—only to see the patterns pinch out, scramble, disintegrate. Whenever I thought I'd managed to explain something in my head it ceased to be true; as a 1986 Geologic Highway Map of Wyoming notes, "All these relationships are inherently inexact and sometimes problematic." Jen, meanwhile, had been memorizing Yeats's "The Second Coming," and I remember catching snippets as we walked across a sudden crop of red, scoriacious bombs, similar to the crunchy "lava rock" used in landscaping. "Things fall apart, the center cannot hold," she muttered. "…Surely some revelation is at hand."

In late afternoon, an interpersonal complaint from Jen caught me off guard. Our looks took on old darkness—passing over the crest of the first mountain we ever climbed together, Mount Wallace, was a joyless, sullen affair. Below, Jen went off to be alone and my pessimism found something else to fixate on: stirrings of illness that I'd almost succeeded in ignoring throughout the day. For once it was an effort to get any dinner down. Trying might've been a mistake. It was followed by one of the worst nights of my life. I was hot and cold, clammy all over, and sick to my stomach, while my brain spun its wheels, finding traction nowhere. The thought of daybreak became my only refuge; at the same time, I was losing the strength to face it. I checked my watch every half-hour or less—each time surer than the last that I'd be hours closer to morning—and each time, devastatingly wrong, the minutes were made to seem longer, the end that much further away. A half-hour before sunrise I teetered to my feet by force of will, desperate to leave the ghastly tent, and got an early start firing up breakfast. I hadn't shared my condition with Jen (the timing seemed too convenient), so we ate in more silence and hard feelings—me taking sips of broth, as our homemade potato-egg scramble, usually a special treat, was even less appetizing than dinner. Though I got myself shuffling along the trail all right, I didn't walk far before I had to jump in the bushes, barely getting my pants down in time. When I returned to my backpack, I had to admit I was sick. Thank goodness it got us past arguing.

It helped that we weren't in a rush to get anywhere. Though we had plenty of busy ideas for the next three days, we could also strip them down to a single day of twenty easy miles into the town of Gardiner. It made sense to me to divide the miles up as much as I could in case I didn't start feeling better, so I kept at it.

I've learned in the past that I prefer to journey toward my home rather than away from it. Let the homing impulse—the *Zugunruhe*, or "migratory restlessness"—kick in and work for you. Even if the difference is nearly insignificant (arriving at an airport with a ticket for home isn't much different from arriving home), knowing in a forlorn moment that your steps take you closer to what you know, rather than further away, functions as a not-insignificant comfort. That day, I slogged to escape the same impartial skies that looked so rapturous the day before.

In about a mile I stepped off the trail again. I sat down on a stump, sunk my head in my hands, and spit out gobs of vile saliva. Jen handed me a ginger chew, said to settle the stomach, but my first taste was more than I could handle. I remember watching it slip out of my mouth in slow motion and into the dirt. After a half hour, perhaps, and no throwing up, I was ready to try walking again. My motivation sprung from the questionable conviction that if I just vomited I'd feel better, and walking felt like it could get me there quick. We had a bit of a hill coming up—I checked later, it was only a couple hundred feet—but I steeled myself for an epic struggle. Immediately it seemed like a rather obvious mistake. My breath came short and hard, I felt dizzy. When we got to the top, I drooped over until my head rested on my knees. We found camp a half mile beyond that. In the few minutes it took Jen to set up the tent, I fell asleep, then woke disoriented and chilled. The next day passed almost exactly the same way.

◊◊◊

With sickness comes insecurity, with insecurity comes regret, and on this occasion, I thought a lot about giardia. This pathogen needs no introduction to most outdoor people: it's a big bad wolf they've been warned about all their lives. The signature blend of gastro-intestinal distress it causes—giardiasis—is publicized at trailheads, in outdoor literature, in gear shops where many forms of water treatment are sold, and as much as anything, by word-of-mouth. So on the one side of the table you have this advisory to always treat your water, with the implication that nasty germs are everywhere. The counter argument is equally potent, and laid out with great conviction in a widely-circulated paper by Dr. Robert L. Rockwell called *"Giardia Lamblia* and Giardiasis with Particular Attention to the Sierra Nevada."

"Drink freely and confidently,"* advises this biomedical engineer, as he himself has done. Upon writing, Rockwell could boast thousands of trips into the Sierra backcountry, spanning a half-century, without ever treating his water or getting sick, and many of his friends could say the same. Like so many others, I found his paper persuasive (the report is not peer-reviewed—just a synthesis of his own research that he published in the Yosemite Association Newsletter—and there are many articles refuting its points), but no more persuasive than stories from people I know who have walked entire long trails across the country, carrying no filtration device, drinking almost anything that comes along. Such reports immediately appealed to some of my preexisting beliefs. Namely, that American culture is pathologically risk-averse (except, perhaps, in the financial markets), and we self-medicate this condition with consumer goods. I've witnessed water-purification debates digress into pure superstition. Some people don't trust ultra-violet pens, or pump filters, or only drink water held at a rolling boil for ten minutes—in some groups everybody has their own method, some of them are executed imperfectly, and nobody gets sick. For a long time, I defended my own insistence on purifying everything with a story about soldiers introducing giardia to North America after returning from Vietnam. That made sense to me: it explained why, only recently, humans would

---

* Elsewhere, Rockwell specifies what he means by "freely." Basically, drink smart. Pick your sources with consideration of what's upstream.

have lost the ability to drink from even the cleanest water sources found in nature, after doing so for millennia. When I finally looked for evidence to confirm this factoid, I didn't find any. *Giardia* has always been here, and within the lives of baby boomers, everybody was still drinking the water.

On our trip I carried a chemical water treatment called Aquamira,* but in our month and a half in the woods, I'd only treated our water a couple times. Now, my addled state of sickness left me plenty of time for misgivings. Perhaps this lesson from Rockwell's paper is the best takeaway:

> Giardiasis has been called a disease of 'somes.' Some people do not contract it even from heavily contaminated sources. Some infestations vanish with no treatment at all. Some people become asymptomatic carriers. Some evidence suggests that some people acquire a natural immunity to some strains. And some strains seem more virulent than others.

So it's always a gamble. In addition to the people I know who never treat and never get sick, I also know people who definitely have gotten giardiasis, and they're all reasonable people. No matter what stance you take on the issue, the evidence is there.

As I lay in the tent, questioning my ability to proceed, I briefly convinced myself that I was done. I'd already skipped five meals in a row. I was weak and miserable. As I told Jen, "Hiking any more than I absolutely have to is unimaginable right now." It was the warmest and nicest late-September I could ever hope for, yet each shadow harbored a menacing chill, each breeze bared me to my weakness.

At the same time, it was becoming increasingly clear that my symptoms were not consistent with giardiasis. On the third evening of sickness, I forced myself to eat an entire whole-wheat bagel, employing long, horizontal rests between bites. Packing up slowly the next morning I waited for the misery to set in. But a half-mile down the trail, I realized I was fine to keep going, so that's what we did. I stopped blaming the

---

* Beloved by many backpackers for its lack of taste and portability, the product makes absolutely no claim to decontaminate water. It is marketed as a way to improve the flavor of stored water.

water and blamed the door handles of the Cooke City Visitor Center instead. And, for the record, I never changed my drinking habits.

◊◊◊

In fact, walking almost felt good again: it put space between me and the bug. We popped out at a trailhead, started down a dirt road, turned off into a campground, picked up another trail, followed it out to the road again, then walked through the community of Jardine—old mining buildings, summer homes, dude ranches. Soon we were in the sun and the sage, a far cry from the grove of whitebark where we started the day. In the middle of a long, straight stretch, Jen peeked over the steep shoulder of the road and announced, "There's a great ditch here!" She was right: it really was a great ditch. An irrigation canal supported an outlying corridor of Douglas fir and juniper just off the side of the road, hidden and unsuspecting. We skidded down the steep shoulder, past the bones of road killed elk and a chunk of steel plumbing, to strip and wash in the water. Sunlight pricked through the canopy; the cold, fast, dark flow made us gasp.

Back on the road, fresh in the warm sun, the bath became a powerful reminder of everything I loved about our trip. The thrill of chance, the "making do," the small discoveries.

I told a story that came to mind. Ten years earlier, when I was nineteen, I went on the first, and what I hope will remain the strangest, odyssey of my adult life. Out of the five months I spent living in my car, driving around the West, rock climbing, and working odd jobs, I spent about seven weeks of it based in a vacant lot in the town of Joshua Tree, California, that climbers called "the Pit." Basically, whoever wanted could camp there for as long as they wanted. I found work washing dishes at a café in the evenings and, after fracturing my ankle falling off a very tall boulder (my granddad paid to have it diagnosed two months later—too late for treatment), I spent the rest of my off-time hobbling around, working, and reading in the desert. I wanted to learn to meditate, but came about it far too desperately. My great journey of excitement and discovery turned into an immersion course in amateur Existentialism. Anyway, one afternoon before work, I was filling water jugs from a spigot that I knew about on the side of a tourist shop when a new Honda Element pulled in beside me. It was covered in stickers that advertised different outdoor manufacturers, jam bands, that sort of thing. The couple that got out both wore dreadlocks, designer corduroy patchwork pants, and tribal-looking jewelry. In other words, they epitomized the mean but sometimes-useful word "trustafarian." Seeing me reminded the girl that they, too, needed water, which she mentioned to her boyfriend.

"We'll go back to the store," he said.

"But we can fill up here!"

"We're not drinking from a *HOSE*," he snarled.

"In plenitude too free/ we have become adept/ beneath the yoke of greed …Lord, I flinch and pray,/ send Thy necessity." These words from Wendell Berry's poem, "We Who Prayed And Wept," give form to my own, wordless little prayer before I take to the road. They remind me why I think travel offers something real to daily life. Uncertainty, poverty, and depravation recontextualize the little neuroses that clog a life of routines. They bring freedom from Berry's "tyranny of things." To move my bones after lying ill, to wash my skin in a ditch along a county road, and for that to make my entire day—I sense what it means to be grateful for everything. The world astounds me.

"Too much safety seems to yield only danger in the long run," wrote Aldo Leopold, and America is transparent proof of that. We have no way to check ourselves. As our way of living proves unsustainable, our death-grip on freedom and security—never enough of either—makes us crazy, contrary, and combative. Most of us assume we'll have more luck colonizing Mars than reining in the selfish interests clearly spelling out our doom. Travel and voluntary poverty rephrase the ordeal from accepting what doesn't feel right to making a stand and figuring out what does.

Across the irrigation canal, across Bear Creek and barely half a mile away from us, a parched bench called Deckard Flats led the eye toward a knot of forested terrain wedged into a collision of jurisdictional boundaries. The Flats are infamous in Montana game management: a bottleneck of terrain on a fall elk migration route, in combination with a tradition of unlimited bull tags, has reduced browtine-to-cow ratios in the northern herd to an appalling 1:50. It's the big game version of shooting fish in a bucket. While an average of ten bulls were being gunned down across the small hunting district for each day of hunting season, those invested in the bloodbath worked deftly to shift popular blame for the travesty onto wolves.

Just above Deckard Flats, a cluster of inholdings wedged into a corner abutting both the Absaroka-Beartooth and Yellowstone Park was about to unveil a new mining plan: 128 exploratory drill holes and 36,000 feet of drilling on the rim of Yellowstone River's Black Canyon. Announced in quick succession with a similar proposal for reopening a large mine in Emigrant Gulch, fifteen miles north, defenders of this forever-embattled landscape soon found they had two new developments to fight off. Yellowstone's history of resource exploitation is, it turns out, anything but history.

As we wound down the last couple road miles into Gardiner, I called my parents on Jen's phone. An upward trajectory of health seemed like the right time to tell them I was sick in the first place. Meanwhile, I took a pictures: of a creepy mountain man-stiff, carved from a log; a faux street sign declaring one lofty private driveway "ABOVE THE REST;" and a picture of the town, looking treeless and hardscrabble, sitting cluttered on the river in a dish of distinctively shaped mountains. Phone in one hand, camera snapping in the other, I gave myself away as a tourist of the twenty-first century. Just outside Gardiner's residential grid, we stopped at a guardrail to watch a bull elk with his harem. The great animal lifted his nose in the smoky sky and unleashed that squeaking, honking whistle-song of the subalpine wilderness. I gawked with the best of them. The first elk we'd seen in ten days were courting in somebody's fertilized backyard.

Part Five. **WHERE WE'RE GOING**

It is in the doing, the being, the becoming that meaning is made. What becomes sacred is the act itself—not what remains.

—Terry Tempest Williams

1

"Back in the land of people," my journal reads. That meant we had to hurry. Get to the post office before it closed, but oh!—ten minutes late. Then to the grocery, where we bought cheese and summer sausage and sorted our things on the edge of the parking lot. A van pulled in, driver and passenger *screaming* at one another. The woman jumped out while the vehicle was still moving and almost face-planted the concrete—stumbling away, she yelled and cussed. Then she turned around and jumped back in, and the two sped off. A low-slung sedan appeared next. Its Washington plates stopped a couple feet from my boots. Three tough-looking kids got out and congregated in the adjacent parking space. As they tapped on their phones, two men joined them from behind the building—I heard low voices, hands flashed between pockets. Not your typical small-town Montana, here was the strange marginalia that accompanies an international model of land conservation-cum-cash cow to rural communities. Around 600 million dollars a year, to be specific.

Then Jen's dad, Mark, pulled in, over from Missoula to join us for two days. We hopped in his car and drove to the Boiling River, a few miles inside Yellowstone's boundary, where an enormous hot spring emerges from a cave to mix with the Gardner River.[*] The parking lot overflowed down both sides of the road. From the outskirts of the line we watched a fifteen-passenger tour van dump a full load into the parking lot—so we weren't surprised to find the springs more crowded than any of us had ever seen. As I sized it up for open water, a chill upstream breeze and all those half-naked bodies convinced me I'd be unwell again in no time.

Ever since the temperature of the hot spring spiked a couple years earlier, the Boiling River has been a lot less hospitable. Soakers endure a gauntlet of clinging, scalding plumes and frigid river water, beating their feet on slick or sharp rocks, before encountering a tolerable mix. In spite of the crowd, nobody was in the spot we liked, and Jen and I relished the heat like we never had before. But soon we had to leave, back to Gardiner and out the other side to the Eagle Creek Campground, to find a camp for the night. All the sites were taken, extras spilled across the surrounding grass, so we kept driving toward Sheep Mountain, passing two separate parties of dog walkers who, instead of walking themselves, idled their pickup trucks along while the dogs ran. The three of us settled for a last-resort spot in the sagebrush—true "sagebrushers," our camp was a demonstration of how Yellowstone's initial car tourists got their nickname. Mark declared, "Camping isn't going to be as fun as I thought it was going to be" (no campfire for the marshmallows)—then it was back to town, pizza at the K-Bar, where there was a long wait for

---

[*] Gardiner, the town, takes its name from the Gardner River. The different spellings can be explained by the fact that both names (after Johnson Gardner, a trapper with the Ashley-Henry group of the 1820s) came very early, and were passed around verbally for some time before they were written down.

indoor seating. We took a metal table on the windy street corner and I put on all the clothes I had, immodestly stepping into long johns while cars drove by. Then I ate way too much pizza. We got back to camp after 9:30, hours later than I'd been awake in days, and, no surprise, I couldn't fall sleep. The next morning, we drove from Gardiner to the Park headquarters in Mammoth, Wyoming, picked up a backcountry permit for the three days we'd be in the park, and drove some more to the Bunsen Peak Trailhead.

Had I retained my health, Jen and I would have followed trails all the way to Mammoth to meet her dad—and had we not proposed this meet-up with the incentive of climbing Electric Peak, we would've walked between the towns on the old gravel entrance road, now closed to vehicles. But things being as they were, an eight-mile gap formed in the route Jen and I were linking up—an asterisk on our claim to have "walked from Lander to Bozeman." This isn't to say we weren't excited that Mark came so far to help us out: we were both excited and honored. Still, what to make of this gap? During all that driving it became a nasty mental sticking point for me. I knew that my satisfaction with our trip should in no way be affected by a technicality (after all, the jog took us almost straight south, when we were actually heading north). Yet it didn't make the omission stop feeling like something—a blemish on an ideal.

In the faith that even the most misdirected feelings contain some germ of truth, I stared out the window and tried to break it down. I asked myself: did the bypass highlight a lingering insecurity that I wasn't capable of walking the entire thing? No. I didn't question our physical capacity of getting up that old roadbed. Then did the purity of walking the entire thing hold some symbolic importance for me? I wanted to say no—but of course it did! I wanted to summarize our entire trip in a beautifully simple sentence, without qualifying or justifying or explaining. I wanted to be able to look at a map and say, "I did it all!" This admission, though unsurprising, seemed important to me: it related to pride and social currency. It competed with—rather than complemented—my guiding values.

Lastly, had anything else been compromised by our motoring, besides a mental artifact worth challenging anyway? Maybe so. The theme of our approach was openness: the theory that every inch of the ecosystem held equal opportunity for inspiration. There weren't worthy places and unworthy places, interesting and uninteresting—there was just one big picture, deserving of equal amounts of attention throughout. And while even that drive up to Mammoth had the potential for transcendence, just as every second of every day equally does, at forty-five miles an hour it offered so much less than walking it would have (so I thought). Not to mention I'd literally traveled that road dozens of times—most recently the night before, back and forth to the Boiling River—but never the old grade tucked above the Gardner River on the opposite side. I couldn't expect some breakthrough over there, but the bottom line was that the beauty of the long hike—the mechanism to see things anew—was deprived of its function.

Realistically, this wasn't a concern worth wasting time on, nor did it explain a certain melancholy to the moment. But the funk got me thinking more generally about how Jen and I try to be intentional about what we do, about our goals, and about our lives together. We try to have reasons. The enemy of intentionality is apathy—the resignation that all this trying doesn't change anything. Apathy ruthlessly contests the *why* of effort, and in my experience, it arises most poignantly from the paradoxes created by compartmentalization in our lives. So many conventions of modern existence preserve form only as an anachronism of intent: the reasons have dissipated long ago, and we are left only with motions, empty and counterproductive.

In such an atmosphere, it's hard to hold an ideal, even a small one. Our attempts lead us to take otherwise meaningless and sometimes ridiculous-looking stands. This isn't just a fear I had on our trip. I have it in my writing, on the job, and in everything else I do with my life: I fear it doesn't matter if I have my reasons, whether I try a certain way, or actually believe in something going into it. I fear that people only see you the way they want to see you, that content is nothing against presentation, that the trickiest causes are all foregone. At that time, I also knew I had an illness still hanging on, a faltering of inner strength. So I kept my chin up and sat along for the ride.

My final takeaway—and an appreciably ironic one at that—was that being challenged with a gap in our route likely provoked greater introspection than walking it would have. A car may have been the most efficient path to what I was looking for, after all.

◊◊◊

The driving ended at a parking lot below Bunsen Peak. The core of another Absaroka volcano, Bunsen is almost ten million years older than Washakie Needles; hill-shaped. During Pleistocene glaciation, the largest ice sheet in North America (non-contiguous with the Continental Ice Sheet capping the North Pole) was centered on the Yellowstone Plateau. Bunsen looks so diminutive because this layer of frosting—over 4,000' thick in the center and flowing outwards—ran about 600' of ice right over the top of the mountain, and pretty well took the edge off of it.

I took pleasure knowing that our trailhead, right at the mountain's base, was the same one where Karsten Heuer and Maxine Achurch began an extraordinary foot journey in 1999, which ended sixteen months later at the edge of the Yukon.* It was lovely to imagine the continuity between that spot and where we started walking, and even lovelier to know that it keeps going, as far as curiosity will take you. Heuer's journey was partly inspired by the nascent concept of ecological connectivity, which emphasizes the importance of not only protected areas, but also wildlife corridors. These are zones that deserve special consideration, inviting wildlife to move between areas of preferred habitat such as (to use the most immediate examples) the Greater Yellowstone Ecosystem, the central-Idaho wilderness block, and Glacier Park country up against the Canadian line. There are no official protections for such places—they exist only in the hopes of concerned citizens, and the secretive code of animal spoor.

Heuer considered all the places along the way from the context of functioning wildlife populations. Grizzly bears and wolverines, which live on each end of his route, rely on large and undisturbed habitats for their survival. By connecting on foot the southernmost ranges of these animals with the biological stronghold of the far north, he ground-truthed the feasibility for these species to interbreed and find genetic

---

* Heuer finished the trip with a different girlfriend.

resiliency. Revisiting his book after we got home, I was struck by the number of parallels I found between our experiences in the Gallatin Range: the first leg of his trip and the last leg of ours.

◊◊◊

After so many days alone together, Jen and I were pleased to have a guest. Mark was more successful at passing along a passion for outdoor adventure to all three of his kids than anyone could realistically hope; we're lucky to share at least one good trip with him each year. It's additionally good for me because, through all that we enjoy sharing, there's some recreationalist-philosophy graph out there that would plot Mark and I near opposite ends. I learn at least as much from being with him as from people I'm in full agreement with. To elaborate: while I banish the concept of exercise from my appreciation of the mountains, and speed and distance count not towards quality, he is a passionate downhill skier and mountain biker, and things don't get better than when he's smashing a personal record by minutes or miles. We can't take things for granted when we talk about why we love the things we do.

This fact manifested quickly while hiking to our campsite on the upper Gardner River. "Bob and I went on a big bike ride this weekend. Oooh…" he trailed off. "I forgot, I wasn't going to tell you about that." Of course, it was too late. This long-anticipated ride took them through portions of the Rattlesnake Wilderness, in violation of the Wilderness Act. (In his defense, the Rattlesnake, just outside his hometown of Missoula, is the only American wilderness that once explicitly allowed bicycles.) Not that Jen and I were scandalized by the thought. We'd debated the issue with him before, and before that, I was pretty well broken-in to the fact that illegal mountain biking in the wilderness is common around the college-town hubs of Montana outdoor communities. The week before I started as a wilderness ranger in the Spanish Peaks, I ran into an old friend from high school: "Just look the other way when you see me riding in there," he instructed me. "I certainly won't," I replied.

Eager to convey the poignancy of our trip so far, Jen and I began relating the last, hungriest days of our walk through the Washakie Wilderness. Many Native American tribes employed fasting to prompt a spiritual experience, and while I hardly could've felt less spiritual during my time of hunger, that's almost how I'd taken to remembering it: a time of cold and emptiness, with ominous powers emanating from the foliage. Jen was recounting the odds and ends that we managed to forage during that time—saccharine-sweet false wintergreen berries, rich and oily pine nuts, and maybe ten other varieties of odds and ends—when her dad blurted out: "Oh, Jen, you'll have to take some pictures of me wearing this hat." He turned around to indicate a colorfully embroidered graphic on his baseball cap that read "Precision Systems." "My friend owns the company. He might put the picture on Facebook." Jen assented, but didn't try to resurrect the picture of hunger and cold and beauty. It was something we'd both have to get used to: the most meaningful things getting lost in translation.

A final memory from that walk had me wondering if our month and a half on the trail estranged me from our culture more than I'd anticipated. While taking a rest, I saw what I thought was a flake of jasper in the grass. Picking it up, I discovered it to be a piece of our dried fruit, with one small bite out of it, that Jen had given it to her dad to try. *Wasted food!* Shocking. I put it in my mouth without hesitation. Would the reaction have been as automatic if I saw half a corndog on the street? I had to wonder.

After we got to our campsite and put up the tents, Jen and Mark took off to climb Electric Peak—by far the highest mountain in the Gallatin Range. Meanwhile, I hung back at camp. It was an agonized decision but one that I was proud of myself for making: I still had a bodily memory of sickness, and I'd literally promised myself the night before (woozy in the hot spring, depleted at the K-Bar) to take it as easy as possible as long as I could. Mark left me magazines and the newspaper to read. After a week wrestling with essays by Camus, it was a perfectly guilty pleasure to kick back in the sun and let my eyes drift over *TIME*'s tawdry infographics.

Then I became fixated on the front page of *The Missoulian* from the previous morning. The headline read "A Little Faster." It seems the

Montana Legislative Session was off to an inspired start: "Nine bills and council proposals had been introduced that addressed speed limit increases" in the first two weeks. The Republican Representative that drafted the one that passed, Mike Miller, was quoted extensively. After noticing that Idaho and Utah already have 80 mph speed zones, whereas Montana drivers were limited to 75, he reached his historic revelation: "I don't believe drivers in other states are more competent or skilled than Montana drivers." As for safety, "We've had the 75 mph speed limit since mid-1999. I believe that in the last 16-plus years, the technology and safety features built into cars have increased enough to justify the maximum higher speed limit."

By regarding safety features as justification for riskier behavior, Miller's rationale summarily defines "risk homeostasis." Here, technology paid itself off by making us safer, so now we're going to return accident levels to where they were before by acting more recklessly. The nearest segment of highway to me at that time—Highway 89, from Gardiner to Livingston—illustrates the tragic side of Miller's fallacy. Between 2002 and 2012, the Montana Department of Transportation cleaned up about 1,600 road-killed "large mammal carcasses" from that corridor—more than one every three days. Because as many as half of wildlife-vehicle collisions go unreported according to the state of Montana (some people take road kill home, and many animals manage to limp into the bushes before succumbing to their injuries), this number greatly lowballs net mortality. Bighorn sheep licking antifreeze along the shoulders of Yankee Jim Canyon, and Yellowstone's northern elk herd—which have their winter range divided in two by the road—are common victims. Local populations of both species are currently declining, biologists are scrambling to find ways to help them recover, and public factions point fingers at everything except themselves. Although that specific road will not be changed to 80 mph, the cultural refusal to slow down remains epidemic; other entrance roads to Yellowstone have comparable statistics. Animals are not equipped with better "technology and safety features" every sixteen years, and neither are human brains. 2015 saw the biggest spike in traffic fatalities in half a century, largely blamed on the distractions of smartphone apps.

Equally galling is Miller's implication that a lower speed of travel (which, to many people, has the primary advantage of conserving gasoline) should be seen as a corollary to the competency of the driver. But then, like so many politicians, Miller won his seat by perfecting the voice of the rat race—a canonical in which everybody goes exactly as fast as they are able, whether or not they have anything to do when they get there. I was interested to read "skeptics and outright opponents of the speed limit bump tend to outweigh proponents." So why were nine of our politicians scrambling to raise it, and nobody trying to lower it? They were pandering to the paranoiac Westerner's resentment of control, and this was the most meaningless yet visible way to grant Montanans more "freedom"—six and two-thirds percent more freedom, to be exact, advertised fire-sale style, on 264 new 4'x5' signs.

To round it out, *The Missoulian* shared that "Kevin Hodge of Dillon thanked the Montana legislature for raising the speed limit. 'There's a lot of wide-open spaces and many miles covered,' Hodge reasoned. 'As a driver of about forty thousand miles a year, I cannot appreciate how much I enjoy higher speed limits.'" Hodge's garbled word choice speaks volumes; I vote to fine people driving forty thousand a year, not encourage them. I threw the paper down. It would help start that evening's fire. While it's affecting to be reminded of these things, this society of ours, it was an awful waste of a gorgeous afternoon. I spent the next two hours losing myself in the trees at half speed—I found the skull of a cow moose, a fen with a great view of Electric Peak, and, carrying no water, I drank by pursing my lips to clear streams, and drawing in from my chest.

◊◊◊

Mark headed out the next day. Jen and I started up a pass, and the weather instantly soured. Electric Peak sits east of the Gallatin crest, but crossing the trailed saddle that drapes its spur actually takes you higher than the divide itself.* Our steadily inclining grade served as an unhappy reminder that I was nowhere near full strength. On top, the view was frozen and grey. We looked across the Yellowstone River toward Dome Mountain, but the light was so dull it was like squinting into a blurry photograph. On the long drop to Sportsman's Lake in Mulherin Creek, I found my first orchid of the trip—a small rattlesnake plantain, its tiny clamshell petals not yet withered. Until then, I hadn't realized just how dramatically orchid habitat is weighted toward wetter ranges west of the Rocky Mountain Front. Though obviously misguided to bloom so late in the fall, this lonesome flower would bloom nonetheless. We'd do well to follow its example. Rain moved in at lunch, then left on a cold wind.

Mulherin (also spelled Mol Heron) Creek happens to host one of the most eccentric legacies in the area. The beginning of this story traces to a brick mansion in Colorado Springs, 1973. Before going to bed one evening, Mark L. Prophet, the coincidentally-named prophet of a syncretic spiritual organization called the Summit Lighthouse, made an unusual demand of his wife Clare: "If anything happened to him she should take [the rest of the family] and go to Montana." And then, of course, something did happen to him: he died of a massive stroke first thing the next morning.

Why Montana? Part of the mythological appeal to Mark Prophet, who began his practice in Pennsylvania, may have been based on the place name's Spanish meaning: "mountain." Prophet's system borrowed heavily from a previous movement known as "I AM," founded by Guy Ballard in the 1930s. Ballard employed mountain imagery liberally throughout his teachings—both symbolically, when speaking of spiritual accomplishment, and literally, as loci of divine power. He taught, for example, that "masters"—enlightened spirits from across the ages whose wisdom he channeled—"lived in invisible caves inside mountains," and that the Grand Teton "was the most spiritual center in North America." (It's basically a literal interpretation of the transcendentalist metaphor of mountains as cathedrals.) Though Ballard

---

* It's common for standout peaks to isolate themselves from hydrologic divides, because their outsized glaciers rapidly chew moats around and behind them. The high Tetons offer a most striking example.

was headquartered on the East Coast, he claimed to visit such prominent power centers on psychic flights with the masters, not unlike Scrooge's forays with the Christmas Spirit.*

Thirteen years passed before Clare Prophet acted on her late husband's instructions. When she did move to Montana, she brought a new religion and hundreds of followers along with her, to a 12,500-acre ranch centered in a secluded vale along Mulherin Creek's lower reaches. Geographic symbolism figured heavily in Prophet's messaging—she rechristened Devil's Slide, a nearby mountainside streaked cinnabar red, "Angel's Ascent;" prosaic Deaf Jim Knob was now "Maitreya Mountain." In photographs of "the Heart of the Inner Retreat," a secluded meadow that largely inspired her decision to purchase that particular ranch, Sportsman's Peak punctuates the background. Meanwhile the northeast slopes of standout Electric Peak, which rises six thousand feet above the Yellowstone River, served as an ever-present touchstone for Prophet and her followers. Among Prophet's most successful publications was a ten-part series called *Climb the Highest Mountain*.

---

* In the "Mysteries of the Yellowstone" chapter of Guy Ballard's book *Unveiled Mysteries* (written under the pseudonym Godfré Ray King), the author puts forth an alternative theory to the origin of the name "Yellowstone." In that narration, the author recounts flying back and forth between the "Royal" (Grand) Teton and 14,000-year-old Yellowstone mines that are sealed within solid cliff walls. After gaining access through these walls under the guidance of Saint Germain, Ballard bears witness to stores of yellow diamonds, "the most beautiful... that have ever been found within this earth" as well as enormous quantities of gold. He continues:

> "The word—'Yellowstone,'" explained Saint Germain, "has been brought down through the centuries—for more than fourteen thousand years. At that time—the civilization of Poseidonis had reached a very high point of attainment because—a Great Master of Light was at the head of the Government. It was only during the last—five hundred years—that the decline took place, and the misuse of her great wisdom held sway. Within the present boundaries of the—Yellowstone—which are still the same, existed the richest gold mine the world has ever known..."

Certainly a more exciting explanation for "Yellowstone" than the most plausible. The competing theory says Yellowstone National Park took its name in translation from *Roche Jaune*, the name given by French trappers to the lower Yellowstone River, which is rimmed for dozens of miles by golden sandstone in the vicinity of Billings, Montana.

Over the next several years, the Church Universal and Triumphant (or the "CUT Ranch," as it is locally known), while ostensibly promoting a blend of Eastern and Western spiritual teachings, took on the most stereotypical hallmarks of a doomsday cult. Church leaders channeled voices, interpreted signs, foretold disaster. The 1988 fires, which burned right up to the boundary of the ranch two years after the church officially moved its headquarters there, dialed up the hysteria. As we've already seen, wildfires make for resonant symbols in even the most pragmatic minds—to CUT followers, the flames embodied a more generalized evil intent on destroying their church. Refusing to leave in the face of incineration, church members made a dire stand; because the 27,000-acre Fan Fire died just in time, they took credit for halting it with their chants. Nevertheless, Prophet's sermons noticeably darkened thereafter. Within a year she initiated the most notorious episode of the church's history—now referred to as "the shelter cycle."

To inventive minds, natural phenomena will always suggest more than face value. To Clare Prophet, the Yellowstone wildfires foreshadowed an imminent nuclear apocalypse. That fall she spurred the construction of a cavernous underground bunker that could host 750 people for seven years and seven months. (If only this valley of the Yellowstone hadn't been named "Paradise" by railroad boosters, would it have happened somewhere else instead?) In impromptu communities such as Glastonbury, dozens of other bunkers invaded the valley, boasting CUT followers from across the globe. Meanwhile, the church legally amassed dozens of high-powered assault rifles, thousands of rounds of ammunition, and two armored personnel carriers. They also ran foul with the law for trying to buy other, even more aggressive weapons—and tank-piercing bullets—under fictitious names. Locals had a right to be suspicious.

The suspense culminated on the night of March 14, 1989, when the foretold disaster failed to materialize. Clare Prophet responded the way that any self-respecting prophet would: she announced that the group's prayers had averted the disaster. While this helped save face among her most committed followers, it certainly didn't win over any doubters, and prompted crises of faith in many more. In a remarkably insightful autobiography by Erin Prophet, *Prophet's Daughter*, Clare's oldest child recounts how, as the prophesied moment came and passed, the church actually began praying *for* a nuclear disaster. While the church tried to recoup their losses and regain credibility, an enormous underground tank of diesel fuel ruptured into Mulherin Creek.

Despite these well-known blunders, the church is still headquartered on the property they call the Royal Teton Ranch just north of the Yellowstone boundary. A holy spot by any standards—one hopes that future visitors find ways to revere such wonders without developing, subdividing, and polluting it to the extent that the Church Universal Triumphant has.

Jen and I made camp at our assigned site on High Lake: an expanse of mud hardpack. The day's rain, sheeting across the surface, had organized loose pine needles into tiny terraces like rice paddies. When I couldn't get our camp stove going (Jen later determined the fuel bottle was over-filled), and because fires weren't allowed where the park required us to camp, I retraced our steps a hundred yards to where the trail meanders outside the Yellowstone boundary. There, an overblown fire ring is scorched into the earth beside a can dump in a rocky pit. Behold the inefficiencies of management units: no national forest employee will hike a dozen miles each way to clean up a single fire ring, and no Park Ranger will touch the mess, because it's technically outside their line.

That evening, after most of the sky cleared off and the sun went down, I watched an isolated thunderhead float across a crisp field of stars. With a mushroomed top, crenellated sides, and frequent flashes lighting amorphous regions of its interior, it resembled nothing so much as an electric jellyfish. The cell quietly grumbled in the windless night— shocking and reviving the world below like one of H.P. Lovecraft's Outer Gods—before passing on, to deplete or enhance itself over the sleeping plains.

◊◊◊

Of all the mountain ranges we walked in 2015, the Gallatins are the most geologically diverse. There you can find a smorgasbord of limestones and shales; volcanic vents, dikes, and lahars; metamorphic basement rocks that approach the vintage of the oldest parts of the Winds. Eclectic topography makes manifest this complicated back-story. The southern range, over twenty miles long, features broad, blocky mountains, abutting the divide, which are favored by grizzly bears and great herds of elk. Moving north out of the park, the ridge rises and falls fitfully along a slender, often-grassy ridge, spitting off a great diversity of watercourses in the process—from steep timbered chutes like Moose Creek, to broad ranching basins like Tom Miner. The northernmost quarter or so of the range forks and forks again into a sharply honed, high relief cluster of Absaroka-style volcanic summits. As a package, the range is varied, distinct, and endearing; a weekend warrior's dream.

The Gallatins are also the only major mountain range bordering Yellowstone that lacks designated wilderness—a distinction that makes its long and narrow footprint feel all the spindlier as it absorbs pressure from the rapidly developing valleys and canyons below. Because the Gallatins have come very close to hosting a wilderness area, but never quite made it over the hump, its heart carries (in eighteen awkward syllables) a special designation: the Hyalite-Porcupine-Buffalo Horn (HPBH) Wilderness Study Area (WSA). What does it mean, "WSA," and how is that different than wilderness? Well, everybody's still trying to figure that out.

As Frederick Swanson recounts in his book, *Where Roads Will Never Reach*, "The leaders of the wilderness movements in the Northern Rockies never constrained their efforts, as some histories imply, to preserving hiking areas and treeless mountain basins. They enjoyed their recreation, to be sure, but for most of them wildlife was key." The Gallatin story testifies to this claim: these mountains were recognized for their importance to wildlife from the very outset of the modern conservation movement. Area outdoors-people in the early 1940s (ranchers, in other words) were the first to request additional protections from the USFS. In 1954, a group of cowpunchers, outfitters, plus a pastor and his family—a group "representative of a significant section of local public opinion"—drew up an outline for what they called the Hilgard Hold Area. This prospective wilderness encompassed high-priority wildlife range in both the Gallatins and the Madison Range (the latter parallels the former, on the west side of deep Gallatin Canyon). In

1958, Olaus Murie, councilman of the Wilderness Society and "father of modern elk management," took an extended trip to the area. The purpose was to both "discuss the mundane and realistic matters" of establishing the hold, and in the meantime, enjoy a five-day pack trip into the high country. The trip was a success: the landscape "idyllic," the local support strong, Murie gave his blessing. Six years later, despite nearly unanimous public support and assurances from the supervisor of the Gallatin National Forest, it would come as a community shock when the 1964 Wilderness Act passed over the Gallatins and Madisons.* The reason wouldn't be addressed for over thirty years.

With no definitive decision-making framework to determine which areas of wilderness character should receive designation or when, the possibility of Gallatin wilderness languished like a dormant seed, awaiting a favorable political climate. And as America lurched ahead with explosive population, prosperity, and industrialization, the window for achieving permanent protection started closing even more rapidly.

By 1977, additional roads tangled the contours of the Gallatins, others had been fended off, and Congress passed the Montana Wilderness Study Act to get things moving again. This act obligated the Secretary of Agriculture to determine in five years whether or not the HPBH and eight other WSAs met the criteria for wilderness, and then to make formal recommendations to Congress—otherwise, it was written, "the wilderness study areas designated by this Act shall, until Congress determines otherwise, be administered by the Secretary of Agriculture so as to maintain their presently existing wilderness character and potential for inclusion in the National Wilderness Preservation System."

When the study finally concluded years later, the HPBH was found ineligible for wilderness status—but not because the land in question didn't possess all the qualities warranting such protection. Rather, national forest land in the Gallatins was peppered with inholdings of private land: about ten percent of the total area. Hastily deeded to the Northern Pacific railroad in 1864 to incentivize the western conquest,

---

* The first round of wilderness designation was anything but comprehensive. The Act created fifty-four different areas, making up nine million acres, in thirteen different states. Montana got five.

financially productive in no obvious way, these alternating sections were rarely used as intended and left a particularly cumbersome legacy to all stakeholders. The WSA inventory came as a reminder for managers to re-up their efforts to swap out and consolidate the checkerboard, which they did—and though it meant the public lost access to many peripheral parts of the forest, the backcountry was gradually secured in the process. It wasn't until 1998 that things could finally move forward.

By that time, the WSA inventory had been scrapped for not following protocol, and nobody planned to start a new one. Likewise, the viability of a 600,000-acre Hilgard Hold Area was lost forever.* In the western half, in the center of the Madison Range, TV anchor Chet Huntley founded a ski hill called Big Sky, which rapidly swelled into thousands of acres of tasteless vacation condos and trophy homes (now the third largest ski resort in America); two more adjacent ski hills were forthcoming. In the eastern half of the former Hold Area, the newly consolidated HPBH—which drapes the Gallatin Crest for 155,000 of its most glorious acres—slouched further into the purgatory where it remains to this day. Still, Congress never "determined otherwise," therefore the HPBH would continue to be managed as wilderness. But for some time that protection applied in only the loosest possible way.

For decades after its designation, motorized and mechanized uses were overlooked in the HPBH, despite the standards of WSAs. It was only a matter of time before advancing wildlife research began to question the impacts of these uses. The HPBH, after all, has been a place for endangered species like the grizzly bear to find refuge from

---

* Four splinters of the Hilgard Hold were salvaged by a 1983 bill that created a disparate but important wilderness called the Lee Metcalf, and thirty-four years later, this is still the most recent wilderness area established in Montana. In 1988, President Reagan vetoed the Montana Natural Resources Protection and Utilization Act. Introduced by a Montana senator and passed by Congress, the bipartisan bill would have created new wilderness, required the completion of wilderness studies in the Gallatin National Forest, and opened up strategic and economically productive forest land to extraction industries. Reagan commented only that, in his opinion, it would "injure the economy of Montana."

explosive exurban development in Big Sky; where elk fenced out of developed valley bottoms find winter forage in places like Porcupine Creek.* Other animals, of which too little is known *to even be considered endangered*—like lynx and wolverines—haunt the HPBH's corners, causing rare sightings to resonate like myth in the valleys below. After consulting the language and intent of the WSA Act, several conservation groups challenged the Forest Service's complacency in court: due to the popularization of rapidly developing recreational technologies, in places where "the imprint of man's work" was once "substantially unnoticeable," imprints were becoming substantially more so.

The District Court that heard the case sided with conservationists. Vehicles should be excluded (with a couple exceptions) from the HPBH, it said, in accordance with the ground rules of the WSA Act. That was in 2009. The weight of that determination fell, of course, on the people who'd gotten used to bringing vehicles there—and the following spring a consortium of interests in private-property rights, resource extraction, mountain biking, and motorized recreation, called Citizens for Balanced Use, appealed the decision. Their argument: "the Wilderness Study Act only authorized the Forest Service to issue an Interim Order that maintained wilderness character, not to enhance it." Though the appeal failed, the cause did not die. Almost ten years later, backlash against environmental protections in the Gallatin Range is still gaining momentum, and becoming more audacious in scope.

Today, the establishment of a Gallatin Range wilderness area is mired in an increasingly polarized discourse, and mountain bikers have gone on the offensive to take on the concept of wilderness altogether. In 2015, Ted Stroll, a retired California attorney, founded a group called The Sustainable Trails Coalition. Within the year, his group would draft "The Human-Powered Wildlands Travel Management Act of 2016" to open wilderness areas to many types of mechanical and motorized equipment, from mountain bikes to chain saws.

---

* After securing title to several sections in Porcupine Creek, Yellowstone Club developer Tim Blixseth theatrically staged a bulldozer at the tributary's mouth. He employed the resultant public outcry as leverage in the ongoing land swaps.

2

In 1961, when Stewart Udall was sworn in as Secretary of the Interior under John F. Kennedy, he promised that "nature will take precedence over the needs of modern man." His meaning should not be confused with Lord Byron's famous line, "I love not Man the less, but Nature more," because Udall did not believe that the interests of the human and non-human needed to be adversarial, nor even distinct from one another. He'd explain, "Plans to protect air and water, wilderness and wildlife, are in fact plans to protect man."* For the sake of our shared future, he framed the relationship as a cooperative one. Udall's philosophy reflects brightly in the legislation passed during his tenure, legislation that continues to guard our collective interests today. He was

---

* This is not to say that all of Udall's achievements are celebrated by dyed-in-the-wool conservationists. In the struggle to ban motors from Yellowstone Lake, for example, he sided with boating clubs and fishing guides. He recognized the need for balance.

there for the Water Quality Act, the Solid Waste Disposal Act, and—among many others—the Wilderness Act of 1964.

Though the Wilderness Act is hardly fifty years old, it safeguards what is as old as time: features and qualities of the landscape that are relatively unaltered by human ambition. In a nation that religiously esteems techno-industrial expansion, this level of protection was bound to be contentious. Its drafters were well aware of that. They knew that intact ecosystems could not be trusted to the temperamental politics of an abstract future—so much had been lost already—so they created this specific congressional protection instead.

It is not wise to separate this world into human places and natural places. This important observation is often employed as a critique of the wilderness idea. In doing so, the critique plants a false assumption, because wilderness is not the end goal toward which all conservation efforts aspire. It is only one land designation on a spectrum, each one equally important, that must work together to achieve a sustainable relationship between human civilization and the natural resources upon which it depends. That is, we need wilderness lands—places where every lesser interest is subordinated to the preservation of the most complex and essential public resources of clean water, clean air, and biodiversity—but we also need buffer lands, in which functioning ecological systems are managed for the sustainable yield of more concrete resources. Other places we need to manage even more intensively, to support the overwhelming needs of the human population. And, of course, we need places where the heaviest impacts of human lifestyle and industry can be concentrated: fully mechanized urban environments. Yes, sadly, the demands of human civilization are such that everything must ultimately be considered by their terms. But as Udall understood, these interests take many forms, and occasionally what we need is the opposite of what we want.

Almost by definition, the functions of wilderness are difficult to measure. For some people, this calls their legitimacy into question; for others, it strikes at an irreducible complexity, and even helps to illuminate their fundamental importance. Wilderness is a way to preserve all the things that we have not yet learned to quantify or synthesize, yet rely upon nonetheless. Throughout the fermentative prehistory of the

Wilderness Act, a lot of red flags were going up in the natural world. Rain fell as acid, bald eagles laid rubber eggs, a hole in the atmosphere allowed the sunlight to sear our skin. All of these costly and dangerous impacts were direct side effects of human industry. The damages were accidental, sure, but that didn't make them any more acceptable. It was becoming increasingly obvious that, no matter how impressive or well-meaning the human talent for innovation, our industriousness was nevertheless capable of almost inconceivable harm. Somehow, we needed to hold ourselves to a higher standard. Wilderness designation is the most binding outgrowth of this resolution.

◊◊◊

In 2009, *Bike Magazine* published an article by its editor, Lou Mazzante that brainstormed ways to include bicycle use in wilderness study areas. The article was long, sleek, and a little bit panicked. It could be seen as a reaction to the failed appeal-of-the-appeal of the Gallatin Travel Management Plan made by Citizens for Balanced Use. Despite his investment in the issue, or perhaps in consideration of it, Mazzante cautioned his readers to keep clarity and not get carried away. As he pointed out, "The rules are clear when it comes to Congressionally designated Wilderness: no roads, no buildings, no mining or logging, no motorized travel, no mechanized transport, and no bikes."

In just a couple years, however, *Bike Magazine* would swing this common sense observation 180 degrees. Mazzante's moderate message was reformulated to "restore Congress' original vision." That is, we were now made to believe that bicycles are *supposed to be* in wilderness. The rhetorical about-face was doctored by the Californian lawyer behind The Human-Powered Wildlands Travel Management Act of 2016 (HPWTMA, or bill S.3205), Ted Stroll. Somewhere in the midst of "400 hours" of research, Stroll found a 1973 Forest Service document that defined "mechanized equipment" as "propelled by a non-living power source," conceivably making an opening for bikes. This key document—with wording that may have carried over from 1966—was created internally by only one of the four agencies that administrate wilderness, at best two years after the Wilderness Act was passed. It does not reflect

WHERE WE'RE GOING 265

the democratic process and it reveals nothing about the intentions of Congress—just some carelessness within the warrens of a very large government bureau. But like deniers of climate change, single-mindedly rooting from mountains of evidence to the contrary, Stroll proceeded to cobble a case together from random outliers, quotes out of context, and the opposite of consensus.

For everyone who does not intend to bicycle in wilderness, or seek to categorically dismantle federal land protections like the Utah senators who picked up Stroll's bill, the Wilderness Act is a more-than adequate guide as to whether or not bicycles belong there. Because, as Mazzante knew well, it is clear on this point. Honed over sixty-six drafts and eighteen hearings, the Act does not mention bicycles specifically, just as it doesn't mention jeeps or bulldozers. Rather, in its very first line, we learn that wilderness is intended to "assure that an increasing population, accompanied by expanding settlement and growing mechanization, does not occupy and modify all areas within the United States." Mountain bikes, which became commercially available seventeen years after the Act, epitomize this trend toward mechanization. It then elucidates: "There shall be no temporary road, no use of motor vehicles... [and] no other form of mechanical transport." The fact that this legislation specifies mechanical transport *in addition to* motorized transport—despite its belabored economy—should be enough to end the debate over the intentions of Congress.

If it's not enough, corroborating evidence is readily available. From Aldo Leopold's sketches of the concept in the 1920s, right up to the final language of the act, wilderness-appropriate recreation is specified as "primitive" almost as often as not. By primitive, it is unlikely its architects meant to include forms of transportation that were not yet invented. And Wallace Stegner, whose "Wilderness Letter" was a seminal document to the passage of the Act, spelled it out even more clearly: these would be places "barred from wheels."

Which brings us to the crux of the matter: the case for the HPWTMA is not about facts. It is about an evolving democratic process in which facts are drowned out by collective feelings of anger and powerlessness, and amplified by the echo chamber of the internet. It is about a process so democratic that what is factual and what is fabricated is ultimately entrusted to the court of public opinion. It is about a society addicted to living beyond its means, coming up against the natural (and already much deferred) constraints of their definition of "freedom," and construing all safeguards and regulations as the enemy. It is about a year when the most powerful country in the world elected the cartoon of a plutocratic demagogue for their president. To understand the momentum behind the bikes-in-wilderness movement, we must look beyond the factual bases of this debate and consider the emotional ones.

◊◊◊

A couple weeks before Jen and I left for the summer, we took a day hike elsewhere in the Gallatin Range. We were talking; I'd just found a low-profile orchid (*Piperia unalascensis*) that I'd learned of recently and wanted to share. But our words broke off at the sound of rubber on dirt. In fact, we literally jumped into the bushes. The mountain biker who flashed between us shouted "THREE MORE!" so we stood back, wearing the same beleaguered expression. Another bike shot by, then another. It was a routine occurrence. They didn't acknowledge us, and their wrap-around helmets and armor prevented us from seeing anything specifically human about them. A minute passed and I started feeling stupid. I pictured the little sign at the trailhead illustrating trail etiquette: bikes yield to pedestrians... a nice thought that I've never seen in practice. So we started walking again, and that's when the last bike appeared, mashing the brakes and skidding into the brush. The girl riding it was livid. "Didn't they tell you to get out of the way?" she demanded. "Yes," I said, and thought about it. "But that's a lot to ask."

There's a reason why bikes are banned from sidewalks in town, along with other vehicles. Part of the danger is simple physics, while part of it appears to be psychological: that same summer, on another trail in the Gallatins, a mountain biker intentionally pedaled directly into a cow moose with calf, breaking his own arm. "If I'm going to be encountered by a moose and I'm going to die," Brian Steddum declared to a reporter, "I'm going to die fighting." Agreeing with Steddum's aphorism is easier than understanding his application of it—taking the leap from wildlife sighting to "Thunderdome." The *Bozeman Daily Chronicle*, in relating his story, clearly explains that Steddum stopped his bike some distance away, and yelled at the stationary moose, before he decided to "die fighting." I've literally had dozens of such encounters on foot, but one is usually more than enough to know that, if it escalates, you'll have only yourself to blame.

    I should take a step back. Here I am, demarcating the impasse of an old-fashioned user conflict. This is a hard one for me, because in so many ways I consider myself a bike advocate. I can boast over 10,000 miles on one of my current rides, and I've had unforgettably glorious days mountain biking around Greater Yellowstone on the other. Even when the members of hiking and biking communities overlap, however, an in-the-moment rub exists between those operating vehicles and those that aren't, just like it does between sometimes-pedestrians driving cars and car owners who happen to be traveling on foot. The playing field is not level: that's why it is regulated. Tight trails with blind turns often require split-second reflexes to prevent parties from physically colliding. Even when they don't, many on horseback have been thrown by a spooked mount, and we're not the only hikers who have found themselves jumping in the bushes. This tension is the biking activist's primary ammunition. Because everyone can walk in places they can't necessarily bike, and the specialist mindset irreducibly bundles identities with hobbies, it creates the illusion of segregation. Bicyclists who demand to be seen as nothing less claim the status of a persecuted minority. They would have you believe that bigotry is what excludes them, personally, from wilderness—and forget that the principles excluding vehicles are fundamental to wilderness, predating the existence of their very sport by nearly a generation.

    While this sense of wronged-ness permeates the biking-in-wilderness community, it is best observed in the voice of one its most prolific writers—a Washington man named Vernon Felton. His pieces ceaselessly goad mountain bikers to simplify the debate into a question of discrimination. He taunts his readers: "You are not welcome here. …You've been banned." He makes authoritative announcements: "We've come to the root of the issue …it's a question of intolerance." Central to his sense of injustice is the Wilderness Act itself. Felton describes this piece of legislation as "dangerous:" a government effort to "aid and abet ...intolerance" and create "second-class citizens."

In taking this stance, Felton and others have succeeded in whipping up a polarizing atmosphere of mutual disgust. Lost is complexity—such as the very important fact that no person is just a mountain biker or just a hiker. The imposed framework forces us to pigeonhole ourselves into one camp or the other, and then to take up arms. More than one mountain biker, answering the call, has concluded that their only remaining hope is to strike preemptively, and otherwise overwhelm their opponents with righteous indignation. They evoke civil disobedience. One advocate, Lance Pysher, advises his peers in a classic statement of the times, "It doesn't matter if you are right or wrong. It's just a matter of how much political force you can bring to bear on the situation." Contemporaneous with the introduction of the HPWTMA, I watched a rash of vandalism break out on the national forests near my home. It wasn't long before I couldn't find a single wilderness sign that hadn't been defaced by bicyclists (it is easy to identify the perpetrators, because on the list of prohibited uses, "bicycles" was the only word getting scratched out). In one case on my ranger district, trail workers spent weeks of cumulative labor resurrecting an overgrown path for mountain bike access, to ameliorate this very issue. When we finished, we placed signs at the junctions of wilderness trails. Mountain bikers ruined those signs in less than a week. All the while, tire tracks keep popping up where they shouldn't have.

Once a conflict becomes this escalated, it is incredibly difficult to back it down. Participants fixate on their wrongs—the low blows, the actions of the few most desperate individuals—and the actual issues become lost. As Justin Farrell summarizes in a sociological study of the Greater Yellowstone,

> Most social actors involved simply miss the fact that they are fighting tooth and nail to promote and defend incommensurable moral orders, obsessively marshalling evidence that is itself meaningless when abstracted from their larger narratives and moral commitments, all the while in so doing obscuring what the debate is ultimately about.

There are many good examples related to this issue coming from both camps: mountain bikers trying to implicate "spring-loaded trekking

WHERE WE'RE GOING 269

poles" (I don't even know what those are) as mechanical transport, and examples of hiker hypocrisy; hikers accusing bicycles of causing excessive trail erosion. But at the end of the day, most telling to me is that we currently have an interest group, billing itself as the future of both the civil rights and environmental movements, all while promoting a form of vehicular recreation. This is the sort of cultural appropriation that, with a unified voice, we must resoundingly disavow.

◊◊◊

Perhaps the first fallacious implication of Bill S.3205 is that wilderness would benefit from popularization, because that would be its primary function. Now, human use is not just appropriate in wilderness, it is vital. Yet no responsible managers are promoting increased use. That's because they aren't selling a product—they're safeguarding a treasure. Crowds endanger not only the integrity of the resource but our ability to experience it,[*] and its own popularity is already wilderness's fastest-growing and most complicated threat. Here, the old Forest Service adage of achieving the greatest good for the greatest number is not as simple as achieving the greatest number—just as the greatest possible number of humans is not a sensible goal for planet Earth. Quota and permit systems are already used in some overcrowded wilderness areas; in those units, the obstacles to "unconfined recreation" go far beyond not riding a bike there. This is why managers speak of the "wilderness experience:" not to put value judgments on user-groups but to understand visitor preferences, so that people can be directed toward places managed for their interests.

Wilderness, like every land designation, is managed for its highest use. It is not meant to offer all things to all people. If riding a mountain bike has anything to do with wilderness character, its riders have little interest in explaining how.[**] Advocates are transparent on this: if

---

[*] Refer to the categories of carrying capacities in Part One.

[**] They have, however, tried to ingratiate themselves by obfuscating the purpose of wilderness. Ted Stroll exemplifies this misunderstanding with qualifications such as this one: "Mountain biking may be richer in flow than any other endeavor." Meaning... what? More

wilderness is not redefined to accommodate mechanized vehicles, then wilderness will have a fervent new enemy. Mountain biker Kurt Gensheimer promises a growing "anti-conservationist movement," while Felton shrugs: "Mountain bikers have been put in a position in which every new Wilderness gained is a wild place lost to them." Felton's admission illuminates an important distinction between mechanized and non-mechanized transport. Mountain bikes are not a tool for experiencing nature—they are a tool for enhancing it. Riders pursue a relationship between the body, a vehicle loaded with sophisticated technology, and a constructed riding surface[*]—two of those players are antithetical to wilderness. We might even infer that this sport discourages the central goal of wilderness: the "preservation and protection [of landscapes] in their natural condition," and conclude that nature for nature's sake is incompatible with mountain biking. Not only does the HPWTMA aim to popularize wilderness, it aims to popularize it with those who are averse to wilderness character.[**]

---

successful inroads have been made by cyclists who cast themselves as the torchbearers of trail maintenance, a public service that has been stunted by federal budget cuts. While doing so, bicyclists regard constructed trails as though they are the institutions that wilderness designation is designed to protect. As I explained in Part Four, such sterile strips of development are exactly the type of "permanent improvement" the Act warns against, and only justified in areas with sufficient pre-existing use. A disused trail is a *good* sign for the prospect of wildness—and this point is thoroughly lost on chainsaw-promoting bicyclists. Other advertised benefits of S.3205, aimed at broadening its support base, are similarly irrelevant—such as welcoming wheelbarrows and strollers. This equipment is comically unsuited to the average wilderness trail.

[*] Some riding styles require more manipulation of the terrain than others. In 2015, my trail crew spent a day deconstructing an illegal mountain bike terrain park in the northern Gallatins. Mountain bikers cut down dozens of green trees and displaced cubic yards of soil to build jumps and other obstacles. There are a number of similar sites on public lands in Montana. As attempts to realize the potential of increasingly high-performance equipment by manufacturing increasingly technical challenges, these terrain parks are symptomatic of the way runaway technology distances us from the offerings of nature. The resultant erosion can be heinous. "It's not like we're motorized," offers Donovan Power, one Montanan apologist for such "freeriders"—as though that's the only criterion for destructiveness. His excuse is a popular ruse. Unfortunately, our crew didn't have the time or resources to fully rehabilitate that site in the Gallatins, as Forest Service crews generally do not.

[**] Of course, mountain bikes may be used to carry riders to places where they plan to stop and seek a "wilderness experience." But then we're talking about efficiency—treating some parts

Even this observation, however, needn't constitute a judgment on any one who enjoys mountain biking. Rather, it's to establish an inevitability, given the nature of the sport: one consequence of pursuing "flow" is that attendant mountain bikers cannot look away from the trail for much more than a split second. Wilderness trails are rocky and winding, and if you look around too much, you'll eat dirt. As long as a person is engaged in this fast-paced, attention-demanding pursuit, the quality of the surrounding environment—the wilderness character, if you will—becomes peripheral at best. This is a sport in which it profoundly does not matter if those endemic flowers keep blooming along the wayside, or if they go extinct.

◊◊◊

As we've seen, deliberately increasing use in wilderness is in itself a prospect with serious implications, contrary to the goals of the Act. But with mountain bikes, this concern is compounded by the fact that vehicles invite different types of impacts, ones that introduce unique concerns.

The appeal of backcountry vehicles, such as mountain bikes, is traveling faster and further. In so doing, they encourage the disruption of more wildlife habitat than would otherwise be possible. Mechanical efficiency shrinks the functional size of wilderness. The correlation between isolation from human presence and environmental health led the Wilderness Act to place a premium on the simple vastness of protected space. It's in there twice, actually—as a human value, because larger areas facilitate "opportunities for solitude," and as a non-human value, because wilderness must be of "sufficient size as to make practicable its preservation and use in an unimpaired condition." The time and energy required to penetrate wilderness is perhaps its greatest asset: it insulates the non-human from evermore-pervasive human disruptions. That's the whole idea. And nothing poses a greater threat to

---

of wilderness as means and others as ends, which is counterproductive. If that's all we're going for, we're better off building a road to every viewpoint, so that everyone can enjoy them.

natural autonomy than humans boosted by high-geared mechanical advantage.

Not only do mountain bikes have an outsized presence as a result of their efficiency, but even if they covered the same amount of ground as foot-travelers, some evidence shows that their impact on wildlife would still be unnecessarily large. The Starkey Project, a study of land use and wildlife interactions on national forest in the American West, is pretty much the most comprehensive study of its kind imaginable. Over twenty-four years it incorporated the work of fifty-plus scientists, and generated over 140 research papers. One thing it tells us is that ungulate tolerance of mountain bikes is about the same as it is for ATVs: they will flee when either type of vehicle approaches within 1500 meters, compared to 500 meters for a hiker or 750 meters for a horseman. In short, the corridor of disruption created by a mountain bike appears to be three times wider than it needs to be.*

---

* Here we can see that, although wilderness-bikers are the ones calling out bigotry, their demands are ultimately more arbitrary and elitist than those who support the Wilderness Act. If wilderness restrictions were simply a matter of human rights, mountain bikers would include other user-groups in their demands. Dirt bikers, for starters, could not only make all the same arguments that mountain bikers are, they have several additional claims to legitimacy: for one, they do not necessarily create more disturbance than bicycles, nor does the language of the Act prohibit them any more explicitly than it does bicycles. Secondly, unlike mountain bikes, they predate the Wilderness Act and were once used as a means of transportation in many now-protected places. And lastly, they offer backcountry access to a much larger segment of the public—those with physical limitations that prevent them from pedaling demanding trails. Instead of including dirt bikes in their demands, however, mountain bikers have thrown them under the bus. Listen to Ted Stroll, justifying bicycles because they are human-powered: "You have to understand that during this time [of the Wilderness Act's passage], there was a great fear that America was growing soft. Americans were suddenly watching TV, they were driving cars everywhere–it was a massive societal shift and Congress wanted to change that." The real reason for wilderness, Stroll tells us, is so that Americans don't all turn into a bunch of dirt-biking softies; it *should*, according to him, be used to manipulate public taste. You have to wonder if the "discrimination" of the Wilderness Act that wilderness-bikers decry may also be what appeals to them: the power to sanction certain forms of recreation and blackball others. In fact, exercise has nothing to do with Congress' decision to pass the Wilderness Act: the reason that I clear wilderness trails with a crosscut and not a chainsaw is not because Congress thinks my arms need more exercise. All in all, the argument behind Bill S.3205 embodies a rather unfortunate cliché we have in the West: that of the intolerant newcomer. The one that high-mindedly pleads for an open-door policy to be let in, but once he is, he locks the door behind him. If bicyclists

This disruption pattern is supported by other wildlife research. Karsten Heuer describes a radio-collared grizzly sow abandoning a foraging circuit after a mountain-biking route showed rapidly increasing use (the self-identifying mountain-biking demographic grew 16% from 2010 to 2015). In a different sort of conflict, an off-duty law enforcement officer in northwestern Montana plowed into a grizzly on his mountain bike in June 2016. "The preliminary investigation ...found that Brad Treat, 38, was riding his bicycle Wednesday afternoon at a high rate of speed when he collided with the bear. The bear attacked Treat and killed him. ...Investigators believe Treat had no time to react or avoid the collision." While it isn't fair to indict bicycling as a mode based on this single incident, because hikers are usually the ones getting attacked (hiking is proportionately more common in grizzly country than biking), it is a good reminder that there are right and wrong ways to confront dangerous wildlife—and speedy surprises make for the worst of all.

When we know that so many wild animals are already facing heat stress, reduced forage, and declining numbers, it would be irresponsible to throw more stressors into the mix without very good reason. And there is not a good reason. There is only an amplified demand, on the part of one user group, to engage protected places only on their own, weighted terms. To concede to such a demand would invert the core value for which wilderness is managed—from natural integrity to popular appeal—and throw out the counsel of science in the process.

◊◊◊

Ted Stroll's rhetoric goes a long way toward showing us just how much his hobby means to him and fellow members of a mostly white leisure class. It also reveals how such attachments serve an ultimately disempowering function. First, experience-enhancing products raise our

---

succeed in changing the act by placing themselves above dirt bikers, dirt bikers will be able to use *every single one* of their arguments to change the Act again, and follow their lead. Especially the argument that they were discriminated against—because they are, and that discrimination is well documented in the activism of mountain bikers.

standards of pleasure. Next, our tastes and estimations of self-worth shift accordingly. Before we know it, we have fewer freedoms because we refuse them, and we recast this internal blockade as an external one. In a self-reinforcing thinking error, Stroll's personal harmony has become contingent on making the rest of the world change, not admitting that his sense of self is an artificial one.* His is an entirely first-world predicament—the failure of materialism—happiness endlessly deferred by the promise of advertisements. Direct extensions of his reasoning would have everyone talking at will on phones in the theater, bringing guns on the airplane, using smartphones on tests, living lives hermetically insulated from unenhanced reality.

Politically, the argument lies somewhere between private property rights and corporate personhood, with a helping of transhumanism thrown in. When Stroll calls himself a "persona non grata" he means that he feels ostracized or shunned—denied full status as a human being. At the same time, everyone can see that he has the same rights as everyone enjoying wilderness on foot—he merely insists on more—forcing us to conclude that a technologically enhanced notion of self is what alienates him, not the 1964 Wilderness Act. I don't support excluding anyone from wilderness. But if there are people out there today who insist on identifying themselves with machines, I will support excluding machines nonetheless.** As we face a future of increasingly elite, wearable technologies, this stance is more responsible than redefining personhood to include however much one can afford to buy. Mechanical advantage, carbon fiber and sophisticated metal alloys, price tags so high they force bike shops to offer payments plans—these materialistic balls and chains are being fobbed off in lieu of natural wonder. When Stroll writes that "traditional environmental organizations… are doing enormous harm to the future of conservation because they work relentlessly to disconnect Americans from traveling

---

* "In our world everybody thinks of changing humanity, but nobody thinks of changing himself." —Leo Tolstoy

** I do not mean to include people who are restricted to wheelchairs in this category. Because wheelchairs are not capable of rolling up and down wilderness trails, horses, rafts, and canoes are all better options for people with mobility issues to enjoy wilderness. Michael Yochim's *A Week in Yellowstone's Thorofare* is the moving story told by one such adventurer.

on public lands," and suggests that wilderness will never be relevant to young people unless we allow mechanization, he is selling the future short. Baby boomers such as Stroll have been proven to be *more* addicted to technology than any other generation—teenagers included. Young people won't appreciate us making preemptive deductions from their heritage in their names. They'd prefer to inherit a world that's intact.

Stroll's argument is both informed and additionally convoluted by its application to wilderness. Wilderness has a complicated relationship with civilization—for almost all of history, it has represented an affront to human authority. The conviction that "unimproved" nature is on some level threatening, even evil, still resides within many cultural presumptions (say, lawn care)—bringing me back to Felton's objection that the Wilderness Act is, in some generalized way, "dangerous." Citizens of the twenty-first century need to find the rectitude to admit that today the tables have turned. Unimproved nature can protect us from our own ruinous overconsumption—unfortunately, as Michael McCarthy warns, "Losses… are now so extensive and ruinous they are coming to define the natural world." Not wildness, serenity, beauty, or bounty. Loss.

Today, the sorts of red flags that prompted the conservation movements of the 1960s have only increased. Disturbing phenomena mar the most seemingly isolated places: there is a raft of garbage in the middle of the Pacific almost continental in scale, ice sheets failing at both poles, consistently unprecedented weather events, ecosystems collapsing almost everywhere we can think to look—all the while, the vanquishment of nature endures as the default human mode. As before, the causes of our planet's deepest wounds are almost too removed and complex to begin to address. They must, therefore, be seen as symptomatic of something profound—a hubristic human tendency—a broken relationship. They are reminders that we have to slow down, reduce our footprint, and pay more attention.

Wilderness, then, safeguards the most ephemeral yet basic resources of survival: water, air, and biodiversity. We entrust to wilderness baselines of ecological data. It is emblematic of a cooperative relationship. And for people who appreciate these things, wilderness incidentally provides opportunities for a unique form of recreation, one that is defined by human deference and self-restraint.

Wilderness is a place to put down our favorite amenities and explore what it means to go without. As our self-images become more intricately tangled with advancing technology, this challenge is bound to feel more and more personal. But for continuing to challenge us while essentially remaining the same, the value of wilderness to our society can only grow. That was true before mountain bikes came along—and it's even truer, now.

It can be shameful, really, to find yourself embroiled in the recreation wars—the arena where hobbies get moralized, privilege is a prerequisite, and the stereotypes all stink. Surely the real work is getting along: promoting inclusiveness, refraining from judgment. I tell myself this, and then I wind up back in the fray. I'm trying not to feel bad about it anymore. Because, for providing insight into the ways our culture regards the environment (by "our culture," I mean the only one for which I am qualified to speak—the culture of the middle-class American West), the recreation wars tell us much about ourselves. And more importantly, about things bigger than ourselves—topics that tend to overwhelm unless approached tangentially.

It's taken me a long time to calm down in the woods. I work hard at it because, whenever I do, I'm reminded of how much I have to learn. This habit is fragile because it competes with the restless attention encouraged by the rest of my day: every combative drive across town, every television firing in my direction, and so many robotic human interactions. At one point, it was important for me to know how many miles I could hike; how fast I could run the Bridger ridge; how deep I could stab into wilderness, while spending as little time as possible doing it. Today, I feel this insistence on performance was unhelpful and misguided. Others feel differently: that athletic prowess polishes competitive instinct and prepares you for the work environment... as though that's the highest purpose we can imagine.

Collectively, we Americans don't hurt for want of freedoms. In fact, we reserve for ourselves more freedoms than anyone deserves: the freedom to cause irreversible harm to this planet, and the power to condemn other people—in this country and any other, now and for the indefinite future—to lives of destitution and tragedy. Always the justification is our own standard of living, even as these freedoms condemn us to feedback loops of exploitation, self-delusion, neurosis, and self-destruction. We destroy the most intricate and precious with habits so deeply entrenched they're mistaken for patriotism. (Another epithet leveled at supporters of the Wilderness Act by wilderness-biking advocates: "un-American.") When Wendell Berry stated in his famous thesis that the ecological crisis is a crisis of character, he meant a character that takes for granted cheap energy, indulgent diversions, and the myth that unadulterated self-interest solves more problems than it creates. This character is not villainous or alien—it's in all of us—but America must assume responsibility commensurate to its role as trendsetter. Not only are our direct impacts disgustingly huge (Americans generate six times the solid waste of the average human), and our indirect influence even bigger (our glamorization of consumption hypnotizes developing economies), collectively we're among the few educated enough to know better. Not that you need any schooling at all to start noticing. Every broken-necked songbird beneath the sheet-glass window, every extinction, every time a modified diesel truck "rolls coal" across your windshield—each of these mainstays of day-to-day life are equally important reminders. None of our cultural presumptions have been sufficiently tested against time. The only reliable guidelines for how to be in this world are extant models of long-term adaptation—what is written in wild DNA, the ways life forms fit the land, natural laws. These are the spheres in which we may sincerely ask how we should live, and what we should value.

It makes me crazy, as each passing month and year on this planet breaks another heat record, to learn mountain bikers, one of the few demographics privileged to regularly enjoy public lands, have teamed up with two Utah senators whose views on the environment are blinded by conservative politics* to dismantle wilderness protections under the guise of "equality." That they're proclaiming themselves the "true conservationists." It makes me crazy that this country just voted high-risk, short-term economic interests over social justice and environmental responsibility. It makes me crazy, and my craziness makes things worse. Because then my reasons don't come through—only the alarm, the sadness, the helplessness. I add my voice to the hysteria that's already in the air. Humans, having squandered their chance to live in beauty, are turning on one another. And yet—and yet, as Jack Turner wrote, "Emotion is still the best evidence of belief and value." A truth is burning through. Everyone feels it, even if we can't agree what it is.

No one doubts that humans, aided by technology, are capable of conquering nature in the sense of racing over it, insulating themselves from it, disrupting its processes. But there is some very legitimate concern that we are not capable of backing off and giving it enough room to function as the life-supporting system we need it to be. Do I really believe that mountain bikers, or trail runners, or hunting guides, are "the problem"? No. Of course not. Rather, I believe that the integrity of the natural world is inestimably important, and that this is the consideration to which we must always return. I take umbrage when recreationalists of any kind (backpackers as often as not), those who find themselves in the favored position to engage the natural environment first-hand and reap its many benefits, threaten it with self-glorifying interests and cheapen the discourse. Mass consumption of nature has no correlation to increasing awareness—in the same way that, as Rebecca

---

* The first Senator who sponsored Stroll's wilderness biking bill, Orrin Hatch, is a "sagebrush rebel" icon who has been at the forefront of land transfer efforts for decades. Despite the fact that public lands tourism is the largest export of his constituency, he clings to the disproven belief that environmental protections leave Utah "forever stunted." And at a time when nine of the previous fifteen years counted among the ten hottest on record, Hatch instructed his voters, "Temperatures have remained steady or cooled over the last decade." In 2015, Senator number two, Mike Lee, introduced S.361: the Disposal of Excess Federal Lands Act. He dismisses climate change as "little more than a cheap public-relations ploy masquerading as a monopoly on scientific knowledge." This prolonged and systematic siege on any and all environmental protections, exemplified by the senators that picked up the wilderness biking bill and shared among other Utah politicians, is what led the international Outdoor Retailer Show to leave Utah after twenty years, and move to Colorado.

Solnit pointed out, winning a pie-eating contest does not make you a food critic.

Of course, all us trail users are supposed to just get along. Take that as you will. To me, "getting along" is not asking a snowshoer to throw a thumbs-up to the posse of 180-horsepower snowmobiles high-marking the mountainside above her ("I'm just happy they're enjoying themselves!")—it's a matter of humans trying to understand their own long-term needs and accommodating other forms of life. If our current environmental crisis really is one of character, we should stop trying to affirm one another in whatever unabashed lifestyles we choose to take up, and instead, take some stands regarding which beliefs and values are going to save us in the long run.

As the rural West continues its exponential growth trajectory the recreation war will intensify. The cacophony of this ultimately petty quibble will provide cover for much graver threats to the landscapes of human survival—becoming, at times, a costly distraction for parties who share much graver mutual concerns. Nevertheless, let us debate. And as we hone our dialogue, let us not lose sight of one another. When user groups choose to push themselves in this way, seeking intellectual challenges just as they seek physical challenges in their sports of choice, they practice channeling their rationality in the aid of emotional ideals. That is more than just play: it is important work. Convincing themselves, if nothing else, of the importance of the land, the water, the nitrogen and carbon cycles—every opinionated sledder, stroller, picnicker and kite-flyer, every pugilistic breather of air and eater of plants will be needed in the great battle that will one day jeopardize everything their previous scrimmages took for granted.

3

Even without full protection, the HPBH remains remote and reasonably pristine. Wilderness-caliber. Scofflaw dirtbike tracks are ever-present along the Crest trail, snowmobilers poach obscure basins where they occasionally die in avalanches, but the traverse that Jen and I made in early October lapsed in suspended isolation. For that, we both thanked and cursed the weather.

Route finding-wise, the Gallatin Crest could appear to be the most straightforward jaunt of our journey: follow the ridge north. Heavy mist will change that. When he was in our position, Karsten Heuer wrote, "I hadn't counted on this, the snow and wet, this freezing drizzle and fog… navigation proved challenging." I felt the same way, and I'd walked most of it at least once before. At one point, when we abandoned the trail down in the creek and the divide forked, Jen and I managed to get a half-mile off route.

Joe Gutkoski, a local hero who worked for the Gallatin National Forest over many decades, recounts how in "1970 or a few years before" (between the Wilderness Act and the WSA Act), the Northern Pacific almost railroaded a logging road from one side of the range to the other. "That area was so susceptible to land flow," he says, referring to the fact that when bentonite—a volcanic soil common in the Absaroka Province—dampens, it creates a greasy, sticky mess. Colloquially it's called "gumbo," and it can give walkers and drivers incredible amounts of grief, just as it did for Jen and me. On a larger scale, it creates widespread instability in the ground. Gutkoski brought attention to obvious failings in the already-surveyed road and it was scrapped. That deflected the momentum toward helicopter logging, before everybody finally realized just how commercially poor the timber really was: heavy on the subalpine fir that means so much to wildlife, and so little to mills and engineers.

Snow fell in gobs as Jen and I crossed this narrowly defeated roadway. The weather kept getting worse—one trail segment that brought us back to the top of the Gallatin Crest sticks in my mind. Only eight-tenths of a mile between junctions, those eight-tenths gave me more than enough time to cycle through a growing litany of complaints.

> *...Stilts of gumbo on my boots; back-sliding on the steep and slimy trail; feet cold and squishy-wet in the sloppy snow; rain pants saturated through to my thighs creating a suction-effect that limits my range of motion in a claustrophobic way—meanwhile, they're falling down at the waist; stomach empty but lacking appetite; shoulders aching from the load—an ache that culminates in a sharp pang connecting somewhere behind my shoulder blade; a burning lump of nausea in the throat, like I need to burp but can't, like I'm gulping from a handle of bad whiskey; glasses fogged and rain-spattered; hands numb, wet, and curled clawlike in the sleeves of my wet jacket; core temperature down... and bringing it all into focus, a piss-poor attitude...*

All this—as we ascended past well-preserved petrified stumps, into a veil of white mist. Was I really that over it? It's hard to say now. All I know is that I was acutely aware of our proximity to Highway 191—the fast track back to town—which lay, at times, only a few miles downhill.

◊◊◊

At the end of a blustery, post-precipitation day on the divide, when deep windows toward the Madison Range opened and closed like yawning mouths, we arrived at Windy Pass. The Pass is a long bench of montane parkland, a camouflage pattern of glades and spruce stands that drapes the crest in a broad dip. While it is a pass in every sense of the word, it doesn't feel that way when you're on it. It retains a confusing element even in the clearest weather—you forget you're on top of the mountains, and not in some blissed-out valley of flower-filled meadows. That day, ground visibility ranged somewhere between fifty feet and a hundred yards, even after the sky began breaking up over our heads and a celestial glow suffused the fog. Jen and I had no clue where we were from the junction we were looking for, so we walked into the middle of a stand of trees, as good as anywhere, and dropped our packs. Then we wandered after one of the many springs. After a day like that, walking without a load is the best kind of rest.

Back at camp I inspected the signs of a recent fire. Flames smoldered deep into the duff, killed saplings, and singed the scaly bases of the big spruce. Fire fighters limbed the trees to keep the fire from spreading. From these piles of branches, now sodden with rain, I selected our firewood. Damp wind snuffed my last eight matches before I finally got a catch with my backup lighter.

Fire remained a focal point of those days. One of precious few corporal pleasures, the warmth never ceased to feel like a miracle. Sometimes, after zoning out in the flames for indeterminate amounts of time, I'd chastise myself for not reading or writing—not "doing something." But I also suspected those evanescent flashes might've concealed what I was looking for as much as anything else. The full but empty-headed absorption that comes from adding small pleasures to real exhaustion might be the best recipe for peace I can come up with.

◊◊◊

Fire is a key accomplice in the debate over how humans became such a thing apart from the rest of nature. There is evidence that we gained power over fire nearly 800,000 ago, when a chart of the *Homo* genus—including branches for extinct species like Neanderthals (which coexisted with *Homo sapiens* for hundreds of thousands of years), Denisovans (whose DNA survives in native Australia and Oceania), Red Deer Cave people (the last surviving relative of humans, existent after *Homo sapiens* migrated to North America), and possibly others—was shaped like a tree instead of rod.

Fire making sprung from a carefully attended set of tools, practiced hand-eye coordination, and some serious consideration of cause and effect. Cooking followed—which, by freeing up more nutrients for digestion, promoted larger, stronger body types. As the potential for fire came to equate the potential of home, its mastery sent human populations dispersing toward the poles. Metallurgy elevated fire-making into high art, putting us on the gadgety path we follow today. It's only fitting, then, that this element—"the first enshrined divinity of mankind," as Joseph Campbell called it—took up major roles in our earliest spiritual systems. Zoroastrianism, the world's oldest-known organized religion, is the most telling example.

Zoroaster is the first-known religious prophet, probably born at least a millennium before Christ. Modern followers still worship at fire temples where live flames, regarded as agents of purity, are employed in rituals ranging from meditation to sacrifice. This does not mean Zoroastrians literally worship fire, as is sometimes suggested. The religion is far less a holdover from animism than the groundbreaking model for the complexity of modern religious practice: the fact that practitioners look to fire isn't nearly as important as what they find there. Although, based on my own experiences with the fickle element, I'm tempted to think that the relationship between the two is no coincidence.

Zoroastrianism emphasizes introspection and personal choice. It is the common ancestor of Christianity and Judaism, Hinduism and Islam. It is credited for originating the concepts of Heaven and Hell, the Messiah, free will—and inspiring western philosophers from Heraclitus to Nietzsche. These connections are still in us: fire and light continue to function as metaphors for belief in secular and parochial language alike. It is valiant, banishing evil from the shadows—and wise, bringing light to what was dark. All summer, the Forest Service trails we followed were all marked with the iconic "i" blaze, meant to symbolize a candle flame or lighthouse—a guiding light. For thousands of years these correlations to safety and salvation were grounded in a utilitarian daily enactment: stoking the hearth. Even in the most modern environments, fire's power can still be accessed rather easily—be that as simple as lighting a candle, laboring over the oven, or tending your wood heat*—but a night in the woods sets you up for a most impactful reminder. There, the myth traces directly to its source.

When I was in high school and seized every opportunity I could to go camping with my friends, I remember declaring that I got tired of watching TV long before I ever got tired of watching fire. That's still true. A fire is a visual portal into the interior realm. It is a place both thoughtless and engaged. To say that it's absorbing is an understatement—it's an all-consuming, non-representational dream. And to look inside there, and feel whole, and feel the warmth of life; to lose the lines between who you are and what's around you and sense something very old and vast inside... it's religious. At least in the only sense that I have known that word.

T. S. Eliot's poem "Little Gidding" (which contains the lines, famous among travelers, "We shall not cease from exploration/ And the end of all our exploring/ Will be to arrive where we started/ And know the place for the first time...") is in itself a discussion of the purifying effects of fire in human culture. The author employs fire as a symbol of World War II: the destruction that precedes creation. The poem is at once a definition of coming home, and a study of what it takes to be able to get there—what we have to go through first.

Jen and I talked about the end of the trip that night. It certainly wasn't far away. She was ready to keep going on forever. I needed to rest, get my health back; I was already looking back on my feet-beating, dusk-to-dawn-ecstatic days a couple weeks earlier like a geriatric remembering his youth.** I'd even let a couple nights pass without

---

* We might even expand this analogy to include the open flame's modern relations: flashing colors of computer screens, purring microwave ovens. Things that mesmerize us.

** Ultra-hiker Heather Anderson wrote, "Women appear to be better suited for walking long distances because it doesn't seem to take the same physical toll on their bodies. The women

bothering to hang our food from bears, though I'm ashamed to admit it. That was another night when, although I was dead tired, I couldn't bring myself to leave the fire until it died. It felt like something that should be done—keep it company—though of course that went both ways. Eventually, my world shrank into a tiny aquarium of warm light, and a dark chill crawled up my spine. When the coals finally crumbled into feathery grey cubes I stood up to the stars, crisp and uncountable, precise and cold, and stiffly hobbled to the tent.

◊◊◊

We still hadn't decided which route to take into Bozeman. The top of Hyalite Peak, a triple divide of watersheds and ridges, was our decision point. In 1999, after Karsten Heuer and Maxine Achurch reached that spot on their way to the Yukon, they dropped down to the Grotto Falls Trailhead to walk busy and narrow Hyalite Canyon for almost fifteen miles of pavement into town. We knew we could figure a better route than that—it was our hometown's backyard, we had to—and yet the best choice eluded us.

The trail to Grotto Falls is the busiest in what local wits call "Hyalite National Park" (it's actually national forest), a complex of forking canyons drained by Hyalite Creek fifteen minutes south of Bozeman. It is, by some determination, the busiest recreation area in Region 1 of the National Forest System. While working there earlier in the summer, I had my first sighting of a backcountry drone,* and my first backcountry selfie-stick, carried intently by a lone man up a path of many waterfalls. As I recalled these thoughts to Jen, we simultaneously realized how much we'd appreciate the obscurest option possible—the road least traveled, if you will—and sprung for a traverse I first did

---

I see at the end of a long-distance hike look fit and badass, but the guys look emaciated." I don't think she could find a better illustration for this theory than a side-by-side comparison of Jen and me in the northern Gallatins.

* It was at work filming a mountain biker. The pilot asked me to wait for the shot so I stood there for some minutes, chainsaw on my shoulder, and watched him fiddle knobs on the controller while staring at a tiny screen. It occurred to me he'd succeeded in turning the place into a video game.

eleven years earlier, which connects the main and east forks of Hyalite Creek over Mount Chisholm. From there, we could continue along the Gallatin-Yellowstone divide for several more miles before dropping into Bozeman Creek, and its network of closed logging roads, ultimately sharing just a few miles with cars before arriving downtown.

I quickly discovered how much better the scramble was suited to my nineteen-year-old weekend warrior self, carrying a daypack, than it was to my weary, under-the-weather, thirty-year-old self. A couple hours passed moving up and down nasty divides on notoriously unstable rock while we hardly changed our position on the map. But at least the sun was out and the rock was fascinating to look at. Hyalite takes its name from the mineraloid hyalite ice (SiO_2), an amorphous form of opal formed where volcanic gases condense on bedrock. The result is a bubbly and utterly transparent shell that fluoresces green under ultraviolet light. A few major outcrops, glazed over dark basalts, lay along our route. Elsewhere, I saw elaborate dendrites (in this case, some dark solution wicked into a cleavage plane) that looked like ferns pressed in the pages of yellowing books. At Fridley Lakes we had the option to set camp or keep going; a brief and frigid plunge in its waters invigorated us to continue up and over the top of Chisholm, the last named summit along our route. At 10,333', that peak has exactly the same elevation as the other highest peak in Hyalite, Mount Bole, miles away—a reminder that the range was originally laid down in neat, horizontal strata by the Northern Gallatin Range Dike Swarm, which capped an existing mountain range in thousands of feet of Absaroka volcanics. Down the other side, we spooked an odd bighorn sheep out of the trees here and there. Their numbers in the Gallatins ranged around 219 that year, in four different herds—still barely outnumbering the more visible mountain goats.

◇◇◇

Our second-to-last camp perched on a small bench below the divide. The forest on the east side was scorched by the 2001 Fridley Fire, one of Bozeman's most memorable: at one point, three firefighters died in a helicopter crash. I remember well the smoke plume—it was apocalyptic—and when it inverted, everything disoriented. We couldn't see the Bridgers on the edge of town. Fourteen years later, only grasses and forbs were growing back; I took advantage of the easy-picking firewood. After dinner and just past nightfall, I walked up to the divide to gather some snow to melt for tea, when a completely unanticipated view of the lights of Bozeman arrested me. *There it is*. A glinting pile of gold dust, pooled at the mouth of the canyon.

I couldn't figure out what to make of this sight—my hometown. As the largest city along our route (and for that matter, the largest city in the entire ecosystem), we hadn't seen anything like it for months. It was beautiful, to be sure—a magnet to the pupil's iron—but it didn't look familiar. It didn't look like a place I'd spent decades of my life. It looked powerful, futuristic, alien—and more than a little dangerous.

For nearly two months we'd found everything we could wish for along the lost ridges and hidden creek bends of the backcountry. We weren't living off the land, of course—not by a long shot—but we lived in and fleshed out a beautiful version of reality that was consistent, believable, and deeply seductive—a version in which the unique attributes of the land and our relationship to them took precedent.

While that was going on, the landscapes of human development had become the least inviting. Valley crossings meant nowhere to go to the bathroom, uncertainties about campsites, contaminated water sources, endless prohibitions. It meant bodies grown stiff from the monotony of roads, where a jarring and stilted trudge took the place of the rolling jointedness that accommodates ceaseless variations of wilderness travel. I could better appreciate the fact that, for nearly every life form on this planet besides scavengers, pathogens, and the domesticated—and certainly for life in general, its web of finely tuned interdependence—the human environment is by far the most deadly. The rules are capricious, the consequences hidden and inconsistent, the bleach, asphalt, and Roundup liberally applied.

Mild Gallatin Valley, with its beacons burning from verdant bottoms through the night, looked like a mirage. A false promise. "All gold is fool's gold:" Edward Abbey wrote that. As Jen and I took on the campy habits of explorers, we'd become unacceptable to so much social decorum, and we responded with something of the outcast's mindset.* I'd accepted those terms; the trade-offs were worth it to me. That distance between the city lights and where I stood, and all the distance that brought me there, was in large part what I'd set out to find. Cities should look strange: I want them to. They shouldn't represent unadulterated comfort or logic or peace, the end goal of all creation, nor the highest purpose. They shouldn't put us at ease. TV commercials should freak us out a little bit. Billboards should outrage our visual paradigm. Cars should remain untrustworthy monsters to be avoided as much as possible; five-acre parking lots should never stop being tragic—we shouldn't stop feeling the entombed earthworms, the sterilized soil.

If we take on these weights too often, the effect can be debilitating. We can only shoulder them by the strength of an independent inner life. Hence the distance: a psychic distance from what we're doing on this world necessitates an occasional physical distance from where we're doing it. It's a lot to take on—more than many people find acceptable—but it's also the challenge that has chosen me, that has given me life, and by accepting it, I know meaning.

After I'd thought all I had to think, I continued to stare. I looked from the bottomless black of the canyon below me, to the lights of a strange town, to the poignancy of the stars.

Then back again.

◊◊◊

Since my sickness in the Absaroka-Beartooth, I'd been struggling to get dinner down. It was a strange feeling to a person who has always prided himself as a utilitarian eater—I generally relish whatever gets me on my way. But that night was especially hard, and two hours after dinner I crawled halfway out of the tent and puked and puked and

---

* "And now I come straight to the point of the philosophy of through trails," Benton MacKaye, the visionary behind the Appalachian Trail and co-founder of the Wilderness Society, wrote in 1927. "It is to organize a Barbarian invasion. It is a counter movement to the Metropolitan invasion."

puked.* It was a cathartic culmination to a week and a half of feeling off. I later learned from my dad that this voiding was a good sign; a quick and volatile reaction that left me feeling much better afterward suggested my body had an association with a toxin, not that it was holding on to a virus.** After the convulsions stopped, feeling much better, I laid back and conked out. For Jen, who had to share a confined space with me, sleep didn't return so easily.

The next day was mostly off-trail in places it felt like no one had ever gone. A skywalk hidden in plain sight. We worked along the ridge until we could drop into the south fork of Bozeman Creek, and from there it would be a few miles down to a decommissioned logging road. Things were wild in there—amazingly lush. Moss carpeted the creek bed. I came away with about a pound of hedgehog mushrooms, white beauties whose gills take the form of teeth. We watched the easy-going creek bottom cut deeper and steeper, and the timber thicken, until we abruptly popped out on the old road. It was an uncanny moment. I snapped a picture of Jen, one step over the threshold, gazing down a narrow corridor defined by walls of regenerating lodgepole pines. We'd fallen into the gravitational pull of the finish.

Late in the day we pitched camp, vagrant-style, in a streamside thicket just below the five-mile bridge. A chill rain set in. It was our last night, but that hardly even registered—we ate while sitting on the sleeping bag in the tent. "Ideas of paradise often involve a place to camp," William Kittredge pointed out. I'd like to add that places to camp, however humble, often involve ideas of paradise. Darkness fell early—sleep so quick to follow.

---

* On about the third heave I remember thinking, "Corn?!" Before dinner we had Corn Nuts as a snack. That's something, to picture stomach contents, tiered like that.

** At first, I took this as reason to believe it had something to do with the dehydrated lake trout in our dinner that night, but when a cultured sample didn't turn up anything a few weeks later, I had to face the reality that the most common of backpacker bugs—an interloper along the fecal-oral route—was more likely than anything else. As gross as it is to say that.

4

We packed up for the last time in a gently descending drizzle, and unceremoniously pushed through dripping cottonwood branches before clawing our way up to the old roadbed. Two miles later, a passing jogger would be the first person we'd see in six and a half days, thus ending a stretch of solitude that can only be explained by miserable weather. Soon the two-track we followed turned into a gravel road, the gravel to asphalt, and the rain blew off to reveal a sky of fathomless blue. We bounced along in sandals, our pants rolled to our shins, steam off the blacktop. Woodland would turn to pasture, pasture to suburb, and then everything snap into the final urban grid.

Wilderness excursions have a richly documented tendency to produce culture shock upon returning to civilization—as you've probably noticed, I didn't escape it on a single leg of our journey. Sometimes it seems like the better the trip goes, the harder things are upon return, and this incongruity might never really resolve itself. It's easy to cite this dilemma as support for the "escape" critique of recreation: like you're being woken back up to reality, when you want to keep sleeping. But just because the relationship between the going and the destination is a source of pain, it needn't indict the venture. That is—if the natural world gives you a rich sense of complexity and wholeness, while your workaday does not, it isn't the natural world that's to blame. In fact, the tension between these worlds may be their greatest value: whether you're working in business or conservation, increasingly we must realize one through the other.

More than sixty percent of Montana households are spattered across what's called the wildland-urban interface. It makes for an exceptionally high dispersal of development, even in the West, and it's a picture of the Gallatin Valley that the *National Audubon Society Field Guide to the Rocky Mountain States* selected to illustrate this environmental crisis.[*] Even when you're not coming out of the woods, it's hard to talk about my hometown without talking about the drawbacks to "success." When you are coming out of the woods, it's dreadful. Again, from Heuer:

> The footprint of development grew with each step out of the mountains. Within a few kilometers we were walking past massive structures of wood, stucco, and glass tucked into the hills. The shiny houses dotted old pastures like an outbreak of thistles, forty buildings parceled side by side on five-acre plots, forty ranchettes crowding an area that had been nothing but a wooded glen with a lone ranch house only a decade before. It wasn't country living—square corners and garish colours poked out of the landscape wherever one looked—but it wasn't quite the city either… For conservationists, who had long extolled the economic advantages of saving wild land to attract tourists and well-heeled settlers, the irony was hard to swallow. The current pace and scale of development had the potential to do as much damage as the wholesale clear-cutting and mining that they'd been fighting for years.

---

[*] "More than 100,000 acres [in Gallatin County] have been developed over the past two decades…"

"Home." Home was changing, quick. Gallatin County ranked as Montana's fastest growing county for most of the fifteen years since Heuer's book; its county seat became a poster child of *Entrepreneur Magazine,* and frequently appeared on the list of America's top ten fastest growing small cities. With an annual growth rate of about five percent, Bozeman's population more than doubled since my family moved there in 1990, and almost half of its residents that fall had been there less than five years.* Worse, many new arrivals had been courted not by the appeal of public-lands-Montana but by private-estate-Montana, a colonial frontier they could cordon off with imported fortunes. This movement was causing the integral buffer zones of Greater Yellowstone to fracture at outlandish rates: things were changing even faster outside Bozeman's city limits than inside of them. Embraced, reveled in, and capitalized on by many, I found the town's popularity, with its accompanying explosions of chain-retail strips and tacky subdivisions, to be blackly and bottomlessly depressing. "Why should Wyoming become more like everywhere else, when everywhere else wishes it were more like Wyoming?" asked the community activist Mike Leon in the 1970s. The way Bozeman courts money it bankrupts everything else.** The wild, healthy context of our trip, which took all of two months to make convincing, already seemed so endangered, so quick to dissolve.

Yet our sense of loss could not be comprehensive. Jen and I were still human, therefore the desire for pizza was not foreign to us. We swung by our friend Nick's basement apartment, just a few blocks from the dear and dingy little place we moved out of in July, and dropped our packs inside his door. Jen made phone calls to meet a few family members who had a free hour that Tuesday afternoon. And just like

---

* By comparison, humankind's exponential growth rate over the past 200 years is only 1.9%. For millennia before that, it averaged about 1/500 of one percent.

** While Greg Gianforte (a mega-millionaire transplanted from New Jersey to Bozeman, infamous first for suing the state of Montana to close a prescriptive fishing easement across his newly-acquired property, infamous second for physically assaulting a "liberal" journalist the day before he was elected to Montana Congress) excoriated Montanans for putting environmental protections ahead of business interests in 2015, directly upriver from him a wastewater pond at a billionaire's club in Big Sky was hemorrhaging into the headwaters of the Gallatin River's west fork.

that, we were strolling with an old friend along streets I've tromped hungrily throughout nearly my entire life—past a park where I once camped on a Wednesday night for a high school sociology report—past the home of a childhood best friend who hosted me on a hundred sleepovers. Strange to realize he'd moved out of state almost twenty years before.

Campus was full of students again, and watching them crowd the expansive grounds of MSU, looking younger than ever, I realized that I never planned to call Bozeman home again. It was too much; it wasn't me. With property values well over the national average, and lower-than-average income levels, Bozeman succeeded all too well in selling its brand—which I summarize by the realtor term "rustic elegance"—on the national level. It became a town of lifestyle tourists and investment properties, a town where you'd have to be stupid to believe the woodsy veneer, a town where I—like many of my college-educated childhood friends—can't imagine ever owning a house without becoming a different person first. Home can't just be the place where you're from: you need to be able to envision a future there, too.

Our destination was a flashy microbrewery in glass and steel, retrofitted into the movie theater of my school days. We all ordered beer. After Jen's mom and sister showed up, Jen and I withdrew behind the screens of small-talk—as usual, there was so much to be said about football practice and golf meets, driver's ed and homecoming (Jen has five younger siblings), and so little to be said about the eccentric worldview we tried to give it all away for. Before we knew it we were being shuttled out to Jen's mom's house, where our trusty packs made a last trip down into the basement bedroom recently vacated by a teenage sister. And there the two of us stayed for the better part of a week. On our first day back in town, I read an entire book and hardly left the back porch.

◊◊◊

It would be natural to suppose that after escaping all the danger attendant upon nearly nine years residence in a wild inhospitable region like the Rocky Mountains where I was daily and a great part of the time hourly anticipating danger from hostile Savages and other

> *sources, I should on arriving in a civilized and enlightened community live in comparative security free from the harassing intrigues of Dames Fortunes Eldest daughter but I found it was all a delusion for danger is not always the greatest when most apparent...*
>
> –*Osborne Russell,* 1848

Journey finished, celebration meal consumed, people got on with their lives. Jen and I were pressed to follow suit. Our arrival rendered obsolete the guiding principles that directed us through so many wonderful days. Now, the ability to route-find or duck a storm was as useful as a dirty sleeping bag. Somebody tell me: when the journey becomes the destination, what do we make of the destination? Because closure doesn't come as long as you're still breathing. The journey mutates, turns inward, intensifies.

In another era, we would have had help in the matter. Traditional cultures ritualized the way back to society with the understanding that it is, unintuitively, harder to come back to people than it is to leave them. For thousands of years, such rites of passage facilitated personal transitions from one social position to another—their functionality is evidenced not just by their longevity, but by their pervasiveness. Similar ceremonies have been documented from Southern Africa to the North American Arctic (they are still used in certain religions, native societies, and a number of enlightened organizations). Almost all of them share the same three phases. *Separation rites* sever a person from their previous role, *liminal rites* cast them into a limbo of identity in order to promote personal development, and *incorporation rites* welcome that initiate back into a new role.

America lacks commonly recognized versions of these rites, and many would argue that's a good thing. Without their normalizing function, we are freer to do things our own way, to "be ourselves."[*] The downside is that their very practical duty often goes unfilled, and almost everyone one day finds themselves in a lonely search for a replacement.

I thought about these things because our trip, in so many ways, was a completely conventional rite of passage. Never mind that the best-

---

[*] To say nothing of the role of such rites in perpetuating a select number of atrocities, such as female genital mutilation.

known rites of passage target people "coming of age"—about half as old as Jen and I were.* In every sphere, from the cradle to the grave, life transitions are marked with ceremony. They address universal needs and desires—and not just those of the initiate, but of the community that claims them.

Jen and I were preparing to make a life transition and we needed to work through what that meant: after six years of seasonal existence, Jen was ready to get a full-time job (I guess you could say that I was not), and we were both ready to leave our hometown, buy a house somewhere. See what it's like. But first we had to do this strange thing— check out, strip away—walk from the freewheeling Wyoming wonderland where we lived to be outside, to our hometown in the north, where we promised to get down to business.

◊◊◊

It is important to remember that, while rites of passage consist of three parts, the parts have different meanings when taken in isolation. For starters, separation rites can be initiated impulsively, by the individual, and for that reason they have never gone away and never will. American culture reinforces the will toward separation by glamorizing tools that liquefy identity—from the motorized rootlessness of the twentieth century to the disembodied connectedness of the internet.** For Jen and me, separation meant exempting ourselves from the workaday of our peers, cleaning out our apartment, putting everything in storage. It didn't matter that we'd only lived in those four hundred square feet of the lower level of a typical student slum for fifteen months: that was the longest I'd lived anywhere in twelve years. It had been our first real place together ("real," of course, being a relative term), a dream through the transient years that preceded it, somewhere to unpack our books and plug in the crockpot. Moving out felt real

---

* The two of us completed cusp-of-adulthood type journeys long before we met. A journey with another person proved is an entirely different, and entirely worthwhile, prospect.

** "Doesn't anybody stay in one place anymore?" Carole King sang in 1971. Today, we might well ask if anybody *exists* in one place, anymore.

enough. I spent my last week in town sleeping on the floor of Nick's apartment, riding my bike to work, watching a TV mini-series, cooking (re: not-cooking) like a bachelor, dismantling my already marginal identity.

Liminality,* the product of separation, is similarly ubiquitous. In its basic form, liminality is a lack of defined social standing—a state of otherness. Taken outside of the tripartite, liminal rites can be a boon or a bane, and they're most frequently both. They represent the openness of freedom that, if obtained without adequate preparation, can expand dangerously and leave the individual helplessly unmoored from meaning. In this sense, liminality seems modern—but it has also seemed modern for thousands of years, infiltrating larger and larger segments of our lives.

Through all the joys of our two-month transience, part of me stayed on guard—a little cautious, a little conscious of myself. I knew that, over the years, I've pursued the wild for personal reasons—as both a coping mechanism and an avoidance. There have been times when my willingness to run to the woods hasn't helped me with my problems, when it exacerbated feelings of isolation and became what might be called addictive. Damaging to relationships. Similar, I imagine, to what Jim Harrison meant when he said, "I had a fairly remote cabin on Lake Superior for twenty-five years… and for a long time I felt that this cabin would strengthen, was strengthening me, for my forays into making a living. But it was just the opposite—the cabin strengthened me for more of the cabin."

There are concerns that come up with a long trip beyond the banalities of safety or money—there is the issue of whether or not you're capable enough to reach the place you're driving for, whether or not you'd know it if you saw it, and whether or not that's really where you want to go. One of my deepest concerns is that the wilderness backpack is essentially an escape, and with them I am running from the more complex, urgent, and possibly more interesting problems of my life. Indeed, some of history's greatest explorers were basically misanthropes, striking forth in a way that might be described as

---

* From Latin *limin*: threshold. Think limbo.

pathological bridge burning, not uncommonly terminal. It's the kind of concern that can never be completely silenced—and right it shouldn't, but lived with and examined on a regular basis.

Even from an environmentalist standpoint, an infatuation with pristine places can be overdone. If it's true that, as Stewart Udall said, "true conservation begins wherever people are and with whatever trouble they are in," and we need to focus our attention to how we live day-to-day, how we keep our homes and what we do for work, then the tunnel-visioned wilderness nut deeply confuses the issue by fetishizing the purity of his experience in the precious few places that humans aren't.

As has been previously examined, hiking for months at a time is no longer the exclusive domain of introverts searching for themselves. It's a "thing"—and it illuminates facets of our culture that we should be proud of. But popularization brings its own challenges: it has become easier to take the intimacy of the ritual for granted, execute it like gameplay, and miss the lessons entirely. To repeat an old line, things that appear to require no explanation are often in the greatest need of one—and when a countercultural act becomes established in the mainstream, a reexamination of its suppositions becomes vital. After succeeding in riding his bicycle across the country, one Missoula friend told me it was a stupid waste of time. He wasn't condemning the act in principle—he was saying how inappropriate it was for himself, given the circumstances. Unsure of what he wanted, he went through the motions of what he essentially treated as a stunt—one that many other people in his socio-economic sphere were already doing—only to finish feeling the same way, his savings gone.

To hear a journey summarized in this way can feel existentially toxic. Many would assume that the dedication required for so much pedaling is necessarily purifying. But the labor and isolating effects of such a trip can also numb or disillusion—and this potential only grows when the ritual ceases to be an act of individual creation, and more of a formulaic social institution. That's because shoving off still doesn't guarantee you anything when you get back, and the biggest challenges remain the least expected.

Of the three types of rites, incorporation rites are by far the trickiest. They cannot be accomplished alone. They require the reformation of a relationship—and in a secular, skeptical, and individualistic society, this depends entirely on circumstance.

The returning traveler—the prodigal son—doesn't simply want to be re-accepted, but re-imagined for what he's become. Today this means that, from the vulnerability of a liminal space, the initiate carries the onus of translating their complex experiences into terms that are socially acceptable. They must bring back not only the ineffable, but a currency for it—and if they fail, they come slamming up against the walls of a capitalist society which requires returns on discoveries… a proving-up on this supposed "personal development" that looks like getting a job and financial independence. Such pressures encourage cheap and motivated readings of experience, Hollywood versions, and may place limits on what types of behavior seem legitimate or acceptable in the future. And if this is beyond the ability of the initiate, or simply incompatible with their discoveries, the liminal space can expand indefinitely, creating an increasingly burdensome legacy of estrangement.

Post-liminal rites are best consummated in a gift economy—a dynamic that can be created between as few as two people—where non-marketable values hold concert with marketable ones, sincerity buys a meal and a bed, and stories fall upon open ears. Driven beneath the surface of a financial system that demands the opposite, the virtues of a gift economy can hardly be relied upon, and the risks of not finding one when you need it can be harrowing. Lewis Hyde warns: "Where commerce is exclusively a traffic in merchandise, the gifted cannot enter into the give-and-take that ensures the livelihood of their spirit;" in saying so, he refers to a rigidly materialistic social pattern which, already institutionalized, is also an increasingly parochial system of belief.

◊◊◊

The way I remember it, one day I was entertaining great feelings of independence on our walk, then, suddenly, I was thirty years old again, crashing in a suburban basement, my weary-looking possessions that couldn't wash clean strewn on the basement floor. There's no question I found some pleasure sating myself in base comforts of the great indoors: I overate all my meals, I sank bonelessly into plush furniture. But the health effects of these indulgences quickly exacerbated their vacuousness.

From this regressive state, the beginning of our story—how and why our hike began—came to seem vitally important. And my inability to determine where the beginning was only made it more precious. I liked to imagine that some transcendent incident, some touch of a fairy-wand, was all it took to lift me from drudging routines to epic mountainscapes—and that all I needed now was to remember this crucial modifier for yet another license on life.

Of course, walking from Lander to Bozeman provided me with enough beauty to last a lifetime or three. But in the wake of such bounty, I lacked an organizing principle to bring it into perspective. Without such a thing, the loveliest dream starts smacking of naïveté as it is forced to answer to the "real world." There's a good reason why Yellowstone Park treasured its dubious campfire creation myth for so long, in which a few soot-smudged pioneers, inspired by geothermals, stir a new icon of democracy (America's Best Idea, no less) from their dying coals. As the mundane subsists on the possibility of greatness, greatness is legitimized by its foundation in the mundane, and it takes a romance between the two to make the resultant bureaucracy palatable. That's why successful companies pay homage to hacker dropouts tinkering in garages when they go public and evil, dictatorships have their revolutionary sweethearts, and Chairman Mao never let go of his peach.

I insisted on a creation myth to the point that my lack of one hardly mattered. The important part was that, somewhere, somehow, the pieces clicked and it was clear what I had to do. My faith in this was like a prayer: that when a thing is right I know it is right and, in a larger sense, my feelings may be trusted at all. Such insistence was a basic denial of everything I learned along the way.

◊◊◊

Soon we secluded to a family cabin. While Jen studied for the NCLEX, I worked six more weeks with the Forest Service. Late in the season as it was, I helped out on projects for other departments with leftover funding; really, what I did was kill things. I set explosives to save the cutthroat trout; I dumped big Doug firs to stimulate aspen regeneration; I buzzed lodgepole pine to prevent their encroachment on willow thickets. It didn't always make a whole hell of a lot of sense. I mean, on the one hand it did—I could've explained the science behind the strategies to anyone who asked.* But I was stuck on a half-baked idea that I didn't have time to hash out—an article from a magazine I found in a bathroom stall. There are two approaches to ecosystem change: adaptation and mitigation. Adaptation "requires responding to the inevitable change in ways that continue to support healthy landscapes;" mitigation tries to delay the effects. I was enlisted in a lot of harsh mitigation—and that entailed burning fossil fuels, and leaving streaks of destruction in my wake. Rarely have I found myself justifying work so baldly, for the sake of my own income. I wanted to learn more before I was forced to do, do, do, ten hours a day, forgetting all my questions.

After offering conversational snippets from our walk to the half-dozen people that seemed interested, I could feel the poignant parts, which I'd boiled into short and exciting anecdotes, sully like Polaroids circulated between too many hands. I started deferring questions with the apology, "It was good, but it's too much to think about right now." As the power and urgency of the experience continued to slip away, I almost took comfort in that—the implications of what we saw out there were simply too powerful, too challenging to everything else I was calling life.

In the process, I abandoned the search for my story. "Is it strange to be back?" they'd ask. (Is this a nice way of saying, "You've been acting rather strange?") "What's weird is how not weird it is," I'd strangely answer. But even that wasn't completely true. It's more that things were failing to be what I thought they would be, and right they should have. What I wanted was for some transformational lens to have

---

* As far as trout and explosives go, constructing waterfalls in streams can isolate imperiled native fish from competitive invasives—in case that's what you're wondering.

inserted itself between who I had been and who I'd become; I wanted to feel like I discovered an answer out there to a question I'd carried for years. Instead, everything was the same in an uncanny way. The early October weather in Bozeman was record-setting hot, in the 80s—about the same as when we left. I rode my bike into town wearing shorts, spooked around libraries, gnashed donuts out of the bag. What little had obviously changed had changed for the worse: I noticed ground broken on three new Bozeman subdivisions.

As for my story, there were still plenty of little clues—interests and desires that went back years, ways I could fit the disparate parts together. Unbidden, unannounced, these small recollections eventually convinced me that a tidy genesis-story wasn't only unnecessary, it would have been a trap. That is: our hike was a long incubated product of a reliable passion, an outgrowth of every year that preceded it. It was who I was before I did it, it was (to hazard an answer to the Zen koan) my face before I was born, and it was who I was now that it was done. There was no secret. There was no trick. There was only the slow, silent, unrecognized work of pursuing what is to be believed, despite the tedium of real life. The work of caring about what is going on around me, whatever that may be.

And—ok, something did change, too, because I could see it on every horizon. My interest, my curiosity, my impetus toward exploration—all of these things came from the land, and the land was still surrounding me.

More than it ever had before.

ACKNOWLEDGMENTS

Thank you to Tammy, Mark, and Sam, for company and support on our walk. Also to Max and Callie, Lynn and Larry, and Denny: friendly faces along the way, who fed us.

◊◊◊

Thank you to my long time friends and trusted bookworms, Alexis and Kindra, for telling me what they think. And to Lawson, for eleventh hour technical help.

◊◊◊

Thank you to my mom, dad, and sister, who believe in the power of writing and the natural world, and are the most enthusiastic readers I ever hope to have.

◊◊◊

Thank you, Jen. This book's for you.

NOTES

Introduction

v **One of the great dreams:** Barry Lopez, *Crossing Open Ground* (Vintage Books, 1989), p. 178.

ix **In 1959, my brother:** Frank C Craighead Jr., *Track of the Grizzly* (Sierra Club Books, 1977), p. 4.

xiii **Wanderer, your footsteps are**: Antonio Machado, trans. Betty Jean Craige, *Selected Poems of Antonio Machado* (Louisiana State University Press, 1979).

Part One

xvi **Wherever we go:** Annie Dillard, *Teaching a Stone to Talk* (Harper & Row, 1982), p. 48.

5 **Tracer dye poured:** National Geographic. *National Geographic Guide to the State Parks of the United States, 4th edition* (National Geographic, 2012).

5 **"550 routes"**: Steve Bechtel, *Lander Rock Climbs* (Elemental Climbing, 2011), p. 9.

9 **"Where man becomes lost"**: Finis Mitchell, *Wind River Trails* (Wasatch Publishers, Inc, 1975), p. 2.

11 **"The Winds may be the Times Square"**: magicdufflepud, "Wyoming, the Wind Rivers, and the Wilderness Paradox." summitpost.org, 9/2/2011.

11 **"Horrendous"**: Orville E. Bach, *Reflections from Yellowstone and Beyond: Forty-Three Years as a Seasonal Ranger* (Blue Willow Press, 2016), p. 36.

13 **In [Western] resource rushes:** Patricia Nelson Limerick, *The Legacy of Conquest* (W.W. Norton and Company, 1987), p. 42

14 **"At a time when too many people":** Tina Deines, "Go Ahead, Wander Your Way." hcn.org, 1/16/2017.

17 **"He soon found that he had undertaken":** Washington Irving, *The Adventures of Captain Bonneville* (1837. University of Oklahoma Press, 1986), p. 126.

17 **"A great part of the interest":** John Charles Fremont, *Memoirs of my Life* (Belford, Clark and Company, 1887), p. 140.

18 **"Explorations furnish a source":** George Black, *Empire of Shadows* (St. Martin's Press, 2012), p. 183.

19 **made allowance for "rare" climbing**: United States Department of the Interior, "Director's Order #41: Wilderness Stewardship." 5/13/2013.

21 **"Quitting is NEVER an option":** Dawn Ballou, "Search continues for man missing in the Wind River Mountains." pinedaleonline.com, 9/11/2006.

21 **"He summoned all of his strength":** Matthew Steven Ward, "Requiem." *Post-War*, August 2006, compact disc.

22 **3.8 billion years of Greenland granite:** Joe Kelsey, *Wind River Mountains* (2nd Edition, Chockstone Press, 1994), p. 32.

22 **"Mountains are not stadiums"**: Anatoli Bourkeev. wikipedia.org, accessed 3/3/2016.

26 **"Rules, like birds"**: Gilbert Ryle, "Knowing How and Knowing That: The Presidential Address" (*Proceedings of the Aristotelian Society*, Vol. 46, 1945-1946), p. 11.

27 **"is marked by an awareness of how":** Jack Turner, *Travels in the Greater Yellowstone* (St. Martin's Griffin, 2009), p. 13.

28 **"HELP! I AM ALIVE":** Molly Loomis, "The Danger of a Life Saving Device." sierraclub.org, 5/29/2015.

28 **1,600 pointless, costly dispatches:** Ibid.

30 **"I think it was Stewart":** Aldo Leopold, *The River of the Mother of God and Other Essays by Aldo Leopold* (University of Wisconsin Press, 1991), p. 228.

36 **Many of us automatically:** Kelsey, p. 22

38 **"Amazing how a huge range"**: Philip R. Knight, *Into Deepest Yellowstone* (PublishAmerica, 2009).

38 **Anthropocentric wilderness inventories:** William H. Ittelson, et al, *An Introduction to Environmental Psychology.* (New York, Holt, Rinehart & Winston, 1974)

39 **"Far from disappearing"**: Jonathan Franzen, *How To Be Alone: Essays* (Picador, 2003), p. 48.

39 **"The claim of individuals, groups":** Alan F. Westin, "Privacy and Freedom" (*Washington and Lee Law Review*, Vol. 25 Issue 1, 3/1/1968).

42 **"Beauty... comes unsought":** Ralph Waldo Emerson, *Nature and Other Essays* (Dover Publications, 2012), p. 16.

44 **"Except as specifically provided":** The Wilderness Act of 1964.

44 **"The wilderness and economics"**: Leopold, 125.

46 **"only the self-deluding"**: C.L. Rawlins, *Sky's Witness: A Year in the Wind River Range* (Henry Holt & Co, 1993), p. 88.

48 **"humanity's irrepressible desire":** Joe Kelsey, *Wyoming's Wind River Range* (American Geographic Publishing, 1988), p. 95.

NOTES

49 **"Industrialist[s] of letters"**: Wendell Berry, *What Are People For?* (Counterpoint, 2010), p. 54.

50 **"boring... unaesthetic... fail"**: Andrew Skurka, "Three Mistakes on the Wind River High Route. Attempt #1." andrewskurka.com, 8/8/2014, accessed 1/10/2016.

50 **"We don't want to make"**: Rawlins, p. 61.

50 **"these places of pilgrimage"**: Terry Tempest Williams, *The Hour of Land: A Personal Topography of America's National Parks* (Sarah Crichton Books, 2016), p. 108.

50 **I've tried to minimize imposing**: Kelsey (1994), p. 4-6.

51 **"absolute best-of-the-best"**: "Chris." Posted comment. "Glaciers & Granite: Wind River High Route thru-hike photos." andrewskurka.com, 9/14/2015, accessed 1/10/2016.

51 **"Increasing haste is a symptom"**: Ernst Jünger, quoted by Sylvain Tesson, *Consolations of the Forest* (Penguin, 2013), p. 70.

52 **"the crowd itself becomes"**: Bernd Heinrich, *The Homing Instinct: Meaning and Mystery in Animal Migration* (Houghton Mifflin Harcourt, 2014), p. 287.

52 **"All that urgency!"**: Mary Oliver, *Swan: Poems and Prose Poems* (Beacon Press, 2012), p. 31.

52 **"a corpse"**: Jack Turner, *Travels in the Greater Yellowstone* (St Martin's Griffin, 2009), p.147.

52 **receding thirty feet a year**: Christine Peterson, "Wyoming Scientists Study Glacier Ecosystem." *Casper Star-Tribune*, 1-23-2011.

Part Two

56 **Hikers, like Midwestern drivers**: Jim Harrison, *Just Before Dark* (Mariner Books, 1999), p. 262.

62 **"Sometimes a lucky hiker"**: Hannah Hinchman, "Badlands Interpretive Trail" (Friends of the Dubois Badlands, 1997). Pamphlet.

62 **"Sometimes walking can be the mind's"**: Robert Macfarlane, *The Old Ways* (Penguin Books, 2013), p. 28.

63 **"four traits specifically helped"**: Lee Goldman, *Too Much of a Good Thing: How Four Key Survival Traits Are Now Killing Us* (Lee, Brown and Company, 2015), p. 5.

64 **"I'm walking through the wilderness wearing"**: Simon Worrall, "Is the Wild West Dead?" nationalgeographic.com, 10/4/2015.

64 **"'Nature' is not nearly so"**: William Cronon, "The Trouble with Wilderness; or, Getting Back to the Wrong Nature." *Uncommon Ground: Rethinking the Human Place in Nature*, ed. William Cronon (W.W. Norton and Company, 1996), p. 25.

65 **"An idea, a relationship"**: Bill McKibben, *The End of Nature* (Random House, 1989), p. 41.

65 **"Nobody ever tamed or domesticated"**: Wallace Stegner, *The Sound of Mountain Water* (1969. Doubleday and Company, 1980), p. 109.

65 **Is it not well done**: Thomas Mann, *The Magic Mountain* (Vintage, 1953), p. 599.

69 **the largest subrange**: summitpost.org/absaroka-range/. Accessed 11/1/2016.

69 **The Absarokas: Wyoming's mysterious**: Lorraine G. Bonney. *Wyoming Mountain Ranges* (Wyoming Geographic Series, 1987).

70 **"It is all, god help us"**: Dillard, p. 99.

71 **"a spinning pinwheel of geology"**: John McPhee, *Annals of the Former World* (Farrar, Straus and Giroux, 1998), p. 257.

71 **"filling valleys on the north side"**: Thomas Turiano, *Select Peaks of Greater Yellowstone: A Mountaineering History & Guide* (Indomitus Books, 2003), p. 270.

73 **"If we are reverent and receptive"**: Alfred Barron, *Footnotes, or Walking as a Fine Art* (1885. Michigan Historical Reprint Series, 2005), p. 102.

75 **"Washakie could see the Iron Horse"**: "Vision of Washakie: Chief of Shoshones." Utah State University Eastern Prehistoric Museum. Brochure.

76 **"The Great Spirit [was telling]"**: Ibid.

77 **I am greatly grieved to report:** Quoted by Grace Hebard, *Washakie, Chief of the Shoshones* (1930. Bison Books, 1962), p. 286.

77 **"The Indian Wars are all over"**: Ibid., p.285.

79 **"I knew an old warrior"**: Frank Linderman, *Plenty-Coups, Chief of the Crows* (1962. Bison Books, 2002), p. 14.

79 **"like George Washington in bronze"**: Quoted by Hebard, p. 265.

80 **massacred 105 women and children:** Dee Brown, *Bury My Heart At Wounded Knee* (Holt, Rhinehart and Winston, 1971), p. 90.

81 **sa:'idïka, which translates, "(he)-eats-dog"**: D. B. Shimkin, "Wind River Shoshone Ethnogeography" (*Anthropological Records* 5:4, University of California Press, 1947), p. 251.

81 **"Washakie and the head men:"** Hebard.

82 **"in all our histories, the true heroes"**: Beaudin, Marc. *Vagabond Song: Neo-Haibun from the Peregrine Journals* (Elk River Books, 2015).

82 **"An inchoate being... erotomania... conjoined good and evil"**: quoted by Barry Lopez, *Giving Birth to Thunder, Sleeping With His Daughter* (Avon Books, 1977), p. xvii.

82 **"Coyote was the father"**: Ella E. Clark, *Indian Legends from the Northern Rockies* (University of Oklahoma Press, 1988).

84 **At seventy-two percent fat:** Steven P. French, Marilynn French, and Richard Knight. "Grizzly Bear Use of Army Cutworm Moths in the Yellowstone Ecosystem" (*Interagency Conference of Bear Research and Management* vol. 9 issue 1, 1994), p. 391.

85 *half* **of her yearly calories:** Dan D. Bjornlie and Mark A. Haroldson. "Grizzly Bears and Army Cutworm Moths" (*Yellowstone Science*, vol. 23 issue 2, December 2015).

87 **"metabolic rate"**: Wallace Stegner, *The Sound of Mountain Water* (1969. Doubleday and Company, 1980), p. 48.

87 **Ultimately, it was market prices:** Rick Reese, *Greater Yellowstone: The National Park & Adjacent Wildlands* (Montana Geographic Series, 1983), p. 82.

88 **"That! If that is not"**: Ernest Thompson Seton, *The Biography of a Grizzly* (1899. Rand McNally, 1969), p. 127.

88 **"The wildest part"**: Ibid., p. 13.

88 **The note's legibility deteriorates:** Tim W. Clark and Denise Casey, *Tales of the Grizzly: Thirty-nine Stories of Grizzly Bear Encounters in the Wilderness* (Homestead Publishing, 1992), p. 139.

89 **"Over the five hundred miles that I walked"**: Gary Ferguson, *Walking Down the Wild: A Journey Through the Yellowstone Rockies* (Simon and Schuster, 1993), p. 48.

90 **Eugene Young counted seventy-six:** Michael J.Yochim, *A Week in Yellowstone's Thorofare: A Journey Through the Remotest Place* (Oregon State University Press, 2016), p. 122.

90 **blames the profusion of recent:** Daniel B. Tyers, "Moose Population History on the Northern Yellowstone Winter Range" (*Yellowstone Science*, vol. 16 no. 1, 2008).

90 **"the arterial worm," blocks blood:** Kindra McQuillan, "What's Killing Moose?" charkooska.com, 2/27/2014.

91 **"how (the ecosystem) breathes"**: Quoted by Todd Wilkinson, "Migrations Serve as Yellowstone's Lungs." *Jackson Hole News and Guide*, 2/4/2015.

NOTES

91 **to "human language"**: Ibid.

92 **"to become one with whatever"**: Peter Matthiessen, *The Snow Leopard* (1978. Penguin Classics, 2008), p. 41.

93 **in their excellent book on regional alpine**: Loendorf, Lawrence and Nancy Stone. *Mountain Spirit: The Sheep Eater Indians of Yellowstone* (University of Utah Press, 2006), p. 178.

95 **researchers found ten times more bones**: Wilfred Husted and Robert Edgar, "The Archaeology of Mummy Cave, Wyoming: An Introduction to Shoshonean Prehistory" (*Midwest Archaeological Center Special Report No. 4*, 2002), p. 165.

95 **fewer than 300 were estimated**: Loendorf and Stone, p. 137.

95 **the most remote place**: Mark Jenkins, "Destination Nowhere." *Backpacker Magazine*, 10/2/2008.

95 **uses the name Thorofare to encompass**: Michael J.Yochim, *A Week in Yellowstone's Thorofare: A Journey Through the Remotest Place* (Oregon State University Press, 2016), p. 19.

96 **"Beautiful as it may be"**: Gary Ferguson, *Hawk's Rest: A Season in the Remote Heart of Yellowstone* (2003. Torrey House Press, 2015), 54.

96 **"Ranger Gordon Reese was contacting"**: Ibid., p. 56.

97 **"loads of peakbaggers"**: Katy Human, "Colorado has 'most remote' area in U.S." *The Denver Post*, 5/3/2007.

99 **"Every direction is south"**: *Into The Cold: A Journey of the Soul*. Directed by Sebastian Copeland, performances by Sebastian Copeland and Keith Heger. KNM Home Entertainment, 2010.

100 **"Silence is not the absence"**: Gordon Hempton, *One Square Inch of Silence: One Man's Quest to Preserve the Quiet* (Atria Books, 2010), p. 2.

100 **"Well, that may be a selling point"**: Human.

100 **When the Nevada Commission of Tourism**: David Robinson, *Real Matter* (University of Utah Press, 1997), p. 151.

101 **The trouble with giving away a place**: Damon Falke on "Reflections West." Year 4, Episode 81. Aired 2015.

102 **It means "danger wood"**: Turiano, p. 253.

104 **the closest thing to a life preserver**: Tom S. Smith et al, "Efficacy of firearms for bear deterrence in Alaska." *The Journal of Wildlife Management*, 2/6/2012.

104 **The round from a panicked shooter**: Christine Page, *A Wall of Protection*. Montana Oudoors, July-August 2014.

104 **in a study of hundreds**: Tom Smith, Steven Herrero, et al. "Efficacy of Bear Deterrent Spray in Alaska." *The Journal of Wildlife Management*, 2008.

104 **"While it might not be advisable"**: Mike Koshmrl, "What Happens When Hunters and Grizzlies Collide?" *Jackson Hole News and Guide*, October 7, 2015.

105 **frisked a man "clearly" suffering**: "Cops See It Differently, Part One." *This American Life*, episode 547, 2/6/2015.

105 **"the southwest Absaroka have long been"**: Turiano, p. 244.

105 **"What I really like about the West"**: Quoted by Kelley McMillan Manley, "Bill Koch's Wild West Adventure." 5280.com, February 2013.

106 **Gary Ferguson tells how one local**: Ferguson (2003), p. 47.

107 **"WYOGA does more than just promote"**: Jesse Rodenbough, wyoga.org. Accessed 12/27/2015.

112 **"rivers of concrete"**: https://volcanoes.usgs.gov/vhp/lahars.html. Accessed 12/11/2015.

113 **twenty or thirty successive fossil:** Willard H. Parsons, *Middle Rockies and Yellowstone* (Kendall/Hunt Publishing Company, 1978), p. 37.
113 **"Beyond the mouth (of Rampart Creek)":** Orrin H. Bonney and Lorraine G. Bonney, *Field Book Yellowstone Park and The Absaroka Range* (1960. Sage Books, 1977), p. 287.
114 **"In the bottoms of the ravines":** Ferguson (1993), p. 192.
116 **"It's a mistake to think of the world":** Rawlins.
117 **"You recognize all things as real":** Ibid., p. 54.

Part Three

122 **It is not nature-as-chaos:** Gary Snyder, *The Practice of the Wild* (Shoemaker and Hoard, 1990), p. 100.
124 **"old house that had been gradually":** Annie Proulx, *Bad Dirt: Wyoming Stories 2* (Scribner, 2004), p. 62.
124 **alone over twenty-one years:** Sarah Maslin, "Gone With the Whimsy." nytimes.com, 2/1/2012.
127 **Free-riding is experienced:** "The Freerider Problem." wikipedia.org, accessed 12/2/2016.
130 **"the first verified lake trout":** nps.gov/yell, accessed 2/19/16.
130 **cutthroat were down over ninety-five percent:** Matt Miller and Kris Millgate, "Gillnets in Yellowstone." nature.org, 8/24/2016.
131 **eighty percent of the lake trout population's diet:** nps.gov/yell, accessed 2/19/16.
132 **not one could be found:** Ibid.
132 **elk calves are more aggressively:** Cathy Newman, "Osprey, Bears, and Especially Cutthroat Trout Suffer Because of Non-native Fish." *National Geographic News*, 1/24/2013.
133 **"nature is not cruel":** Jonathan Menjivar, quoted on "This American Life," episode 545, 1/23/2015.
133 **"Is there not ample evidence of:"** Jan E. Dizard, *Going Wild: Hunting, Animal Rights, and the Contested Meaning of Nature* (University of Massachusetts Press, 1999), p. 138.
133 **"In such a world of conflict":** Albert Camus. camus-society.com/albert-camus-quote, accessed 11/7/2016.
135 **"the epicenter of the whitebark":** Jesse Logan, "Spooked by the Ghost Forests of Yellowstone." mountainjournal.org, accessed 9/6/2017.
137 **"As my thesis work continued":** Margaret M. Hiza, "The Geologic History of the Absaroka Volcanic Province." *Yellowstone Science*, vol. 6 no. 2. Spring 1998.
137 **"an unfamiliar intersection of geology":** Tim Cahill, *Lost in My Own Backyard* (Crown, 2004), p. 109.
138 **"The summit has never been attained":** Scientific American, 3/30/1918, p. 272.
142 **In 2015, thirty-five grizzly mortalities:** https://www.usgs.gov/data-tools/2015-known-and-probable-grizzly-bear-mortalities-greater-yellowstone-ecosystem. Accessed 11/11/2016.
144 **"volcanic. It has fire":** Emily Ballew Neff, *The Modern West: American Landscapes 1890-1950* (Yale University Press, 2006), p. 239.
145 **"When I am in my painting":** Jackson Pollock, jackson-pollock.org/quotes. Accessed 3/20/2017.
145 **These ancient volcanoes are similar:** Hiza.
146 **I have found where ye dikelets:** Joseph Iddings, quoted in Turiano, p. 157.

NOTES

146 **explains this "dazzling center"**: Bonney and Bonney, p. 75.

150 **"The old Lakota was wise"**: Peter Matthiessen, *In the Spirit of Crazy Horse* (1980. Penguin Books, 1992), p. 489.

152 **all that I had not seen**: Rudyard Kipling, *American Notes* (1891. University of Oklahoma Press, 1982.), p. 112.

152 **"I saw a large, ancient Indian"**: Peter Nabokov and Lawrence Loendorf, *Restoring a Presence: American Indians and Yellowstone National Park* (University of Oklahoma Press, 2016), p. 184.

154 **In one illustrative incident**: Mark Barringer, *Selling Yellowstone: Capitalism and the Construction of Nature* (University Press of Kansas, 2002), p. 163.

155 **"clearly proved that our rapacious"**: Wallace Stegner, *Marking the Sparrow's Fall*. (Henry Holt and Company, 1998), p. 137.

155 **"If people could be got into"**: John Muir, "The National Parks and Forest Reservations" (*Sierra Club Bulletin*, vol. 1 no. 7, 1896) p. 282.

155 **"Does it matter how the parks fit"**: Timothy Egan, "Unplugging the Selfie Generation." *National Geographic*, October 2016.

156 **up 16.6% from 2014**: https://irma.nps.gov/Stats/SSRSReports/Park SpecificReports/Annual Park Recreation Visitation, accessed 3/12/2016.

156 **[Muir] could not have known**: Jack Turner, *The Abstract Wild* (The University of Arizona Press, 1996), p. 36.

157 **"Rangers are often overwhelmed"**: Todd Wilkinson, "Yellowstone and Beyond: Are the National Parks Being Loved to Death?" *The Christian Science Monitor*, 7/24/2016.

157 **When the symbols provided**: Joseph Campbell, *Myths to Live By* (Bantam Books, 1972), p. 89.

157 **every dollar currently invested**: Dayton Duncan, "Are We Loving Our National Parks to Death?" nytimes.com, 8/6/2016.

158 **"as if it had been under siege"**: Nelson, Glenn. "The Park Service Centennial Celebration's Damage to the Lands." hcn.org, 12/23/2016.

158 **"Yellowstone won't be saved"**: Wilkinson, 7/24/2016.

159 **"for the enjoyment... of future generations"**: http://www.pbs.org/nationalparks/history/ep3/4/, accessed 9/9/2016.

159 **The Gallatin BMA is closed**: https://www.nps.gov/yell/planyourvisit/bear-management-areas.htm, accessed 9/9/2016.

161 **1.1% of Yellowstone's 2015 visitors**: https://irma.nps.gov/Stats/SSRSReports/ParkSpecificReports/OvernightStays, accessed 4/1/2016.

162 **"In ever manner conceivable"**: Turner (1996), p. 28.

167 **"These comparatively invisible things"**: Alfred Barron, *Footnotes, or Walking as a Fine Art* (1885. Michigan Historical Reprint Series, 2005).

168 **"When we live our lives pursuing"**: Paul Rezendes, *Tracking and the Art of Seeing: How to Read Animal Tracks and Sign* (Collins Reference, 1999), p. 62.

169 **"Everything is related to everything:"** Waldo Tobler, "Tobler's First Law of Geography." wikipedia.org, accessed 4/15/2016.

169 **From the breakaway at the northeast**: Robert J. Carson, *East of Yellowstone: Geology of Clarks Fork Valley and the Nearby Beartooth and Absaroka Mountains* (Keokee Books, 2010), p. 20.

169 **Based on thermodynamic**: Ibid., p. 21.

169 **"things that are beyond us"**: Frank Linderman, *Plenty-Coups, Chief of the Crows* (1962. Bison Books, 2002).

171 **had a dude ride scheduled:** Jeff Henry, *The Year Yellowstone Burned: A Twenty-Five Year Perspective* (Taylor Trade Publishing, 2015), p. 45.

171 **another change was made:** Ibid., p. 46.

171 **"the balance of nature in any":** Aldo Leopold to Charles Kraebel, January 18, 1927. Letter.

172 **"carrying capacity was reduced":** Irwin D. Rasmussen. "Biotic Communities of Kaibab Plateau, Arizona" (*Ecological Monographs* no. 3, 1941), pp. 229-275.

173 **"Fire control by the federal":** Stephen J. Pyne, "Flame and Fortune" (*Forest History Today*, 1996), pp. 8-10.

174 **160,000 new acres of flame:** Henry, p. 144.

175 **"It just looked like another":** Tom Howard and Clair Johnson, "Singed but Spared: Gateway Residents Bitter Over 'Let it Burn' Policy." *Billings Gazette*, 8/9/2003.

175 **"destroyed by the very people":** Alan Simpson, quoted in *Wildfire: A Reader*, Ed. Alianor True (Island Press, 2013), p. 141.

176 **more than a quarter of homes built:** Eric Sagara, Emmanuel Martinez and Ike Sriskandarajah, "Wildfires Spark Where Growth is Sprawling." hcn.org, 10/11/2016.

177 **"Disturbance is just frequent enough":** Robin Wall Kimmerer, *Gathering Moss: A Natural and Cultural History of Mosses* (Oregon State University Press, 2003), p. 67.

177 **"Creation of a mosaic":** Ibid., p. 68.

177 **"subjected to crown fires":** Dennis H. Knight, "The Yellowstone Fire Controversy" (*The Greater Yellowstone Ecosystem: Redefining America's Wilderness Heritage*, ed. Keiter, Robert B. and Mark S. Boyce, Yale University Press, 2001), p. 88.

177 **"The thing that struck me the most":** Henry, p. 67.

178 **"points of no return, beyond which":** Elsie LeQuire, "Climate Change Tipping Points: A Point of No Return?" *Fire Science Digest*, May 2013.

179 **The Tree of Ténéré:** https://en.wikipedia.org/wiki/Tree_of_Ténéré, accessed 11/2/2015.

179 **"about three times as many plant":** Paul Schullery, *Mountain Time: A Yellowstone Memoir* (1984. Roberts Rinehart Publishers, 1995), p. 4-5.

179 **"The fire regime on the Yellowstone":** Yochim, p. 134.

182 **"Climate regulation, composition":** Micheal McCarthy, *The Moth Snowstorm* (New York Review Books, 2016)

182 **concept of wilderness as a psychological:** Wallace Stegner, "Wilderness Letter." *Marking the Sparrow's Fall* (Holt Paperbacks, 1999), p. 111.

183 **"Wilderness is said to discriminate":** Broughton Coburn and Leila Bruno, *Ahead of Their Time: Wyoming Voices for Wilderness* (Wyoming Wilderness Association, 2004), p. 63.

Part Four

186 **Nobody ever headed in that:** William Kittredge, *The Nature of Generosity* (Vintage Books, 2000), p. 13.

188 **"the hottest acronym":** John Branch, "A Real Adventure: Sorting Out All the F.K.T.s." nytimes.com, 8/5/2015.

188 **Jonathan Thompson would write:** Jonathan Thompson, "Is Tech Ruining the Wilderness?" High Country News, 7/20/2015.

189 **How often we speak of the great:** Sigurd Olson, *The Singing Wilderness* (1956. University of Minnesota Press, 1997).

NOTES 313

190 **"Only daring and insolent men"**: Henry David Thoreau, *The Maine Woods* (1864. Quality Paperback Book Club, 1997), p. 84.

190 **"There was really a danger of"**: Ibid., p. 98.

190 **"one more person to get"**: Scott Jurek, "Reflections on the Appalachian Trail." scottjurek.com, accessed 11/7/2015.

190 **"this was a slugfest now"**: Megan Michelson, "A Ghost Among Us." *Backpacker Magazine*, 9/25/2014.

190 **"There seem to be just as many"**: Jennifer Pharr Davis, "On the Longest Hiking Trails, a Woman Finds Equal Footing." nytimes.com, 11/3/2015.

191 **"Doing the [A.T.]"**: Katharine Q. Seelye, "As Hikers Celebrate on Appalachian Trail, Some Ask: Where Will It End?" The New York Times, 8/29/2015.

192 **"Cycles of prosperity and recession"**: Limerick, p. 28.

193 **a low-profile man noted for**: Burton Harris, *John Colter: His Years in the Rockies* (1952. Bison Books, 1993).

194 **In the year of 1835**: Osborne Russell, *Journal of a Trapper*, edited by Aubrey L. Haines (Bison Books, 1967), p. 88.

195 **"The main band of marauding"**: Joel C. Janetski, *Indians in Yellowstone National Park* (University of Utah Press, 2002), p. 93.

195 **the miners started shoveling**: Ralph Glidden, *Exploring the Yellowstone High Country: A History of the Cooke City Area*, 3rd Edition (Cooke City Community Council, 2007), p. 88.

195 **some believe he arrived**: Kelly Hartman, quoted in "History Article." *Life Between Mountains (Annual Museum Newsletter)*, Cooke City Montana Museum, summer 2017.

197 **A vista divorced from the open**: Sigurd Olson, *The Listening Point* (1958. Knopf, 2012).

198 **All you have to do is dig**: Jonathan Thompson, "Silverton's Gold King Reckoning." *High Country News*, 5/2/2016.

200 **Crown Butte projected a total**: Marc Humphries, "New World Gold Mine and Yellowstone National Park." *CRS Report for Congress #96-669*, 8/27/1996.

202 **refused to sell to the government**: Kurt Repanshek, "Land Deal Closes the Book on New World Mine Proposed on Yellowstone National Park's Doorstep." nationalparkstraveler.org, 6/15/2010.

204 **"Mr. Duret had been credited"**: Doris Whithorn, *Twice Told Tales on the Upper Yellowstone, Vol. 2* (Doris S. Whithorn, 1994), p. 37.

204 **"well-stocked with forest, carrying"**: John Leiberg, *Forest Conditions in the Absaroka Division of the Yellowstone Forest Reserve* (Government Printing Office, 1904).

206 **The subject of walking is**: Rebecca Solnit, *Wanderlust: A History of Walking* (Penguin Books, 2001), p. 5.

207 **"A fundamental mismatch [exists]"**: Gretchen Reynolds, "Born To Move." *The New York Times*, 11/23/2016.

207 **"the bond of fifty-thousand"**: Michael McCarthy, *The Moth Snowstorm: Nature and Joy* (New York Review Books, 2016), p. 59.

208 **"My work really is just about"**: Richard Long, "Heaven and Earth: room guide. Room 8." tate.org.uk. Accessed 4/8/2016.

209 **The actuality of things cannot**: Gary Snyder, *The Practice of the Wild* (Shoemaker and Hoard, 1990), pp. 155; 160-1.

211 **Mere ways through the forest**: foresthistory.org/research-explore/us-forest-service-history/policy-and-law/recreation-u-s-forest-service/hiking-in-america/trail-building-national-forests/, accessed 11/8/2017.

213 **"Stay on Trail":** David Robertson, *Real Matter* (University of Utah Press, 1997), p. 11.

213 **"The Great Burn needs silence":** Nicholas Littman, "Passing Through." *The Montana Quarterly*, Summer 2017.

216 **related to a great spectrum:** "Siouan Language," wikipedia.org, accessed 4/1/2016.

217 **No Vitals had a premonition:** Keith Algier, *The Crow and the Eagle: A Tribal History from Lewis and Clark to Custer* (Caxton Printers Ltd., 1993), p. 22.

218 **"There are few groups that put more":** Lawrence Loendorf, "Vision Quest Structures." www.priormountains.org, accessed 4/22/2017.

218 **"a powerful tribe of mountaineers":** Edward Curtis, *The North American Indian, Vol. 4* (1907. Taschen, 2015).

218 **"The Crow country is a good country":** Chief Arapooish. Collected by Colin Calloway in *Our Hearts Fell to the Ground: Plains Indians Views on how the West was Lost* (Bedford Series in History & Culture, 1996), p. 74.

218 **"While twenty-six tribes":** W. Andrew Marcus et al, *Atlas of Yellowstone* (University of Oregon, 2012), p. 17.

219 **"I am obliged to remark":** Jerry Bagley, *The First Known Man in Yellowstone* (Old Faithful Eyewitness Publishing, 2000), p. 83.

220 **"neatly clothed in dressed deer":** Russell, p. 29.

220 **"furtive, wretched and misshapen":** Harris, p. 43.

220 **"ranged from the Lemhis, rich":** Ibid.

221 **"Some people think: Why":** Lois Wingerson, "High Life in the High Mountains?" (*American Archaeology*, vol. 13 no. 4, Winter 2009-2010), p. 18.

221 **"The high elevations of the Winds":** Matthew Stirn, quoted by Blake de Pastino. "13 Ancient Villages Discovered in Wyoming Mountains May Redraw Map of Tribal Migrations." westerndigs.org, November 5, 2013.

221 **"If the women worked 20 hours":** Wingerson, p. 16.

222 **stronger compression strength:** Lawrence Loendorf and Nancy Stone, *Mountain Spirit: The Sheep Eater Indians of Yellowstone* (University of Utah Press, 2006), p. 124.

222 **Spirits were not all equal:** Loendorf and Stone, p. 38.

223 **"The Sheepeaters possessed few":** Harris, p. 109.

223 **"unparalleled levels of physiological":** Laura L. Scheiber and María N. Zedeño, *Engineering Mountain Landscapes* (University of Utah Press, 2015), p. 1.

223 **"Feeble in mind and diminutive in stature":** Hiram Chittenden, *The Yellowstone National Park* (University of Oklahoma Press, 1964), p. 11.

224 **[Ethics columnist Randy] Cohen:** Craig Childs, *Finders Keepers: A Tale of Archaeological Plunder and Obsession* (Little, Brown and Company, 2010), p. 20.

226 **"It's been here for eight hundred":** Ibid., p. 59.

227 **Wildness cannot be collected:** Kimmerer, p. 139.

229 **they named it the Method of Loci:** Sarah C. Rich, "The Architecture of Memory." *Smithsonian Magazine*, 8/6/2012.

229 **the hippocampi of these drivers:** Simon Garfield, *On the Map* (Profile Books, 2012), p. 412.

230 **"My body has ripened":** C.L. Rawlins, *Sky's Witness: A Year in the Wind River Range* (Henry Holt & Co, 1993), p. 238.

231 **"A road, I've been thinking":** David Lynch, *Mulholland Drive* (Universal Pictures, 2001), director's notes.

231 **Now a promise made:** Robert W. Service, *The Spell of the Yukon and Other Verses* (Edward Stern and Company, 1907).

NOTES

232 **"Without stories, we're not much"**: Kittredge, p. 63.

232 **"psychologically, the great wash"**: Ann H. Zwinger and Beatrice E. Willard, *Land Above the Trees: A Guide to American Alpine Tundra* (The University of Arizona Press, 1972), p. 4.

233 **"is also the surrounding territory"**: Bernd Heinrich, *The Homing Instinct: Meaning and Mystery in Animal Migration* (Houghton Mifflin Harcourt, 2014), p. xi.

233 **"circling near their lofts in"**: Ibid., p. 75.

235 **Utah introduced mountain goats**: Krista Langlois, "Non-native Goats in Utah's La Sal Mountains. *High Country News*, 12/22/2014.

236 **"all these relationships are inherently"**: Quoted by C.L. Rawlins, *In Gravity National Park* (University of Nevada Press, 1998).

238 **laid out with great conviction**: Robert L. Rockwell, "Giardia Lamblia and Giardiasis with Particular Attention to the Sierra Nevada." *Sierra Nature Notes 2*, January 2002.

239 **Giardiasis has been called**: Ibid.

241 **"In Plentitude too free/"**: Wendell Berry, "We Who Prayed and Wept." *New Collected Poems* (Counterpoint, 2012), p. 245.

241 **"Too much safety seems"**: Aldo Leopold, *Sand County Almanac*, (1949. Ballantine Books, 1986), p. 141.

Part Five

244 **It is in the doing**: Terry Tempest Williams, *The Hour of Land: A Personal Topography of America's National Parks* (Sarah Crichton Books, 2016), p. 166.

246 **Gardiner, the town, takes its name**: Lee Whittlesey, *Yellowstone Place Names* (Wonderland Publishing Company, 2006), p. 112.

249 **an extraordinary journey in 1999**: Karsten Heuer, *Walking the Big Wild: From Yellowstone to Yukon on the Grizzly Bear's Trail* (Braided River, 2004).

252 **"I don't believe drivers in other states"**: Quoted by Kim Briggeman, "A Little Faster." *The Missoulian*, 9/28/2015.

252 **1,600 road-killed "large mammal"**: "Study, film address vehicle/animal collisions in valley." *The Livingston Enterprise*, 12/13/2013.

252 **2015 saw the biggest spike**: Neal Boudette. "Biggest Traffic Spike in 50 Years? Blame Apps." nytimes.com, 11/15/2016.

253 **"Kevin Hodge of Dillon"**: Briggeman.

254 **"If anything happened to him she"**: Erin Prophet, *Prophet's Daughter: My Life with Elizabeth Clare Prophet Inside the Church Universal and Triumphant* (Lyons Press, 2010). p. 17

254 **employed mountain imagery liberally**: Godfré Ray King, *Unveiled Mysteries* (1934. Martino Fine Books, 2011).

254 **"lived in invisible caves"**: Prophet, p. 33.

254 **"was the most spiritual center"**: Ibid., p. 49.

255 **The word—'Yellowstone,' explained Saint Germain**: Godfré Ray King, *Unveiled Mysteries* (Saint Germain Press, 1935).

258 **"The leaders of the wilderness"**: Frederick H. Swanson, *Where Roads Will Never Reach: Wilderness and Its Visionaries in the Northern Rockies* (The University of Utah Press, 2015), p. 5.

258 **"representative of a significant"**: *Hyalite-Porcupine Buffalo Horn Wilderness Study Report*. United States Department of Agriculture, 1985.

NOTES

259 **"father of modern elk management"**: wikipedia.org/wiki/Olaus_Murie. Accessed 11/5/2016.

259 **"discuss the mundane and realistic"**: Swanson, p. 10.

259 **"the wilderness study areas designated"**: Montana Wilderness Study Act of 1977.

260 **but not because the land in question**: *Hyalite-Porcupine Buffalo Horn Wilderness Study Report*.

261 **"the imprint of man's work"**: The Wilderness Act of 1964.

261 **"the Wilderness Study Act only"**: Quoted by Laura Lundquist, "Federal Judge: Forest Service Can Improve Wilderness Areas." *Bozeman Daily Chronicle*, 6/26/2012.

262 **"nature will take precedence"**: Quoted by Matt Schudel, "Steward L. Udall, 90, interior secretary, was Guardian of America's Wild Places." *Washington Post*, 3/21/2010.

264 **"The rules are clear when"**: Lou Mazzante, "This Land is My Land." *Bike Magazine*, 2009.

264 **"restore Congress' original vision"**: Ted Stroll, "It's Inevitable. There will be Bikes in Wilderness." hcn.org, 3/29/2016.

265 **"There shall be no temporary"**: The Wilderness Act.

265 **"barred from wheels"**: Wallace Stegner, *The Sound of Mountain Water* (1969. Doubleday and Company, 1980), p. 38.

266 **"If I'm going to be encountered"**: Michael Wright, "Bozeman Man Survives Run-In with Moose." *Bozeman Daily Chronicle*, 6/10/2015.

267 **"You are not welcome here"**: Vernon Felton, "Banned In the USA, Part 1." pinkbike.com, 3/18/2016.

267 **"We've come to the root"**: _____, "Sucker Punched." *Bike Magazine*, 11/22/2015.

268 **"dangerous... aid and abet"**: _____, "The Ban on Mountain Biking in Wilderness Areas is More Than Misguided; It's Dangerous." theintertia.com, 8/10/2016.

268 **"It doesn't matter if you are"**: Quoted in "Sucker Punched."

268 **most social actors involved**: Justin Farrell, *The Battle for Yellowstone* (Princeton University Press, 2015), p. 12.

269 **"Mountain-biking may be richer"**: Ted Stroll, "It's Inevitable: There Will be Bikes in Wilderness." *High Country News*, 3/29/2016.

270 **"anti-conservationist movement"**: Kurt Gensheimer, "The Quest to Allow Mount Biking in Federally Designated Wilderness." adventuresportsjournal.com, accessed 3/9/2016.

270 **"Mountain-bikers have been put"**: Vernon Felton, "Taking the Wilderness Debate to Washington D.C." bikemag.com, 2/8/2016.

270 **"It's not like we're motorized"**: Donovan Power, quoted by Alex Sarkariassen in "Biking Bad: Freeriders Push the Limit, with the Law in Pursuit." *Missoula Independent*, 5/31/2012.

271 **"opportunities for solitude... sufficient size"**: The Wilderness Act.

272 **vehicle approached within 1500 meters**: Michael J. Wisdom et al, "Effects of Off-road Recreation on Mule Deer and Elk" (*Transactions of the 69th North American Wildlife and Natural Resources Conference*, 2004), p. 540.

272 **"You have to understand"**: Quoted in "Sucker Punched."

273 **Heuer describes a radio-collared**: Heuer, p. 99.

273 **"The preliminary investigation"**: Sam Wilson, "Grizzly Death Inquiry Suggests New Safety Measures to Protect Bears, Mountain Bikers." *Hungry Horse News*, 3/8/2017.

274 **"persona non grata"**: Quoted by Vernon Felton, "Taking the Wilderness Debate to Washington D.C." bikemag.com, 2/8/2016.

NOTES

274 **"In our world everybody thinks of changing humanity"**: Leo Tolstoy, *Some Social Remedies* (Free Age Press, 1901), p. 29.

274 **"traditional environmental organizations"**: Quoted in Felton, "Taking the Wilderness Debate to Washington D.C."

275 **proven to be *more* addicted**: Ira Wolfe, "Digital Addiction: Are Baby Boomers Calling The Kettle Black?" thehuffingtonpost.com, 3/29/2017.

275 **losses... are now so extensive**: McCarthy, p. 122.

277 **"un-American"**: Steffen Gronegger, "US Wilderness Act: Banning Bikes is Un-American." enduro-mtb.com, 2/11/2015.

278 **"Emotion is still the best"**: Turner (1996), p. 22.

278 **"Temperatures have remained steady"**: Orrin Hatch, "Climate Change 101," http://web.archive.org/web/20091201233001/http://hatch.senate.gov/public/index.cfm?FuseAction=Issuepositions.Home, accessed 1/12/2017.

278 **"little more than a cheap"**: Mike Lee, https://www.facebook.com/senatormikelee/posts/1158826760815682, accessed 1/12/2017.

279 **as Rebecca Solnit pointed out**: Rebecca Solnit, *Wanderlust: A History of Walking* (Penguin Books, 2001), p. 127.

280 **"I hadn't counted on this"**: Heuer, p. 13.

281 **"That area was so susceptible"**: Joe Gutkoski, interview with Phil Knight. "The Road Not Taken," *Outside Bozeman Magazine*, Summer 2006.

283 **"the first enshrined divinity"**: Campbell, p. 35.

284 **"We shall not cease from exploration/"**: T. S. Eliot, "Little Gidding." www.columbia.edu. Accessed 3/2/2016.

284 **"Women appear to be better"**: Heather Anderson, "On the Longest Trails, a Woman Finds Equal Footing." *The New York Times*, 11/3/2015.

286 **ranged around 219 that year**: Frank Lance Craighead, *Wilderness, Wildlife, and Ecological Values of the Hyalite-Porcupine-Buffalo Horn Wilderness Study Area* (The Craighead Institute, November 2015).

287 **"All gold is fool's gold"**: Edward Abbey, *Good News* (Plume, 1980), p. 25.

288 **"And now I come straight"**: Benton MacKaye, quoted by Larry Anderson in *Benton MacKaye: Conservationist, Planner, and Creator of the Appalachian Trail* (John Hopkins University Press, 2002), p. 215.

289 **"Ideas of paradise often"**: Kittredge, p. 173.

289 **"More than 100,000 acres"**: Peter Alden and John Grassy. *National Audubon Society Field Guide to the Rocky Mountain States* (Knopf, 1999).

291 **The footprint of development grew**: Heuer, p. 19.

293 **It would be natural to suppose**: Russell, p. 90.

296 **"I had a fairly remote cabin"**: Gary Snyder, Jim Harrison, and Paul Ebenkamp, *The Etiquette of Freedom* (Counterpoint, 2010), p. 19.

298 **"Where commerce is exclusively"**: Lewis Hyde, *The Gift: Creativity and the Artist in the Modern World* (1979. Vintage Books, 2007), p. xix.

300 **"requires responding to the inevitable"**: Elsie LeQuire, "Climate Change Tipping Points: A Point of No Return?" *Fire Science Digest*, May 2013.

Made in the
USA
Columbia, SC